Mrs Beeton's
CHRISTMAS BOOK

Mrs BEETON's
CHRISTMAS BOOK

PRACTICAL IDEAS FOR CREATING
THE TRADITIONAL CHRISTMAS

★

RECIPES · DECORATIONS · GIFTS · GAMES · CAROLS

Compiled by Pamela Westland

WARD LOCK

First published in Great Britain in 1989
by Ward Lock Limited, 8 Clifford Street
London W1X 1RB, a Cassell Company

Designed by Anita Ruddell

Step by step artwork by Tony Randell
Photography by Jhon Kevern
Home economist: Stella Joyce
Stylist: Alison Meldrum

Text filmset/set in Horley Old Style
by Tradespools Ltd, Frome, Somerset

Printed and bound in Italy by Rotolito of Milan

British Library Cataloguing in Publication Data

Beeton, Mrs, *1836–1865*
    Mrs Beeton's Christmas book.
    1. Food: Christmas dishes, ——Recipes
    2. Christmas activities, ——Collections
    I. Title
    641.5'66

ISBN 0-7063-6788-X

CONTENTS

★

INTRODUCTION

★

The Christmas festival occupies a very special place in the year. For many it is the only time when whole families can be together, and it provides an excellent opportunity to entertain friends and neighbours. Yet, if everything is to run like clockwork from the beginning, a plan of action is needed

Drawn from Mrs Beeton's Classic *Cookery and Household Management*, but brought right up to date and expanded, *Mrs Beeton's Christmas Book* gathers together information and advice, techniques, skills, recipes, and a wealth of ideas, to help with organizing every aspect of the Christmas activities.

The first section is devoted entirely to Christmas feasting. Will your choice for Christmas dinner be traditional turkey or goose, or something a little different; what selection of accompaniments and side dishes will you offer, and how will you cater for a vegetarian? If you are thinking of giving a party, or having people to stay, how much preparation will be involved, and how can you fit it in among all the other things that have to be done? The pages of the comprehensive food section provide all the ideas and help you need, together with advice on pre-planning and advance preparations, which are the secret of all successful entertaining.

Christmas is a time for children, and the sections on decorations and entertainments are packed with ideas to delight the younger members of the household. Different ways of decorating the tree are suggested, and instructions are given for making all sorts of decorations, gift wrapping, cards and tags, and stockings. The words and music for a collection of carols is included, as are the twin legends of Santa Claus and Father Christmas. To make sure that your Christmas parties go off with a bang, there are notions for making, filling and trimming crackers. And to get you and your guests in the party mood there are games galore for all ages.

CHRISTMAS RECIPES

★

Planning to entertain family and friends over the Christmas holiday is a gret deal easier now than it was when Mrs Beeton first wrote her manual in the 1850s. There is a tempting and wholesome range of canned, packaged and freeze-dried goods; freezers in the kitchen (instead of the ice-house in the garden); and a wider selection of fresh foods from all over the world. Make a list of the daily menus and the shopping you need to do, and prepare as much as possible well in advance.

ADVANCE PREPARATIONS

Not many people have the flair for organization and the speed around the kitchen that are needed to leave all the Christmas cooking until the last minute and sail through the whole event serenely. It really does pay to plan the food for the principal days – Christmas Day and Boxing Day, and the times when you will have house-guests or are giving a party – as far in advance as possible.

Make soups and sauces, pies and patés, desserts and bread dough, preserves and potted meats; everything that will freeze or store in perfect condition. Even chop fresh herbs (and freeze them in water in ice-cube trays); make breadcrumbs, and other garnishes and toppings. Every little helps.

Make lists of the shopping you need to do, and get in as much as you can well ahead of time.

In order not to waste time hunting for things in the freezer, make a list of the dishes that are ready and waiting and if possible group them together in one drawer or basket.

KEEPING FOOD HOT

All over the holiday, whether you have extra people staying in your home or are cooking for a party, keeping food hot can be a problem. Here are some tips to help you serve all the components of a meal piping hot.

Cooked or partly cooked food waiting to be added to a dish can either be left at room temperature or put in a container in a bain-marie (a dish or pan of hot water).

Leave casseroles and oven-baked dishes in the oven with the heat turned right down, or turn off the heat if there is sufficient residual heat.

Leave cooked garnishes in a container in a bain-marie.

Open-baked dishes should be lightly covered with greaseproof paper or foil which can be greased if necessary. Cover pastry goods and stacked pancakes (separated with rounds of greaseproof paper) in the same way.

Place pasta, rice and plainly cooked vegetables in a steamer or in a strainer over very hot water.

Sauces, and dishes in sauces, are best kept hot in a bain-marie. The food container should be sufficiently deep and/or lightly covered to prevent water splashing or dripping into it. Cover the top of the dish closely with greaseproof paper to prevent condensation dripping on to the sauce.

Fried food should be served at once, but if it must be kept hot it should be put on soft kitchen paper on a baking tray, uncovered, in a cool oven.

CHECKING APPLIANCES

Well before the Christmas rush starts in the kitchen, it is a good idea to check all the appliances and tools you are likely to need. If some, the ones you seldom use, are stored away, get them out and look them over.

Check that all the plugs and cords are in working order. And be sure to have a few spare fuses ready for emergencies.

Check that all the attachments you are likely to need, the mincer, juice extractor, dough hook and so on, are ready to hand. Nothing is more infuriating than having to search for a vital attachment when you are half-way through a recipe.

Check that all your kitchen and carving knives are really sharp, and ready for all the chopping, cutting and slicing they will be called upon to do.

An electric or manual knife sharpener is a very useful tool if you do not have the knack of sharpening knives on a steel.

Check that you have all the baking pans and dishes in the sizes you need, especially one large enough for the turkey or other main meat course.

Some kitchen equipment shops will hire out cake tins and dessert moulds in special party shapes; you need to book your requirements well in advance.

FREEZER LORE

The storage life, in a modern freezer, for some of the foods it is useful to have during the holiday period:

Cakes, pastry and bread

TYPE OF FOOD	FREEZER STORAGE LIFE	THAWING/ COOKING
Biscuit dough	2 months	Thaw in refrigerator for 45 minutes. Bake at 190°C/ 375°F/gas 5 for 10 minutes
Bread	1 month	Thaw at room temperature for 4 hours
Breadcrumbs	3 months	May be used without thawing
Bread dough	2 months	Unseal bag, thaw at room temperature for 6 hours
Cakes, uniced	4 months	Thaw at room temperature for 2–3 hours
Cakes, iced	4 months	Thaw at room temperature for 3 hours
Cheese cakes	1 month	Thaw in refrigerator for 8 hours
Choux pastry, baked, but unfilled	1 month	Thaw in wrappings at room temperature for 2 hours
Crumpets and muffins	1 month	Thaw in wrappings at room temperature for 30 minutes before toasting
Fruit pies (brush bottom crust with egg white to avoid sogginess)		
baked	4 months	Thaw to serve cold, or reheat
uncooked	2 months	Bake from frozen at 200°C/400°F/gas 6
Pastry cakes, baked	4 months	Reheat or fill with hot filling
unbaked	4 months	Bake frozen cases for time recommended for type of pastry

TYPE OF FOOD	FREEZER STORAGE LIFE	THAWING/ COOKING
Meat dishes	2 months	Thaw in wrapping in refrigerator for 3 hours. Bake at 180°C/350°F/gas 4 for 40 minutes
Meat pies	2 months	Thaw in refrigerator for 6 hours to eat cold, or bake at 190°C/375°F/gas 5 for 1 hour
Pasta dishes	1 month	Bake at 200°C/400°F/ gas 6 for 45 minutes
Paté	1 month	Thaw in refrigerator for 6 hours
Pizza	1 month	Thaw at room temperature for 1 hour. Bake at 190°C/375°F/gas 5 for 20 minutes
Rice dishes	1 month	Heat in double boiler, stirring well and adding additional ingredients
Sauces, savoury (do not freeze if thickened with eggs or cream)	1 month	Heat in double boiler. Taste for seasoning
Sauces, sweet (thickened with cornflour, not flour)	1 month	Heat in double boiler
Soup	2 months	Heat in double boiler
Steamed and baked puddings	2 months	Thaw at room temperature for 2 hours and steam for 45 minutes, or bake from frozen at 190°C/375°F/gas 5 for 45 minutes

Fruit

TYPE OF FOOD	FREEZER STORAGE LIFE	THAWING/ COOKING
Fruit purée, cooked or raw	4 months	Thaw for 3 hours at room temperature
Fruit packed dry with sugar, or in syrup	12 months	Thaw for 3 hours at room temperature or cook while frozen

Fish

TYPE OF FOOD	FREEZER STORAGE LIFE	THAWING/ COOKING
Oily fish	2 months	Thaw large fish in refrigerator; cook small ones from frozen
Shellfish	1 month	Thaw in container in refrigerator and serve cold, or add to cooked dish
Smoked fish	2 months	Thaw in refrigerator to eat cold, or cook from frozen
White fish	3 months	Thaw large fish in refrigerator; cook small ones from frozen

Meat poultry and game

TYPE OF FOOD	FREEZER STORAGE LIFE	THAWING/ COOKING
Cubed and minced meat, offal and giblets	2 months	Thaw in wrappings in refrigerator for 3 hours
Steak, chops and sliced meat	6–12 months	Thaw in refrigerator or cook slowly from frozen
Joints (pork) (lamb and veal) (beef)	6 months 9 months 12 months	Thaw in refrigerator for 4 hours per 500g/1lb
Sausages and sausagemeat	1 month	Thaw in refrigerator for 2 hours
Chicken, guinea-fowl, turkey	12 months	Thaw in wrappings in refrigerator (see page 26 for time chart)
Duck, goose, pheasant, hares, rabbits	6 months	Thaw in wrapping in refrigerator
Ham and bacon (sliced) (joints)	1 month 3 months	Thaw in wrappings in refrigerator

Vegetables

TYPE OF FOOD	FREEZER STORAGE LIFE	THAWING/ COOKING
Vegetable purée	3 months	Heat in double boiler
Avocado pears (mashed with lemon juice)	2 months	Thaw in refrigerator for 3 hours
Courgettes	2 months	Heat from frozen in double boiler
Other vegetables	6–12 months	Cook in boiling water for 8–10 minutes

☆ 9

TYPE OF FOOD	FREEZER STORAGE LIFE	THAWING/ COOKING
Savoury snacks		
Sandwiches (do not remove crusts)	1 month	Thaw at room temperature and remove crusts
Scones and drop scones	2 months	Thaw in wrappings at room temperature for 1 hour. Or bake frozen scones at 180°C/350°F/gas 4 for 10 minutes
Cooked and other prepared dishes		
Casseroles and stews	2 months	Heat in double boiler, or thaw and bake in casserole at 180°C/350°F/gas 4 for 1 hour
Flans, sweet and savoury	2 months	Thaw at room temperature for 3 hours
Ices, sorbets, moulded desserts	3 months	Allow to soften slightly in refrigerator

STORECUPBOARD CHECK LIST

At this time of year more than any other, it is reassuring to add a few of the basic and versatile canned and dry packaged foods to your usual supplies. They are useful when unexpected guests arrive, when you decide to add an unplanned dish to the menu, or have simply run out of freezer and refrigerator space.

Canned and dried goods have a long storage life, and so are not wasted if they do not get used over the holiday. From this comprehensive list, pick out the items you are most likely to need.

Baking ingredients
☐Plain, self-raising and wholewheat flour; ☐other flours such as scofa and granary; ☐bicarbonate of soda; ☐baking powder; ☐cream of tartar; ☐arrowroot; ☐cornflour; ☐pastry, cake and bread mixes; ☐dried yeast.

Beverages
☐Coffee beans or ground coffee; ☐instant coffee; ☐decaffeinated coffee; ☐tea, Indian, Ceylon and other types; ☐a selection of herbal teas; ☐one or two 'bedtime' drinks.

Biscuits and snacks
☐A selection of plain and fancy biscuits including digestive and ginger snaps; ☐a selection of biscuits for cheese; ☐wafers for ice cream; ☐sponge finger biscuits; ☐trifle sponge cakes; ☐crisps, plain and flavoured; ☐potato sticks.

Canned fish and meat
☐Tuna fish; ☐mackerel fillets; ☐pilchards; ☐sardines; ☐anchovies; ☐salmon; ☐ham.

Cereals
☐Have a selection of your family's favourite brands, including muesli, and a packet of variety mini-packs for visitors.

Dairy foods
☐Cream, single, double and soured; ☐yoghurt, plain, Greek-style and flavoured; ☐milk, including UHT; ☐eggs; ☐a selection of hard British cheeses; ☐a selection of blue cheeses; ☐a selection of cream cheeses.

Dried fruits
☐Apricots and prunes; ☐dates and figs; ☐vine fruits – currants, raisins and sultanas.

Fresh fruit and vegetables
☐Apples, dessert and cooking; ☐bananas; ☐clementines; ☐grapefruits; ☐grapes; ☐lemons; ☐oranges; ☐pears.

☐Brussels sprouts; ☐cabbage, green, red and white; ☐carrots; ☐leeks; ☐mushrooms; ☐onions; ☐spinach.

☐Nuts; – almonds, brazils, chestnuts, hazelnuts, pecans, walnuts.

Fruit and vegetables, canned
☐Artichoke hearts; ☐bean sprouts; ☐celery hearts; ☐pimentoes; ☐pulses such as red kidney beans, chick peas, and flageolets; ☐sweetcorn, 'baby'; ☐tomatoes.

☐Cherries, red and black; ☐chestnuts, whole; ☐chestnut purée, unsweetened; ☐grapefruit segments; ☐guavas; ☐mandarin orange slices; ☐mango slices; ☐pineapple cubes and slices.

Oils and vinegars
☐Olive, sunflower and walnut oils; ☐cider, malt, tarragon, red wine and white wine vinegars.

Preserves
☐Clear and set honey; ☐redcurrant, cranberry and mint jellies; ☐marmalade; ☐a selection of mini pots of jam.

Pulses, rice and pasta
☐A selection of dried pulses such as butter beans, haricot beans, red kidney beans (fast-boil them for 10 minutes), flageolets, chick peas,

lentils; ☐long-grain and short-grain white and brown rice; ☐regular, wholewheat or buckwheat spaghetti; ☐regular or wholewheat pasta shapes.

Seasonings

☐Dried herbs such as oregano, mint, rosemary, thyme; ☐ground spices such as cayenne pepper, cinnamon, cloves, ginger, mace, paprika, turmeric; ☐whole spices such as cloves, coriander seeds, nutmeg, cinnamon sticks, ginger root, black and white peppercorns, vanilla pods; ☐sea salt and table salt; ☐lemon juice; ☐vanilla, almond, peppermint and other flavourings; ☐dried onion flakes; ☐garlic paste.

Soups, sauces, stocks

☐Condensed soups such as consommé, mushroom, oxtail and tomato (you can dilute them with stock); ☐meat and yeast extract; ☐a selection of canned or packet sauces such as curry, sweet and sour, chilli; ☐hot pepper sauce; ☐soy sauce; ☐Worcestershire sauce; ☐chicken, meat and vegetable stock cubes.

Sweeteners

☐Artificial sweetener; ☐caster, demerara, granulated, icing and muscovado sugar; ☐coffee crystals.

HOUSEHOLD CHECK LIST

Stock up in plenty of time with all the occasional, heavy and cumbersome household goods you are likely to need. This relieves the pressure on shopping expeditions closer to the holiday, and leaves you more capacity – and energy – to shop for fresh items at the last minute.

Kitchen 'stationery'

☐Aluminium foil; ☐clingfilm; ☐disposable party beakers, plates and dishes; ☐freezer bags; ☐freezer marker pen; ☐freezer tape; ☐kitchen paper roll;☐ greaseproof paper; ☐greaseproof paper bags; ☐non-stick baking powder; ☐paper cake-cases; ☐paper doilies; ☐paper napkins; ☐paper sweet-cases; ☐plastic bags in various sizes; ☐twist ties.

Electricity needs

☐Batteries for torches, radio, camera flash unit and other equipment; ☐electric light bulbs; fairy light bulbs; ☐fuses for appliance and wall plugs; ☐fuses and fuse wire for the electricity circuit.

Household goods

☐Air freshener; ☐borax powder (to remove stains); ☐carpet and upholstery stain remover; ☐cleaning powders and liquids; ☐dishwasher powder; ☐dishwasher rinse liquid; ☐firelighters; ☐furniture polish; ☐household cloths; ☐household soap; ☐lavatory rolls; ☐sink brush; ☐toilet soap; ☐washing-machine powders and liquids; ☐washing-up liquid.

SHOP EARLY

☆ 11

THE CHRISTMAS LARDER

★

As the pace of Christmas activities quickens, it is reassuring to have a larder stocked with preserves, sauces and potted meats to reduce the amount of last-minute cooking and food preparation. These traditional foods have an important role in many of the meals throughout the holiday and several of the suggestions also make perfect Christmas gifts for friends, and popular additions to the home-produce stall at seasonal charity fairs.

MRS BEETON'S
MINCEMEAT

200 g/7 oz cut mixed peel, chopped
200 g/7 oz raisins
200 g/7 oz preserved ginger, chopped
200 g/7 oz cooking apples, grated
200 g/7 oz shredded suet
200 g/7 oz sultanas
200 g/7 oz currants
200 g/7 oz soft light brown sugar
50 g/2 oz blanched almonds, chopped
large pinch each of mixed spice, ground ginger and ground cinnamon
grated rind and juice of 2 lemons and 1 orange
150 ml/¼ pint sherry, brandy or rum

Combine all the ingredients in a large bowl. Cover and leave for two days, stirring occasionally. (This prevents fermentation later.) Pot in sterilised jars, cover with waxed discs and screw-on lids, and label. Store in a cool, dry place.

MAKES ABOUT **1.8 kg/3½ lb**

VEGETARIAN
MINCEMEAT

200 g/7 oz raisins
100 g/4 oz sultanas
100 g/4 oz currants
100 g/4 oz dried apricots, chopped
100 g/4 oz cut mixed peel, chopped
3 × 15 ml spoons/3 tablespoons honey
4 × 15 ml spoons/4 tablespoons brandy
1 × 2.5 ml spoon/½ teaspoon each ground cinnamon, grated nutmeg and salt
200 g/7 oz thick apple purée, fresh, frozen or canned
grated rind and juice of 1 lemon and 1 orange

Combine the dried fruits and peel. Put the remaining ingredients into a small saucepan and bring to the boil slowly. Stir the mixture and pour over the fruits. Mix well and leave to cool.

Pot in sterilised jars, cover with waxed discs and screw-on lids, and label. Store in a cool, dry place for up to three weeks, or in the refrigerator for up to four weeks.

MAKES ABOUT **1 kg/2¼ lb**

QUICK CANDIED PEEL

orange, grapefruit or lemon peel
granulated sugar (see method)
caster sugar (see method)

Scrub the peel with a clean brush. Soak it in cold water overnight to extract some of the bitterness.

Cut the peel into long strips, 5 mm/¼ in wide. Put the strips into a saucepan, cover with cold water and bring slowly to the boil. Drain, add fresh water and bring to the boil again.

Weigh the cooled peel and put into a pan with an equal quantity of granulated sugar. Just cover with boiling water, and boil gently until the peel is tender and clear. Cool, strain and toss the peel in caster sugar on greaseproof paper. Spread on a wire rack to dry for several hours.

Roll the peel again in caster sugar. When completely dry, store in covered jars. Use within three to four months.

Mrs Beeton advised her readers, in a 'seasonable' footnote, to make mincemeat ⟨ about the beginning of December ⟩.

KUMQUAT
CONSERVE

450 g/1 lb kumquats
2 × 15 ml spoons/2 tablespoons salt
450 g/1 lb granulated sugar

Put the kumquats into a saucepan, cover with water and add the salt. Cook gently until the fruit is tender, then drain. Cover with fresh water and leave overnight.

On the following day, put the sugar into a pan with just enough water to dissolve it. Cook over a low heat for 5 minutes without stirring, until a syrup is formed. Drain the fruit carefully, add to the syrup and boil quickly for about 1 hour, taking care to prevent it boiling over.

Test the syrup on a cold saucer for set, and when ready put the conserve into warm, sterilised jars, cover immediately and label. Store in a cool, dry place.   MAKES ABOUT **800 g/1¾ lb**

CRANBERRY &
APPLE JELLY

1 kg/2¼ lb apples
700 g/1½ lb cranberries
granulated sugar (see method)

Slice the apples without peeling or coring, and put into a pan with the cranberries and enough water to cover. Simmer gently until thoroughly mashed. Strain through a scalded jelly bag. Leave to drip for 1 hour.

Measure the extract, return it to the cleaned pan and heat gently. Add the required quantity of sugar (usually about 800 g/1¾ lb for each litre/ 1¾ pints of extract). Stir over a low heat until dissolved, then boil steadily until setting point is reached. To test for this, spoon a little of the syrup on to a cold saucer. Leave to cool, then push a finger over the surface, which should wrinkle. Remove the jelly from the heat and skim. Pot in warm, sterilised jars, cover and label. Store in a cool, dry place.

CRANBERRY SAUCE

125 ml/4½ fl oz water
150 g/5 oz granulated sugar
200 g/7 oz cranberries

Put the water and sugar into a saucepan and stir over a low heat until the sugar has dissolved. Add the cranberries and cook gently for about 10 minutes, until they have burst and are tender. Leave to cool.

Serve with roast turkey, chicken or game.
      MAKES ABOUT **300 ml/½ pint**

APPLE SAUCE

450 g/1 lb apples, sliced
2 × 15 ml spoons/2 tablespoons water
15 g/½ oz butter or margarine
grated rind and juice of ½ lemon
granulated sugar (see method)

Put the apples into a saucepan with the water, butter or margarine and lemon rind. Cover and cook over a low heat until the apple is reduced to a pulp. Beat until smooth, and rub through a sieve or purée in a blender. Reheat the sauce with the lemon juice and sugar to taste.

Serve hot or cold with roast goose, duck or pork. Sweetened apple sauce is also delicious served with steamed puddings.
      MAKES ABOUT **375 ml/13 fl oz**

PRUNE SAUCE

200 g/7 oz prunes
250 ml/8 fl oz water
strip of lemon rind
25 g/1 oz sugar
pinch of ground cinnamon
1 × 15 ml spoon/1 tablespoon rum or brandy (optional)
lemon juice to taste

Soak the prunes in the water overnight. Put them into a saucepan with the lemon rind and cook gently until tender. Remove the stones and lemon rind. Rub the prunes through a sieve or purée in a blender until smooth. Reheat and add the sugar, cinnamon, rum or brandy if used, and lemon juice to taste.

Serve hot or cold with roast goose, pork, venison or mutton. The sauce is also good with steamed apple pudding.
      MAKES ABOUT **375 ml/13 fl oz**

RAISIN SAUCE

75 g/3 oz soft dark brown sugar
25 g/1 oz flour
1 × 15 ml spoon/1 tablespoon mustard powder
salt and pepper
350 ml/12 fl oz boiling water
4 × 15 ml spoons/4 tablespoons vinegar
50 g/2 oz raisins
25 g/1 oz butter

Mix the dry ingredients in the top of a double saucepan or in a bowl placed over simmering water. Stir in the boiling water and the vinegar gradually to prevent lumps forming. Cook slowly for 15–20 minutes. Add the raisins, and continue to cook for 5 minutes. Beat in the butter a little at a time.

Serve hot, with ham or pork.
      MAKES ABOUT **400 ml/¾ pint**

CHESTNUT SAUCE

200 g/7 oz chestnuts
375 ml/13 fl oz chicken stock
pinch of ground cinnamon
strip of lemon rind
25 g/1 oz butter
salt and pepper
5 × 15 ml spoons/5 tablespoons single cream

Make a slit in the rounded side of the chestnut shells, and boil or bake (page 20) them for 15–20 minutes. Remove the shells and skins while hot.

Put the chestnuts into a saucepan with the stock, cinnamon and lemon rind. Simmer gently for 30 minutes, or until the chestnuts are very tender. Remove the lemon rind.

Rub the chestnuts and the liquid through a sieve, or purée in a blender. Return the purée to the pan, add the butter, and season to taste. Stir in the cream just before serving.

Serve hot, with roast turkey or chicken.

MAKES ABOUT **375 ml/13 fl oz**

ANCHOVY BUTTER

100 g/4 oz unsalted butter, softened
8 anchovy fillets
1 × 2.5 ml spoon/½ teaspoon lemon juice
black pepper

Cream the butter until light. Pound the anchovy fillets to a paste, or purée them in a blender with a little of the butter. Beat the anchovies into the creamed butter, and add the lemon juice, a few drops at a time, to avoid curdling. Season to taste with pepper.

Leave to stand at room temperature for at least 30 minutes before using, so that the flavour matures.

Press the butter into small pots and store in the refrigerator, but do not freeze.

Serve on toast as canapés, or on grilled fish or steak.

MAKES ABOUT **125 g/5 oz**

CUMBERLAND RUM BUTTER

100 g/4 oz soft light brown sugar
100 g/4 oz unsalted butter, softened
2 × 15 ml spoons/2 tablespoons rum
1 × 2.5 ml spoon/½ teaspoon grated orange rind
pinch of grated nutmeg

Beat the sugar into the butter gradually until well blended. Beat in the rum, a few drops at a time, taking care not to allow the mixture to separate. Stir in the orange rind and the nutmeg.

Pile the butter into a dish and leave to become firm before serving. If storing in the refrigerator, bring the butter to room temperature before using.

MAKES ABOUT **250 g/8 oz**

BRANDY BUTTER

200 g/7 oz caster sugar
100 g/4 oz unsalted butter, softened
1–2 × 15 ml spoons/1–2 tablespoons brandy

Beat the sugar into the butter gradually until the mixture is pale and light. Beat in the brandy to taste, a few drops at a time, taking care not to allow the mixture to separate.

Chill before using. If the mixture has separated slightly after standing, beat well before serving.

If liked, a stiffly whisked egg white can be stirred into the mixture to give a softer texture.

MAKES ABOUT **325 g/11 oz**

ORANGE BUTTER

2 oranges
4 sugar lumps
175 g/6 oz unsalted butter, softened
about 25 g/1 oz caster sugar
1 × 15 ml spoon/1 tablespoon orange juice
4 × 5 ml spoons/4 teaspoons orange-flavoured liqueur (optional)

Pare the rind of the oranges and grind or grate it with the sugar lumps. Put into a bowl, and work in the butter and caster sugar until well blended. Stir in the juice and liqueur, if using, a few drops at a time, taking care not to allow the mixture to separate, until they have been fully absorbed.

Serve Orange Butter as an alternative to rum or brandy butter. It is especially good with mince pies.

MAKES ABOUT **250 g/8 oz**

THE BOAR'S HEAD – A CHRISTMAS CUSTOM

' *The Boar's head, in ancient times, formed the most important dish on the table, and was invariably the first placed on the board upon Christmas-day, being preceded by a body of servitors, a flourish of trumpets, and other marks of distinction and reverence, and carried into the hall by the individual of next rank to the lord of the feast. At some of our colleges and inns of court, the serving of the boar's head on a silver platter on Christmas-day is a custom still followed; and till very lately, a boar's head was competed for at Christmas time by the young men of a rural parish in Essex.* '

MRS BEETON (1861)

Fresh figs in sherry, clementines in vodka, dried apricots in madeira (all on p.16) and Mrs Beeton's mincemeat (p.12).

CLEMENTINES
IN VODKA

1 kg/2¼ lb clementines
100 g/4 oz caster sugar
600 ml/1 pint water
½ vanilla pod
2 × 15 ml spoons/2 tablespoons orange flower water
300 ml/½ pint vodka

Remove the leaves, stalks and flower-ends from the clementines. Prick them all over with a darning needle – this helps the syrup to penetrate the skins.

Put the sugar, water and vanilla pod in a saucepan over a low heat, and stir occasionally. When the sugar has dissolved, add the clementines, increase the heat, bring to the boil and simmer, uncovered, for about 25 minutes, until the fruit is tender. Remove the vanilla pod.

Drain the fruit, reserving the syrup. Pack the fruit into two warm, sterilised jars. Divide the vodka between them, then fill up the jars with the syrup. Seal the jars and reverse them gently to blend the liquids.

TO STERILISE JARS

Wash and thoroughly rinse jars and drain them well. Immediately before using, put them in the oven at 110°C/225°F/gas ¼ for 10 minutes. Alternatively, stand the jars on a trivet in a large saucepan, cover them with cold water, bring to the boil and boil for 5 minutes. Drain well before using.

Store in a cool, dry place. The fruit is at its best when it has matured for at least four weeks.

FILLS TWO (700 g/1½ lb) JARS

DRIED APRICOTS
IN MADEIRA

450 g/1 lb whole dried apricots
100 g/4 oz caster sugar
strip of orange peel
1 litre/1¾ pints water
150 ml/¼ pint medium Madeira
1 × 15 ml spoon/1 tablespoon almond-flavoured liqueur

Put the apricots, sugar, orange peel and water into a saucepan over a low heat, and stir occasionally. When the sugar has dissolved, increase the heat, bring to the boil and boil, uncovered, for 10 minutes. Reduce the heat and simmer for a further 30 minutes.

Drain the fruit, reserving the syrup. Pack the fruit into two warm, sterilised jars. Divide the Madeira and liqueur between them, then fill up with syrup. Seal the jars and reverse them to blend the liquids. Store for at least 2 weeks.

FILLS TWO (450 g/1 lb) JARS

FRESH FIGS
IN SHERRY

12 fresh green or black figs, quartered
100 g/4 oz caster sugar
about 400 ml/¾ pint sweet sherry

Pack the figs into two warm, sterilised jars. Sprinkle on the sugar and pour on enough sherry to cover the fruit. Close the jars and shake them from time to time to dissolve the sugar.

Store the jars in the refrigerator for up to four weeks.

FILLS TWO (350 g/12 oz) JARS

PICKLED PRUNES

450 g/1 lb dried prunes
350 g/12 oz soft light brown sugar
400 ml/¾ pint water
250 ml/8 fl oz cider vinegar
1 × 5 ml spoon/1 teaspoon allspice berries
1 × 5 ml spoon/1 teaspoon whole cloves
1 cinnamon stick
3 × 15 ml spoons/3 tablespoons brandy

Put all the ingredients except the brandy in a saucepan. Bring to the boil slowly, stirring occasionally until the sugar has dissolved. Simmer for about 45 minutes until the fruit is tender and plump.

Lift out the prunes with a perforated spoon and pack them into warm, sterilised jars. Strain the pickling liquid, discarding the spices, and pour over the fruit to cover. Divide the brandy between the jars. Close them and tip them gently to distribute the spirit.

Store in a dry, cool place. Serve with roast goose, duck or pork, or with cold meats.

FILLS TWO (450 g/1 lb) JARS

LONG-TERM STORAGE

Fruits preserved in a blend of syrup and alcohol will keep for several weeks since both the sugar and the fortified wine or spirit act as preservatives.

For longer-term storage, extending the shelf life up to a year, close the preserving jars and, if using screw-on lids, undo them by a quarter-turn. Stand them on a trivet in a large saucepan, cover them with cold water, bring to the boil and boil for 20 minutes. Remove the jars, tighten the lids and leave to cool. Label and store in a cool, dry place.

MRS BEETON'S
PATE MAISON

3 bay leaves
8–10 back bacon rashers, rinds removed
100 g/4 oz pig's liver, trimmed
100 g/4 oz fresh belly of pork, skinned and trimmed
200 g/7 oz cold, cooked rabbit pieces
200 g/7 oz pork sausagemeat
1 onion, chopped
25 g/1 oz fresh white breadcrumbs
1 egg
1 × 15 ml spoon/1 tablespoon milk
5 × 15 ml spoons/5 tablespoons brandy
salt and pepper

Put the bay leaves in the base of a 1.25 litre/2 pint oblong ovenproof dish. Line the dish with the bacon rashers, reserving two or three to cover the top.

Chop the liver, pork and rabbit coarsely and mix with the sausagemeat. Add the onion and breadcrumbs to the mixture. If you have a blender you can process these ingredients to a coarse paste.

Beat together the egg, milk and brandy. Work into the dry ingredients and season to taste.

Turn the mixture into the lined dish, cover with the reserved bacon rashers and then with a lid or foil. Stand the dish in a pan with hot water to come half-way up its sides.

Set the oven at 180°C/350°F/gas 4. Cook the pâté for 1 hour.

When cooked, put a heavy weight on the pâté and leave to cool. To serve, remove the bacon rashers from the top and turn out of the dish.

MAKES ABOUT **1 kg/2¼ lb**

JELLIED
CHICKEN LIVER PATE

100 g/4 oz slightly salted butter
1 small onion, chopped
1 garlic clove, crushed
450 g/1 lb chicken livers, trimmed
3 × 15 ml spoons/3 tablespoons brandy
1 × 15 ml spoon/1 tablespoon port or Madeira
2 × 5 ml spoons/2 teaspoons French mustard
pinch of ground mace
pinch of ground cloves
salt and pepper
about 3 × 15 ml spoons/3 tablespoons aspic jelly or jellied canned consommé

Melt 50 g/2 oz of the butter in a large frying pan, add the onion and garlic and fry gently until softened but not coloured. Add the chicken livers to the pan and fry, turning them frequently, for about 6 minutes until browned but not crisp.

Scrape the contents of the pan into a bowl. Pour the brandy and port or Madeira into the frying pan, stir well and then add to the chicken liver mixture. Add the remaining butter, the mustard and spices and season well. Mash or pound and then sieve the mixture, or purée in a blender to a smooth paste.

Turn the pâté into an earthenware dish or pot, leaving 1 cm/½ in headroom. Cover loosely with greaseproof paper and leave in the refrigerator or a cool place until firm.

Meanwhile, melt the aspic jelly or consommé and let it cool until almost setting. Spoon it over the pâté and leave in the refrigerator or a cool place to set for at least 24 hours.

Serve the pâté the same day, or store it in the freezer.

MAKES ABOUT **1.5 kg/3 lb**

TO CLARIFY BUTTER

Put the butter into a saucepan, heat it gently until it melts, then continue to heat it slowly without browning until all bubbling ceases. This shows the water has been expelled. Remove from the heat and skim off any scum that has risen to the top. After a few minutes gently pour the clear butter into a bowl or jar, discarding the sediment.

Clarified butter is used to seal potted fish, cheese and meats, and to fry and grill fish, chicken, veal and other dishes.

POTTED HERRING FILLETS

2 (200 g/7 oz) cans herring fillets (in any sauce), drained
50 g/2 oz butter
pinch of cayenne
pinch of ground mace
salt and pepper
melted clarified butter

Mash the herring fillets. Melt the butter in a small saucepan and add the fish, spices and seasoning. Stir until heated through but not fried. Cool slightly, then turn into small pots and cover with clarified butter. Leave until the butter is firm, then cover with foil.

Serve as a pâté, on canapés or in sandwiches.

MAKES ABOUT **400 g/14 oz**

POTTED CHEESE

2 eggs
200 g/7 oz strong hard cheese or mixed cheeses, grated
1 × 15 ml spoon/1 tablespoon butter
2 × 15 ml spoons/2 tablespoons prepared mustard
4 × 15 ml spoons/4 tablespoons single cream
pinch of cayenne
salt
melted clarified butter

Beat the eggs until they become liquid. Mix together the cheese, butter, mustard, cream, cayenne and salt to taste. Put the mixture into a saucepan and heat to simmering point slowly. Add the beaten eggs and cook very gently until the mixture thickens.

Turn into a chilled container or small pots, and cool quickly. Cover with clarified butter. Leave the butter to set, then cover with foil.

Terrine of duck, Pâté Maison (p.17) and Potted cheese.

The potted cheese will keep in the refrigerator for two or three weeks. Serve it on canapés, as a sandwich spread or as an after-dinner savoury.

MAKES ABOUT **400 g/14 oz**

★

TERRINE OF DUCK

450 g/1 lb raw boneless duck meat
100 ml/4 fl oz brandy
2 shallots
200 g/7 oz belly of pork, skinned and trimmed
275 g/10 oz raw chicken meat, skinned
shredded rind of 1 orange
pinch each of dried thyme and savory
salt and pepper
3 eggs, beaten
450 g/1 lb streaky bacon rashers, rinds removed
3 bay leaves

Mince or grind the duck meat and put it in a bowl with the brandy. Stir well, cover and leave for 4–5 hours.

Chop the shallots and mince the pork and chicken, or process in a blender. Stir in the orange rind, herbs and seasonings, and finally the eggs. Mix thoroughly.

Line a 1.5 litre/3 pint ovenproof dish with the bacon rashers, reserving enough to cover the top. Press in the meat mixture, level the top and arrange the bay leaves in the centre. Cover with the reserved bacon, then with foil. Stand the dish in a pan of hot water to come half-way up its sides.

Set the oven at 180°C/350°F/gas 4. Cook the terrine for 1 hour, or until it has begun to shrink slightly from the sides of the dish. Remove the foil and the bacon and return the terrine to the oven for 15 minutes to brown it slightly.

Put a weight on the cooked terrine and, when it is cool, store in the refrigerator for at least 12 hours. Serve it, cut in slices, from the dish.

MAKES ABOUT **1.5 kg/3 lb**

CHRISTMAS EVE

★

On Christmas Eve the food preparation needs only the finishing touches, the presents are wrapped and your home has an extra sparkle. It is time to relax with family and friends in anticipation of tomorrow's festivities. Hand- and heart-warming mulled wine and other drinks could be served, perhaps with roasted chestnuts, mince pies, sausage rolls and fancy sandwiches.

MULLED·WINE

500 ml/18 fl oz water
6 cloves
½ cinnamon stick, lightly crushed
pinch of grated nutmeg
thinly pared rind of ½ lemon
1 bottle (70–75 cl/1¼ pt) claret
granulated sugar

Put the water into an enamel or stainless steel saucepan and heat gently; then stir in the spices and lemon rind. Heat to boiling point and simmer for 10 minutes. Strain the liquid into a bowl and add the wine. Sweeten to taste with sugar.

Return the liquid to the pan and heat without boiling. Serve immediately.

FILLS TEN WINE GLASSES

THE CLOVE.

BISHOP

12 cloves
1 large orange
1 bottle (70–75 cl/1¼ pt) port
granulated sugar

Press the cloves into the orange and put it in an ovenproof bowl. Cover tightly with foil.

Set the oven at 180°C/350°F/gas 4. Roast the orange until lightly browned. Cut it into eight pieces and remove the pips.

Pour the port into an enamel or stainless steel saucepan, add the pieces of orange and heat gently to simmering point. Sweeten to taste with sugar and simmer gently for 20 minutes, taking care not to let the liquor boil.

Strain through a fine sieve and serve immediately.　　FILLS TWELVE SHERRY GLASSES

TO SERVE MULLED DRINKS

Mulled wine and other drinks are at their best served piping hot. Serve the drinks in heatproof glasses or in standard glasses which, to avoid breakage, have been warmed. A silver teaspoon placed in each glass in turn as the steaming wine is poured also helps by taking up some of the heat.

MULL.

★

ROASTING CHESTNUTS

Chestnuts, available from October to January, are the perfect fireside snack to serve with drinks. To cook them, prick the skins with a sharp knife to prevent them bursting, spread them on a baking tray and cook them at 220°C/425°F/gas 7 for 10 minutes. More traditionally, put the chestnuts on a trivet or shovel over a glowing fire. Peel the nuts and serve them hot, dipped in salt.

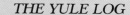

WHISKY PUNCH

thinly pared rind and juice of 3 lemons

1 litre/1¾ pints boiling water

1 bottle (75 cl/1¼ pt) whisky

200 g/7 oz lump sugar

Strain the lemon juice and put it into a bowl with the lemon rind. Pour the boiling water over it, then add the whisky and stir in the sugar. When the sugar has dissolved, strain the liquid and serve at once.

FILLS FIFTEEN WINE GLASSES

THE CHRISTINGLE SERVICE

The special children's Christingle service, which has been customary in Scandinavian and other European countries for over a century, is now being held in an increasing number of British churches. Each child is given an orange pierced with thin sticks bearing sweets, and a candle to symbolise the light which Christ brought to the world.

SPIRITUOUS

❛ PUNCH: – Punch is a beverage made of various spirituous liquors or wine, hot water, the acid juice of fruits, and sugar. It is considered to be very intoxicating; but this is probably because the spirit, being partly sheathed by the mucilaginous juice and the sugars, its strength does not appear to the taste so great as it really is. ❜

MRS BEETON (1861)

NON-ALCOHOLIC
FRUIT PUNCH

1 litre/1¾ pints red grape juice

thinly pared rind and juice of 3 oranges

6 cloves

4 cm/1½ in piece cinnamon stick, lightly crushed

granulated sugar

2 eating apples, thinly sliced

Put the grape juice, orange rind and juice and spices into an enamel or stainless steel saucepan and heat to boiling point. Simmer over a low heat for 10 minutes. Add the sugar and stir occasionally until it has dissolved. Strain the liquid and discard the orange rind and spices.

Add the apple slices, and serve immediately.

FILLS TEN WINE GLASSES

THE YULE LOG

Christmas Eve was traditionally the day for hauling in the Yule Log. The wood had been cut down some time in advance and left to dry. The log – usually ash in England and birch in Scotland – was lit in the hearth from a piece saved from the previous year. It was the custom in many households for the lady of the house to keep the kindling piece under her pillow, as a year-round precaution against fire.

THE CHRISTMAS DINNER

★

The menu is a comprehensive one, offering the host or hostess a wide choice of dishes within the traditional framework, and the meal will be a long and relaxed one. Set the scene for the occasion by arranging the table as attractively as possible, following the general guidelines given here and adding your own individual touches with candles and flowers.

CHRISTMAS DINNER

★

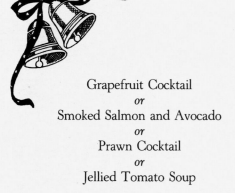

Grapefruit Cocktail
or
Smoked Salmon and Avocado
or
Prawn Cocktail
or
Jellied Tomato Soup

★

Mrs Beeton's Roast Turkey
with Savoury Stuffings, Bacon Rolls and
a Selection of Sauces
or
Roast Goose with Prune Stuffing
and Sage and Onion Forcemeat Balls
or
Mrs Beeton's Roasts Ribs of Beef
with Yorkshire Pudding and Horseradish Cream
or
A selection of Savoury Vegetarian Dishes

★

Brussels Sprouts with Chestnuts
Glazed Carrots
Green Peas with Bacon
Braised Celery

★

Lemon Sorbet

★

Rich Boiled Christmas Pudding
or
Standard Plum Pudding
or
Vegetarian Plum Pudding
with
Pouring Cup Custard
or
Sweet Mousseline Sauce

★

Mince Pies
with Cumberland Rum Butter
or
Orange Butter

★

Oranges in Caramel Sauce
or
Glacé Fruit Bombe

★

Cheeseboard

★

Petits Fours

★

Liqueurs

★

Coffee

★

LAYING THE TABLE

Arrange the cutlery and glasses well ahead of the meal, polishing each piece with a soft, dry cloth as you put it in position so that every item sparkles in the lamp or candlelight.

Allow, if possible, 50–60 cm/20–24 in for each place setting, measuring from the centre of one plate to the centre of the next. Lay the knives, blades pointing inwards, on the right of the setting and the forks on the left, in the order in which they will be used. The first to be used will therefore be on the extreme right or left, and the last next to the plate.

The soup spoon, if soup is to be served, is placed on the outside right, next to the fish knife or meat knife. The dessert spoon and fork can either be laid in neat alignment across the top of the setting, with the spoon handle to the right and the fork handle to the left, or at the side of the plate, spoon on the right and fork on the left; either arrangement is correct.

Fruit knives and forks can be laid across the top of the setting with the dessert spoon and fork, or at the side. Alternatively – and if space is limited – they can be handed round with the dessert plates.

The small knife for bread may be placed next to the dinner plate, on the right-hand side, or vertically across the side plate, which should be on the left of the place setting.

Line up the cutlery as neatly and closely together as practical, with the handles about 1 cm/½ in from the edge of the table.

Allow one cruet set for each four places and the same number of butter dishes, each with its own small butter-knife.

PLACING THE GLASSES

Glasses should be arranged in a straight line across the top of the right-hand cutlery, in the order of use; for example, a glass for white wine on the right, then one for red, and a port or liqueur glass on the left. If you include a tumbler

The evergreen wreath (p.106), homemade cracker (p.130) and fanned napkin (p.120) all add to the festive dining table.

or stemmed glass for water, place this before the liqueur glass. The last glass should be placed just above the meat knife.

If you are using just one wine glass, place it anywhere above the right-hand cutlery.

THE MENU

If someone in the family is able to write artistically, or to set out a typewritten page decoratively, why not provide a menu for the meal? Guests may not only like to see the bill of fare – and leave space for the courses to follow; they may also like to take home the menu as a memento of a happy occasion.

Equally, if yours is to be a large dinner party, it is a good idea to place a small name card at each place setting. This obviates the need for the frantic 'now, who goes where?' thought process as guests move towards the table.

THE FIRST COURSE

★

Repared in advance and waiting in the refrigerator, the first course of your Christmas dinner should be – in terms of quantity – little more than a token. Make it easy to serve, light, refreshing and, most of all, appetising. Here is a selection of delicious and simple dishes to whet your appetite as you plan your meal of the year.

JELLIED TOMATO SOUP

1 large honeydew melon
400 ml/¾ pint chicken stock
4 spring onions, trimmed and chopped
5–6 celery leaves, chopped
500 ml/18 fl oz tomato juice
few drops of Worcestershire sauce
4 cloves
pinch of granulated sugar
1 × 5 ml spoon/1 teaspoon lemon juice
salt
cayenne
4 × 15 ml spoons/4 tablespoons water
2 × 15 ml spoons/2 tablespoons gelatine
80 ml/3 fl oz soured cream
mint sprigs to garnish

Remove the seeds from the melon and scoop out the flesh with a ball scoop. Chill the melon balls and the chicken stock.

Put the chopped spring onions and celery leaves into a saucepan with the tomato juice, Worcestershire sauce, cloves, sugar and lemon juice. Season with salt and cayenne, half-cover the pan and simmer for 10 minutes. Strain the liquid into a bowl.

Put the water in a basin and sprinkle the gelatine into the liquid. Stand the basin over a

pan of hot water and stir the gelatine until it has dissolved completely. Add a little of the tomato liquid and stir well. Pour the gelatine mixture into the remaining tomato liquid and mix well. Add the chilled chicken stock, stir well, and leave to set.

To serve, whisk the jellied soup until frothy. Pour into a chilled bowl and gently stir in the melon balls. Swirl on the soured cream and garnish with mint.   SERVES EIGHT

GRAPEFRUIT COCKTAIL

4 large, firm grapefruit
¼ ripe Charentais or Ogen melon
1 (225 g/8 oz) can pineapple cubes, drained
2 oranges, peeled and segmented
8 maraschino cherries, halved
caster sugar
80 ml/3 fl oz medium-dry sherry
8 mint sprigs

Cut the grapefruit in half crossways and remove the pips. Snip out the cores with scissors. Cut out the segments, reserving the shells, and cut away the membranes.

Put the flesh in a bowl. Cut the melon flesh into 2 cm/¾ in cubes. Add the melon, pineapple and orange to the grapefruit flesh, sweeten if desired and stir in the sherry. Cover and chill before serving.

Pile the fruit into the reserved grapefruit shells. Brush the mint with a little juice from the fruit, sprinkle lightly with sugar and use to garnish. Serve chilled.   SERVES EIGHT

SMOKED SALMON
& AVOCADO

shredded lettuce leaves
225 g/8 oz thinly sliced smoked salmon, cut into finger strips
2 large, ripe avocados, stoned, peeled, sliced and tossed in lemon juice
bunch of watercress sprigs
2 lemons, quartered
snipped chives to garnish

Arrange the lettuce leaves to cover a serving dish. Make a wheel pattern with the avocado slices and smoked salmon fingers. Arrange the watercress around the outside and the lemon quarters in the centre. Sprinkle with chives to garnish.   SERVES EIGHT

★

'THE MELON: — This is another species of the cucumber, and is highly esteemed for its rich and delicious fruit. It was introduced to this country from Jamaica, in 1570; since which period it has continued to be cultivated. It was formerly called Musk Melon.'
MRS BEETON (1861)

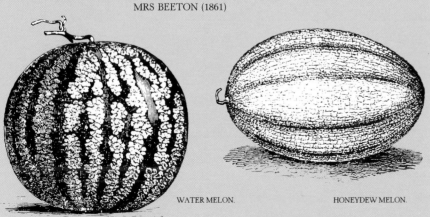

WATER MELON.   HONEYDEW MELON.

PRAWN COCKTAIL

8 lettuce leaves, shredded
150 ml/¼ pint mayonnaise
2 × 15 ml spoons/2 tablespoons tomato purée
large pinch of cayenne or few drops of Tabasco sauce
salt (optional)
2 × 5 ml spoons/2 teaspoons tarragon vinegar (optional)
400 g/14 oz peeled cooked prawns
8 whole cooked prawns to garnish

Place a little shredded lettuce in each of eight individual glass serving dishes. Mix the mayonnaise with the tomato purée, cayenne or sauce and season with salt and vinegar if liked. Stir in the peeled prawns. Taste the sauce and add more seasoning if needed.

Pile the prawn mixture into the glasses and garnish with the whole prawns.

Serve with very thinly sliced brown bread and butter rolled into cylindrical shapes.
SERVES EIGHT

SMOKED SALMON

To serve on its own: Use a good, long, very sharp knife to cut paper-thin slices. Serve it with lemon wedges, cayenne pepper, and brown bread and butter. Alternatively, form thicker slices into cornets, and secure with a cocktail stick if necessary.

★

THE TURKEY
★

As the centrepiece of the Christmas dinner table and the culinary highlight of the season's festivities, the turkey rightly takes pride of place. For this reason, the bird must be cooked to perfection and grandly garnished.

MRS BEETON'S
ROAST TURKEY

1 turkey
stuffing such as Herb Forcemeat (page 28) for neck end
stuffing such as Sausagemeat Stuffing (page 28) or Chestnut Stuffing (page 28) for tail end
salt and pepper
5–6 fat bacon rashers
fat for basting
450 g/1 lb pork chipolatas
watercress to garnish

Wipe the bird inside and out with a clean, damp cloth. Stuff the neck end with a stuffing such as Herb Forcemeat and put the other chosen stuffing inside the body.

Truss the bird (see direction), season the skin all over with salt and pepper and lay the bacon rashers over the breast.

Set the oven at 220°C/425°F/gas 7. Melt the fat in a roasting tin, place the bird in the tin and roast for 15–20 minutes, then reduce the heat to 180°C/350°F/gas 4. (For the overall cooking time, see chart.)

Separate the chipolatas and prick the skins with a fork or knife-blade. Add them to the fat in the pan about 30 minutes before the end of cooking time.

About 20 minutes before serving, remove the bacon and allow the breast to brown and the skin to become crisp. Test that the bird is cooked. To do this, pierce the thick part of a thigh with a fine skewer. The juices should run clear, and show no trace of pink.

When the bird is cooked, remove the trussing string. Place the turkey on a warmed serving dish and garnish with watercress. Surround the bird, if desired, with a selection of baby vegetables, arranging them in neat piles to make a colourful garnish.

Note A 6 kg/13 lb turkey will just fit comfortably into an oven with an interior capacity of 0.07 cubic metres (42 × 40 × 40 cm)/0.09 cubic yards (16½ × 15¾ × 15¾ in). If the oven is smaller than this, or if you wish to cook a larger bird, it can sometimes be done by removing the legs and cooking them separately. You can reassemble the bird, for the sake of appearance, using fine wooden skewers and perhaps placing a line of small watercress sprigs where the legs are rejoined.

THAWING TIMES FOR A FROZEN TURKEY

It is most important to thaw frozen poultry thoroughly before cooking it. When a large bird is concerned, this means planning well ahead. Remove the turkey from any box and place it, still in the polythene bag, on a large dish. Remove the bird from the bag and extract the giblets and neck as soon as possible – this speeds up thawing. Keep the turkey covered with foil once the bag is removed, to prevent it drying out on the surface.

WEIGHT	Thawed at room temperature 18°C/65°F	Thawed in refrigerator 4°C/40°F
	Hours	*Hours*
2.5–3 kg (5–6 lb)	18–20	40–50
3–3.5 kg (6–8 lb)	20–23	50–60
3.5–4.5 kg (8–10 lb)	23–26	60–66
4.5–5.5 kg (10–12 lb)	26–29	66–70
5.5–7 kg (12–15 lb)	29–31	70–74
7–8 kg (15–17 lb)	31–33	74–78
8–9.5 kg (17–20 lb)	33–35	78–82
9.5–11.5 kg (20–25 lb)	35–40	82–86

ROASTING TIMES FOR TURKEY

Follow this chart of recommended roasting times for a turkey which is cooked with stuffing.

WEIGHT	Cooking time: 15–20 minutes at 220°C/425°F/gas 7 and then at 180°C/350°F/gas 4
	Hours
2.5–3 kg (5–6 lb)	3–3½
3–3.5 kg (6–8 lb)	3½–4
3.5–4.5 kg (8–10 lb)	4–4½
4.5–5.5 kg (10–12 lb)	4½–5
5.5–7 kg (12–15 lb)	5–5½
7–8 kg (15–17 lb)	5½–6
8–9.5 kg (17–20 lb)	6–6½
9.5–11.5 kg (20–25 lb)	6½–7½

TRUSSING THE TURKEY

The purpose of trussing a bird is to make it look attractive and to secure the stuffing.

The easiest way to truss is with a large needle and stout thread. Needles designed specifically for trussing can be bought at kitchen shops.

Put the bird on its back and hold the legs together to form a V-shape pointing towards the neck end. Insert the threaded needle into one leg, just above the thigh bone; pass it through the body and out at the same point on the other side. Leave plenty of thread on either side.

Turn the bird breast-downwards and carry the thread through the elbow joint of the wing on each side.

Twist the end of the wing under the neck to hold the flap of skin in place; tie the ends of the thread loosely together.

Loop the thread over the ends of the drumsticks and draw them together, tying off round the 'parson's nose'. To make this easier, a slit may be cut in the flesh above the original vent cut and the 'parson's nose' pushed through.

When the bird is trussed, the skin should still be complete if possible, to prevent any fat escaping from the bird during cooking, as this can result in dryness.

QUANTITIES TO ALLOW

When buying a whole turkey, allow 350–450 g/12 oz–1 lb per person for a bird weighing up to 7.5 kg/16 lb; 450–550 g/1–1¼ lb per person for a bird weighing 7.5–10.5 kg/16–23 lb. A larger bird, weighing 10.5–11.5 kg/23–25 lb will give sixteen to twenty generous servings.

Remember that a frozen turkey loses about five per cent of its weight on thawing. If you buy a fresh bird, allow from 1.5 kg/3 lb weight for the head, feet and innards.

The roast turkey complete with bacon rolls (p.29) and brussels sprouts.

HERB FORCEMEAT

200 g/7 oz soft white or brown breadcrumbs
100 g/4 oz shredded suet or melted margarine
large pinch of grated nutmeg
1 × 15 ml spoon/1 tablespoon chopped parsley
1 × 5 ml spoon/1 teaspoon dried mixed herbs
grated rind of 1 lemon
salt and pepper
2 eggs, beaten

Mix the breadcrumbs with the suet or melted margarine. Add the nutmeg, herbs and lemon rind and season to taste. Stir in the beaten egg to bind the mixture.

Use the forcemeat to stuff the neck end of a turkey or (making half the quantity) a chicken. Alternatively form the mixture into 24 or 32 balls and bake at 180°C/350°F/gas 4 for 15–20 minutes, or fry in deep or shallow fat until golden.   MAKES ABOUT **350 g/12 oz**

SAUSAGEMEAT
STUFFING

liver of the turkey, washed and trimmed
1 kg/2¼ lb sausagemeat
100 g/4 oz soft white breadcrumbs
2 × 15 ml spoons/2 tablespoons chopped parsley
2 × 5 ml spoons/2 teaspoons dried mixed herbs
1 × 2.5 ml spoon/½ teaspoon grated nutmeg
1 × 2.5 ml spoon/½ teaspoon ground mace
2 eggs, beaten
salt and pepper

Chop the liver finely and mix it with the sausagemeat and breadcrumbs. Add the herbs and spices and season to taste. Stir in the beaten egg to bind the mixture.

Use to stuff the tail end of a turkey.
          MAKES ABOUT **1.25 kg/2½ lb**

RICE & CRANBERRY
STUFFING

450 g/1 lb long-grain rice, washed and drained
1 litre/1¾ pints chicken stock
200 g/7 oz margarine
2 large onions, chopped
2 × 15 ml spoons/2 tablespoons chopped parsley
1 × 5 ml spoon/1 teaspoon dried thyme
1 × 5 ml spoon/1 teaspoon dried sage
pinch each of ground cloves and grated nutmeg
salt and pepper
350 ml/12 fl oz Cranberry Sauce (page 13)

Put the rice and stock into a large saucepan. Bring to the boil and stir once. Cover the pan and simmer for 15 minutes, or until the rice is tender and the stock has been absorbed. Turn the rice into a bowl.

Melt the margarine in the pan and fry the onion until it is tender. Add the cooked rice, herbs and spices and season to taste. Stir in the Cranberry Sauce. Leave to cool before using.

Use to stuff the tail end of a turkey.
          MAKES ABOUT **1.5 kg/3 lb**

CHESTNUT
STUFFING

800 g/1¾ lb chestnuts or 550 g/1¼ lb shelled or canned chestnuts
125–250 ml/4½–8 fl oz Chicken or Giblet Stock (opposite)
50 g/2 oz butter
1 large mild onion, chopped
salt and pepper
pinch of ground cinnamon
1 × 2.5 ml spoon/½ teaspoon granulated sugar

If using fresh chestnuts, make a slit in the rounded side of their shells and boil them for 20 minutes. Remove the shells and skins while hot.

Put the chestnuts in a pan with just enough stock to cover them. Heat to boiling point, reduce the heat, cover and simmer until the chestnuts are tender. Drain and reserve the stock. Rub the chestnuts through a fine wire sieve into a bowl.

Melt the butter in a small saucepan and fry the onion over moderate heat until translucent but not turning brown. Add to the chestnuts. Season to taste and stir in the cinnamon and sugar. Stir in just enough of the reserved stock to make a soft stuffing.

Use to stuff the neck or tail end of a turkey, and place another stuffing in the body.
          MAKES ABOUT **800 g/1¾ lb**

QUANTITIES OF STUFFING FOR TURKEY

This table gives a rough guide to the total weight of stuffing – a choice, perhaps, of a herb forcemeat and a chestnut and sausagemeat stuffing – appropriate for turkeys of varying weights.

WEIGHT	Total quantity of stuffing
2.5–3 kg (5–6 lb)	300–350 g (10–12 oz)
3–3.5 kg (6–8 lb)	350–450 g (12 oz–1 lb)
3.5–4.5 kg (8–10 lb)	450–550 g (1–1¼ lb)
4.5–5.5 kg (10–12 lb)	550–700 g (1¼–1½ lb)
5.5–7 kg (12–15 lb)	700 g–1 kg (1½–2¼ lb)
7–8 kg (15–17 lb)	1–1.25 kg (2¼–2½ lb)
8–9.5 kg (17–20 lb)	1.25–1.5 kg (2½–3 lb)
9.5–11.5 kg (20–25 lb)	1.5–2 kg (3–4 lb)

The exact quantity of stuffing required will vary to some extent with the type of stuffing. One uses less of a light fluffy stuffing which needs room to swell than of a dense mixture such as sausagemeat. As a general guide 700 g/1½ lb sausagemeat and 450 g/1 lb forcemeat will stuff an average-sized 6 kg/13 lb turkey.

DO'S AND DON'TS

You can make any stuffing a day or two in advance and store it in a covered container in the refrigerator, or further ahead if you freeze it.

When making stuffing just before you need to use it, always allow it to cool completely before packing it into the turkey or other bird.

It is recommended that you pack the stuffing into the bird immediately before cooking. It is not advisable, for reasons of health and hygiene, to stuff the bird the day before.

BACON ROLLS

Cut the rinds from streaky bacon rashers, cut each rasher in half crossways and roll up. To fry, secure the outer end with a wooden toothpick inserted along each roll. To grill, thread the rolls on short skewers. Put in a dry frying pan or under a moderate grilling heat, and fry or grill for 3–5 minutes, turning frequently, until crisp.

Allow two bacon rolls (2 half-rashers) per person.

CHESTNUT SAUCE

200 g/7 oz chestnuts
375 ml/13 fl oz chicken stock
pinch of ground cinnamon
small strip of lemon rind
25 g/1 oz butter
salt and pepper
5 × 15 ml spoons/5 tablespoons single cream (optional)

Make a slit in the rounded side of the chestnut shells and boil them for 20 minutes. Remove the shells and skins while hot. Put the chestnuts in a saucepan with the stock, cinnamon, and lemon rind. Heat to simmering point, and simmer gently for 30 minutes or until the chestnuts are very tender. Remove the lemon rind.

Rub the chestnuts and the liquid through a sieve, or purée in a blender. Return the purée to the pan, add the butter, and season to taste. Heat gently for 2–3 minutes. Stir in the cream, if used, just before serving.

MAKES ABOUT 375 ml/13 fl oz

GIBLET STOCK

1 set of giblets, washed and trimmed
2 onions, quartered
1 carrot, trimmed and quartered
1 celery stick, thickly sliced
2 bay leaves
6 peppercorns
salt (optional)
600 ml/1 pint water

Put all the ingredients into a saucepan and heat to boiling point. Cover the pan, reduce the heat and simmer gently for 1 hour.

Leave the stock to cool slightly, then, using a large spoon, skim off the fat. Strain the stock, cool and chill until required.

MAKES ABOUT 500 ml/18 fl oz

THICKENED GRAVY

pan juices
2 × 15 ml spoons/2 tablespoons plain flour
500 ml/18 fl oz hot water from cooking vegetables, or Giblet Stock (above)
6–8 × 15 ml spoons/6–8 tablespoons red wine (optional)
2 × 15 ml spoons/2 tablespoons red currant jelly
salt (optional)
pepper

After roasting the turkey, pour off most of the fat from the roasting tin, leaving 5 × 15 ml spoons/5 tablespoons of fat and sediment in the tin. Sift the flour over the fat and blend thoroughly with the pan juices. Stir and cook until browned.

Gradually add the hot liquid, stirring all the time and stir until boiling. Boil for 3–4 minutes. Stir in the wine if used, and the red currant jelly. Season with salt if needed (this will depend on the saltiness of the stock used) and pepper.

Strain the gravy into a warmed gravy-boat, and serve very hot. Stir well just before serving.

MAKES ABOUT 600 ml/1 pint

BREAD SAUCE

450 ml/¾ pint milk
1 large onion, about 200 g/7 oz, chopped
3 cloves
blade of mace
6 peppercorns
2 allspice berries
2 bay leaves
75 g/3 oz dried white breadcrumbs
2 × 15 ml spoons/2 tablespoons butter
salt and pepper
3 × 15 ml spoons/3 tablespoons single cream (optional)

Heat the milk very slowly in a saucepan with the onion, spices and bay leaves. Cover the pan and infuse over a gentle heat for 30 minutes. Strain the liquid and return it to the pan.

Stir in the breadcrumbs and butter and season to taste. Heat to just below simmering point and maintain that temperature for 20 minutes. Stir in the cream, if used.

Serve with the turkey, or with roast chicken.

MAKES ABOUT 450 ml/¾ pint

CARVING A TURKEY

As Mrs Beeton noted in her *Book of Household Management* (1861), the only art in carving a turkey consists 'in getting from the breast as many fine slices as possible; and all must have remarked the very great difference in the large number of people whom a good carver will find slices for, and the comparatively few that a bad carver will succeed in serving.'

These instructions may also be used for carving chicken, capon and guinea-fowl.

1 Insert a carving fork firmly in the breast of the bird. On each side, make a downward cut with a sharp knife between the thigh and the body, then turn the blade outwards so that the joint is exposed. Cut through it with either poultry shears or a sharp carving knife. Put the legs to one side.

2 With the fork still inserted in the breast, remove the wings by cutting widely, but not too deeply, over the adjacent part of the breast, to give the wing enough meat without depriving the breast of too much flesh.

3 The breast can be sliced from the carcass as a whole. Alternatively, it can be separated from the back by cutting through the rib bones with poultry shears or a sharp knife.

Carve the brown meat off the legs, if liked, working downwards in thin slices, following the direction of the bone.

To complete the carving of a large bird whose breast and back have been separated, place the back on the dish with the rib bones facing downwards; press the knife firmly across the centre of it, and raise the neck end at the same time with the fork to divide the back into two.

4 Remove the two 'oysters' (choice morsels of dark-coloured flesh) from the shallow hollows beside the thigh sockets. To do this, the tail part of the back must be stood on end and held firmly with the fork.

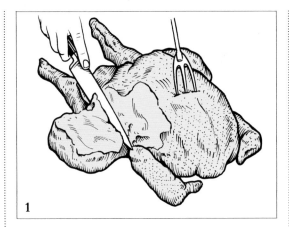

1

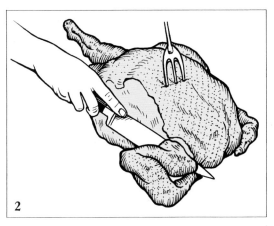

2

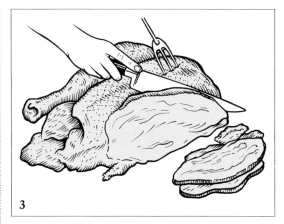

3

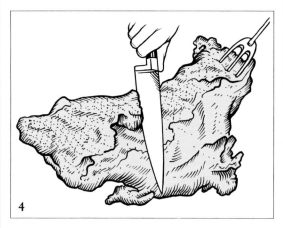

4

TO CARVE A LARGE TURKEY

1 Holding the bird steady with one carving fork, use a second one to bend each leg outwards and downwards, exposing the joint. Cut through it with poultry shears or a sharp carving knife. Put the legs to one side. Remove the wings in the same way. Do not take off any breast meat with the wing joints.

2 Carve the breast meat on the carcass, cutting downwards, parallel with the breastbone.

3 The legs (thighs and drumsticks) should be carved downwards in thin slices, following the direction of the bone. Alternatively, the drumsticks can be reserved for another meal. Serve both white and dark meat to each person, together with a portion of each of the stuffings.

4 To obtain these, slit the skin vertically down the centre of the vent and neck ends, open out the slits and serve the stuffings with a spoon.

5 When the breast meat has been cleared, remove any remaining stuffing to a warmed plate. Detach the wishbone. With the knife or shears, cut horizontally all round the bird through the thinnest part of the rib bones, and lift off the top part of the carcass. Turn the bird over, and carve any remaining meat off the back and sides parallel with the bone.

> **ENGLISH TURKEYS:** — *These are reared in great numbers in Suffolk, Norfolk, and several other counties, whence they were wont to be driven to the London market in flocks of several hundreds; the improvements in our modes of travelling now, however, enable them to be brought by railway. Their drivers used to manage them with great facility, by means of a bit of red rag tied to the end of a long stick, which, from the antipathy these birds have to that colour, effectually answered the purpose of a scourge.*
>
> MRS BEETON (1861)

In a clockwise direction: *bacon rolls (p.29), bread sauce (p.29), rice and cranberry stuffing (p.28), glazed carrots (p.76), chestnut stuffing (p.28), sage and onion forcemeat (p.32), and brussels sprouts with chestnuts (p.38).*

☆ 31

ALTERNATIVES TO TURKEY

★

Goose has a strong claim to being the traditional favourite Christmas bird, and many people prefer the very special quality of its succulent meat to turkey. Alternatively, Christmas is the perfect occasion to serve a big, mouth-watering joint of beef such as sirloin or forerib. And, if you are catering for a vegetarian, the wide variety of fresh vegetables now available at Christmas makes this easy.

ROAST GOOSE
WITH PRUNE STUFFING

1 large goose, with giblets
1 onion, quartered
1 litre/1¾ pints water
½ lemon
salt and pepper
350 g/12 oz prunes, soaked and drained
450 g/1 lb cooking apples, roughly chopped
1 × 15 ml spoon/1 tablespoon flour
2 × 15 ml spoons/2 tablespoons red currant jelly

Simmer the giblets and onion in the water until reduced by half. Strain, skim the fat from the top and set the stock aside.

Weigh the goose and calculate the cooking time at 20 minutes for every 450 g/1 lb. Cut away any visible excess fat. Rinse the inside of the bird, rub the skin with lemon and season with salt and pepper. Prick all over the skin many times with a darning needle.

Stone and chop the prunes. Mix with the apple and season. Pack the fruit into the bird.

Set the oven at 230°C/450°F/gas 8.

Place the goose on a trivet in a roasting tin in the oven. Reduce the temperature immediately to 180°C/350°F/gas 4, and cook for the calculated time.

When the goose is cooked, remove it to a heated serving dish and drain the fat, retaining the juices in the pan. Stir in the flour, gradually pour on the reduced giblet stock, bring to the boil, and stir in the red currant jelly. Season to taste.

Serve with Apple Sauce (page 13) and Sage and Onion Forcemeat Balls (right).

SERVES SIX TO EIGHT

The Cravat Goose

TO CARVE GOOSE

The breast – considered by far the tastiest meat – is carved in thick, wedge-shaped slices. Make the first cut down along the breastbone and, with the blade of the knife slanted slightly towards the centre, make a series of cuts down the breast, parallel to the first cut. Remove the slices by cutting upwards towards the breastbone.

If the bird is large, carve only the breast and save the legs and wings for cold or re-heated dishes.

★

SAGE & ONION
FORCEMEAT

2 small onions, sliced
4 young sage leaves or 1 × 2.5 ml spoon/½ teaspoon dried sage
100 g/4 oz soft white breadcrumbs
50 g/2 oz butter or margarine
salt and pepper
1 egg, beaten (optional)

Put the sliced onions into a saucepan with a little water and parboil. Drain and chop the onions finely. Scald the fresh sage leaves, if used, and chop them finely. Mix the chosen sage together with the onions and breadcrumbs. Melt the butter, add to the stuffing and season to taste. Mix thoroughly.

If the stuffing is to be shaped into forcemeat balls and fried in deep or shallow fat, add enough beaten egg to bind the mixture and shape it into balls.   MAKES ABOUT **175 g/6 oz)**

ROAST BEEF

| a joint of sirloin of beef |
| salt and pepper |
| beef dripping (about 25 g/1 oz per 450 g/1 lb of meat) |

Weigh the meat to calculate the cooking time, and select the method of roasting – quick or slow roasting (see below). Tie the meat into a neat shape if the butcher has not already done so, and wipe and trim.

Place the joint, fat side up, on a wire rack in a shallow roasting tin. Season the meat, and rub or spread it with dripping. Place the roasting tin in the oven and cook for the required time, basting the joint occasionally.

Transfer the cooked meat to a warmed serving dish, remove any string and secure with a metal skewer if necessary. Keep hot. Drain off the fat from the roasting tin and make a gravy from the pan juices in the tin.

Serve with Yorkshire Pudding (page 36) and Horseradish Cream (page 36).

TO CARVE A SIRLOIN OF BEEF

To carve a sirloin on the bone, first cut out the fillet or undercut and carve it into slices.

Then turn the sirloin over, so that it rests on the bone, and carve the meat across the width of the joint and straight down towards the blade of the bone. These slices are thicker than those from a boneless joint.

To carve a boned and rolled sirloin, cut a thick slice first from the outside of the joint leaving the surface smooth; then carve thin, even slices.

ROASTING TIMES

JOINT	Quick Roasting: 230°C/450°F/gas 8 reducing to 190°C/ 375°F/gas 5, after 10 minutes	Slow Roasting: 170°–180°C, 325°–350°F gas 3–4	Meat thermometer temperatures
Beef (with bone)	15 minutes per 450 g/1 lb, plus 15 minutes extra	25 minutes per 450 g/1 lb, plus 25 minutes extra	rare – 60°C/140°F
Beef (without bone, rolled)	20 minutes per 450 g/1 lb, plus 20 minutes extra	30 minutes per 450 g/1 lb, plus 30 minutes extra	medium – 68–70°C/ 154–158°F well-done – 75–77°C/ 167–171°F

THE GOOSE.

' The turkey is good, and the capon's fine,
The partridge is quite to my taste;
Off a couple of fowls I sometimes dine,
Or pigeons baked in a paste;
But not one of these could me induce
To forsake my favourite fat roast goose.

Stuff her with onion, mixed with sage,
Nicely baste and carefully roast,
Serve with brown gravy and apple sauce
And let me dine as a guest or host;
Let me be both, it will better suit me,
For a goose and I are good company. '

MRS BEETON'S CHRISTMAS ANNUAL (1868),
"Moralities in Rhyme"

MRS BEETON'S
ROAST RIBS OF BEEF

2.5 kg/5 lb forerib of beef
flour for dredging
50–75 g/2–3 oz clarified dripping
salt and pepper

Ask the butcher to trim the ends of the rib bones so that the joint will stand upright. Wipe but do not salt the meat. Dust lightly with flour.

Set the oven at 230°C/450°F/gas 8. Melt 50 g/ 2 oz of the dripping in a roasting tin and roast the joint for 10 minutes. Baste well, reduce the heat to 180°C/350°F/gas 4, and continue to roast for 1¾ hours for rare meat, or 2¼ hours for well-done meat. Baste frequently during cooking, using extra dripping if required.

When cooked, salt the meat lightly. Transfer the joint to a warmed serving dish. Pour off most of the fat in the roasting tin, leaving a sediment. Pour in enough water to make a thin gravy, then heat to boiling point, stirring all the time. Season with salt and pepper. Strain the gravy into a warmed gravy-boat.   SERVES SIX TO EIGHT

MERRY ENGLAND

❛ *The fire, with well-dried logs supplied,*
Went roaring up the chimney wide;
The huge hall-table's oaken face,
Scrubb'd till it shone, the day to grace,
. . . .
While round the merry wassel bowl,
Garnished with ribbons, blithe did trowl,
There the huge sirloin reek'd; hard by
Plum-porridge stood, and Christmas pie;
Nor fail'ed old Scotland to produce,
At such high tide, her savoury goose. ❜
SIR WALTER SCOTT

Above: Lentil turnovers and peppers with apple (both p.37).

Right: Roast goose with prune stuffing (p.32).

YORKSHIRE PUDDING

100 g/4 oz plain flour
large pinch of salt
1 egg
250 ml/8 fl oz milk
lard or dripping

Sift the flour and salt into a bowl, make a well in the centre and add the egg. Stir in half the milk, gradually working the flour down from the sides. Beat vigorously until the mixture is smooth and bubbly. Stir in the remaining milk.

Set the oven at 220°C/425°F/gas 7. Put a small knob of fat in each deep patty tin and put in the oven until the fat is smoking hot.

Stir the batter just before using, and half-fill the tins. Bake for 20–25 minutes, depending on the depth of the tins.

The puddings should rise high above the tins, and be almost hollow shells. Do not underbake them, or they will collapse as they are taken out of the oven.

MAKES EIGHT TO TWELVE
INDIVIDUAL PUDDINGS

HORSERADISH
CREAM

250 ml/8 fl oz double cream
4 × 15 ml spoons/4 tablespoons fresh grated horseradish
2 × 15 ml spoons/2 tablespoons lemon juice
4 × 5 ml spoons/4 teaspoons caster sugar
1 × 2.5 ml spoon/½ teaspoon prepared mustard
salt and pepper

Whip the cream lightly until semi-stiff. Carefully fold in the other ingredients. Chill until ready to serve.

MAKES ABOUT 300 ml/½ pint

> ❛ HAZEL NUT AND FILBERT:—
> *The common Hazel is the wild, and the Filbert the cultivated state of the same tree. The hazel is found wild, not only in forests and hedges, in dingles and ravines, but occurs in extensive tracts in the more northern and mountainous parts of the country. It was formerly one of the most abundant of those trees which are indigenous in this island.* ❜
>
> MRS BEETON (1861)

SAVOURY
NUT RISSOLES

50 g/2 oz margarine
50 g/2 oz wholemeal flour, plus extra for dusting
250 ml/8 fl oz vegetable stock
salt and pepper
pinch each of dried thyme and powdered sage
1 × 15 ml spoon/1 tablespoon tomato purée
1 × 15 ml spoon/1 tablespoon milk
100 g/4 oz wholemeal breadcrumbs
50 g/2 oz ground hazelnuts
2 × 15 ml spoons/2 tablespoons grated Gruyère cheese
1 egg, lightly beaten
oil for deep frying

Melt the margarine in a saucepan, stir in the flour and cook gently for 4–5 minutes, until lightly coloured. Stir in the stock gradually, and simmer for 5 minutes. Add the seasoning, herbs, tomato purée and milk, and cook for another 5 minutes, stirring gently. Re-season if required.

Remove the pan from the heat and stir in 75 g/3 oz of the breadcrumbs, the nuts and the cheese. Mix well, and leave to cool.

On a floured surface, form the mixture into large cork- or round-shaped pieces. Dip them in the egg, and coat them with the remaining crumbs.

Heat the oil to 180–185°C/350–360°F, when a 2.5 cm/1 in cube of day-old bread will brown in

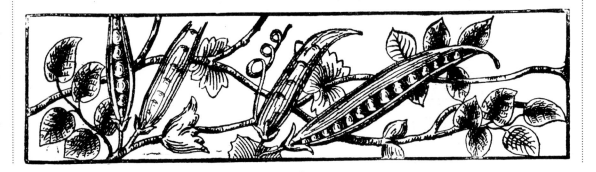

50–55 seconds. Fry the rissoles for 3–4 minutes, until they are golden brown on all sides. Remove them from the oil with a perforated spoon and toss them on absorbent kitchen paper to dry.

SERVES FOUR

VEGETARIAN FORCEMEAT BALLS

1 × 15 ml spoon/1 tablespoon pine kernels, chopped
100 g/4 oz soft wholemeal breadcrumbs
1 × 15 ml spoon/1 tablespoon wholemeal flour
1 × 15 ml spoon/1 tablespoon vegetable cooking fat
1 × 2.5 ml spoon/½ teaspoon chopped parsley
1 × 2.5 ml spoon/½ teaspoon dried mixed herbs
1 × 2.5 ml spoon/½ teaspoon grated lemon rind
salt and pepper
1 egg, beaten
oil for deep frying

Mix together the pine kernels, breadcrumbs, flour, fat, herbs and lemon rind and season to taste. Mix to a stiff paste with the egg and roll into balls.

Heat the oil to 170–175°C/335–345°F and fry for 3–4 minutes until golden brown.

MAKES TWELVE

PARSLEY.

LENTIL TURNOVERS

200 g/7 oz lentils, washed and drained
50 g/2 oz margarine
25 g/1 oz button mushrooms, chopped
25 g/1 oz flour
150 ml/¼ pint vegetable stock
1 × 15 ml spoon/1 tablespoon double cream
Shortcrust Pastry, using 200 g/7 oz flour (page 46)
oil for deep frying

Boil the lentils in unsalted water until soft – the time will depend on the type of lentils used. Drain them, and mash them with 25 g/1 oz of the margarine.

Melt the remaining margarine in a saucepan, add the mushrooms and cook for 1–2 minutes. Stir in the flour, add the stock gradually, and bring to the boil, stirring all the time. Cook for 1–2 minutes. Add the lentils, cream and seasoning. Leave to cool completely.

Roll out the pastry very thinly on a lightly floured surface and cut into eight 12 cm/5 in rounds. Divide the filling between the rounds, moisten the edges, and fold over to form half circles. Press the edges together and seal firmly with your fingertips.

Heat the oil to 180–185°C/350–360°F, when a 2.5 cm/1 in cube of day-old bread will brown in 50–55 seconds. Fry the turnovers for 3–4 minutes, until they are golden brown on all sides. Remove them from the oil with a perforated spoon and toss them on absorbent kitchen paper to dry.

Serve immediately; or cool the turnovers completely, pack them into sealed containers and freeze.

Reheat the turnovers from frozen by frying them again in hot, deep oil, in the oven or the microwave.

SERVES FOUR

PEPPERS WITH APPLE

4 large green peppers
salt
25 g/1 oz margarine, plus extra for greasing
25 g/1 oz wholemeal flour
250 ml/8 fl oz milk
salt and pepper
1 large cooking apple, chopped
100 g/4 oz Gruyère cheese, grated
1 small red pepper, trimmed and chopped
1 large tomato, thickly sliced

Cut the tops from the green peppers, discard the membranes and seeds but keep the caps. Blanch the peppers and caps in boiling, salted water for 3 minutes. Drain them thoroughly.

Melt the margarine in a small saucepan, stir in the flour and cook over gentle heat for 2–3 minutes, stirring constantly. Do not let the flour colour. Draw off the heat and stir in the milk gradually. Return to the heat, bring to the boil and simmer until the sauce thickens, stirring occasionally. Season to taste. Stir in the apple, cheese and red pepper.

Trim the bases of the green peppers so that they stand evenly, but do not cut right through the flesh to make a hole. Spoon the filling into the peppers and replace the caps. Place them in a lightly greased baking dish.

Set the oven at 150°C/300°F/gas 2. Cook the stuffed peppers for 30 minutes. Alternatively, cook them at 180°C/350°F/gas 4 for 25 minutes.

Garnish with the sliced tomato.

SERVES FOUR

VEGETABLES

★

Choose the vegetables you serve with the Christmas dinner as much for their variety of colour and texture as for their flavour. Prepare any chopped bacon, ham and chestnuts in advance and store in small containers in the refrigerator, and have well flavoured stock ready for braising vegetables. Then there will be no temptation, on the day, to serve vegetables 'just boiled' after all! Remember to omit all meat trimmings, and use only vegetable stock, when cooking for vegetarians.

BRUSSELS SPROUTS
WITH CHESTNUTS

1 kg/2¼ lb Brussels sprouts
salt
12–16 cooked chestnuts (page 20), or canned chestnuts, drained
75 g/3 oz cooked ham, chopped
4 × 15 ml spoons/4 tablespoons single cream
salt and pepper

Cut a slice off the base of each sprout and remove outer leaves. Wash the sprouts thoroughly. To cook large sprouts more quickly and evenly, cut a cross in the base.

To boil sprouts, add a few at a time to the minimum amount of boiling, salted water to ensure that the water does not leave the boil. Cook for 5–7 minutes according to size, or until they are just tender. Do not overcook – sprouts readily lose nutrients, colour, texture and flavour. Drain thoroughly.

Cut each chestnut into quarters. Put the sprouts, chestnuts and ham into a casserole. Stir in the cream and season with salt and pepper.

Set the oven at 180°C/350°F/gas 4. Cover the sprouts and cook for 15 minutes.

Alternatively, if oven space is limited, put all the ingredients into a saucepan, cover and simmer very gently for 15 minutes.

Serve immediately.

Note For extra flavour, you can boil the sprouts in chicken or vegetable stock. Drain, and reserve the stock for soup or a sauce.

SERVES SIX TO EIGHT

CHESTNUT.

' ORIGIN OF THE CARROT: — *In its wild state, this vegetable is found plentifully in Britain, both in cultivated lands and by waysides, and is known by the name of birds-nest, from its umbels of fruit becoming incurved from a hollow cup, like a birds-nest . . . when cultivated, it is reddish, thick, fleshy, with a pleasant odour, and a peculiar, sweet, mucilaginous taste.* '

MRS BEETON (1861)

CARROTS
WITH LEEKS

450 g/1 lb carrots
350 g/12 oz leeks
50 g/2 oz butter
large pinch of salt
150 ml/¼ pint medium-dry cider
4 × 15 ml spoon/4 tablespoons double cream

Top and tail, and scrape the carrots, then cut them into slices. Trim, slice and thoroughly wash the leeks.

Heat the butter in a saucepan. Add the carrots, leeks, salt and cider. Cook gently without a lid, for 12–15 minutes, or until the carrots and leeks are tender, shaking the pan frequently to ensure the vegetables are evenly cooked and don't stick to the bottom of the pan.

Remove the vegetables with a perforated spoon and keep them warm. Boil the liquid rapidly for about a minute, then remove the pan from the heat and stir in the cream. Replace the vegetables and turn them in the sauce until they are thoroughly coated. Put in a warmed serving dish.

SERVES SIX TO EIGHT

★

GREEN PEAS
WITH BACON

2 streaky bacon rashers, without rind, chopped

700 g/1½ lb fresh shelled or frozen peas

25 g/1 oz butter

½ small onion, finely chopped

1 × 5 ml spoon/1 teaspoon flour

250 ml/8 fl oz chicken or vegetable stock

pinch of granulated sugar

pinch of grated nutmeg

salt and pepper

Fry the bacon in a non-stick frying pan until it is crisp and dry. Remove from the pan and set aside.

Boil or steam the peas until they are just tender. Melt the butter in a pan and fry the onion gently until golden. Stir in the flour and cook, stirring constantly, for 1 minute. Add the bacon, peas, stock, sugar and nutmeg. Cover the pan and simmer gently for 10 minutes. Season to taste before serving.   SERVES SIX TO EIGHT

‘ SAVOYS AND BRUSSELS SPROUTS: — *When the Green Kale, or Borecole, has been advanced a step further in the path of improvement, it assumes the headed or hearting character, with blistered leaves; it is then known by the name of Savoys and Brussels Sprouts. Another of its headed forms, but with smooth glaucous leaves, is the cultivated Cabbage of our gardens; and all its varieties of green, red, dwarf, tall, early, late, round, conical, flat, and all the forms into which it is possible to put it.* **’**

MRS BEETON (1861)

BRAISED CELERY

15 g/½ oz dripping or margarine

2 onions, chopped

1 carrot, trimmed and sliced

½ turnip, peeled and diced

25 g/1 oz fat bacon, chopped

4 small celery heads

chicken or vegetable stock

1 × 5 ml spoon/1 teaspoon meat glaze, if available

1 × 15 ml spoon/1 tablespoon chopped parsley

Melt the dripping or margarine in a pan, add the vegetables, except the celery heads, and bacon, cover and fry gently for 10 minutes.

Trim the celery heads, discarding any discoloured outer stalks. Cut off the tough tops of the stalks and reserve these for soup or stock.

Add enough stock to half-cover the vegetables. Bring to the boil, and spoon over the celery. Cover the pan with foil, then with a lid. Cook over a gentle heat for 1½ hours, or until the celery is very tender, basting with the stock from time to time.

Remove the celery from the stock with a perforated spoon and put in a warmed serving dish. Drain the cooking liquor into a small pan and add the meat glaze, if available. Boil rapidly until the liquor is reduced to a thin glaze, and then pour it over the celery. Sprinkle with chopped parsley.   SERVES EIGHT

BOWER'S PATENT FISH, POUL-
TRY OR VEGETABLE STEAMER.

VEGETABLES.

STEAMING

When hob space is limited, it may be more convenient to steam vegetables in layers, one above the other. With a purpose-made steaming saucepan, a metal 'steaming fan' used in an ordinary saucepan, a Chinese-style bamboo steamer, or even a colander fitted over a pan of simmering water, several different vegetables can be cooked over a single heat source.

Sprinkle the vegetables lightly with salt, cover them with a tightly fitting lid and keep the water at a steady simmer. These simple guidelines result in perfectly cooked vegetables which (providing you do not overcook them) retain the maximum texture and colour.

THE PLUM PUDDING

★

In Mrs Beeton's day, Christmas plum puddings – made even then with dried vine fruits, not with prunes or plums – were packed into elaborately decorative moulds or simply rolled in a cloth, and brought to the table as fluted or castle shapes, or glistening, shiny-black spheres. Topped with a sprig of holly, flamed with warmed brandy and served with brandy butter and custard, the pudding then, as now, was an important feature of the meal.

RICH BOILED CHRISTMAS PUDDING

200 g/7 oz plain flour
pinch of salt
1 × 5 ml spoon/1 teaspoon ground ginger
1 × 5 ml spoon/1 teaspoon mixed spice
1 × 5 ml spoon/1 teaspoon grated nutmeg
50 g/2 oz blanched almonds, chopped
400 g/14 oz soft light or dark brown sugar
250 g/9 oz shredded suet
250 g/9 oz sultanas
250 g/9 oz currants
250 g/9 oz raisins
200 g/7 oz cut mixed peel
175 g/6 oz day-old white breadcrumbs
6 eggs
80 ml/3 fl oz stout
juice of 1 orange
4 × 15 ml spoons/4 tablespoons brandy, or to taste
125–150 ml/4½ fl oz–¼ pint milk
fat for greasing

Grease four 600 ml/1 pint heatproof basins. Sift together the flour, salt and spices into a mixing bowl. Add the almonds, sugar, suet, sultanas, currants, raisins, peel and breadcrumbs.

Beat together the eggs, stout, orange juice, brandy and 125 ml/4½ fl oz of the milk. Stir this mixture into the dry ingredients, adding more milk if required, to give a soft dropping consistency.

Fill the mixture into the prepared basins and cover with greased paper and a scalded, floured cloth if you wish to boil the puddings, or with greased paper or foil if you wish to steam them.

Put the puddings into deep boiling water and boil steadily for 6–7 hours, or half-steam them (see note) for the same length of time. Remove the puddings and leave to cool completely. Cover with clean, dry cloths, wrap in greaseproof paper and store in a cool place.

To reheat, boil or steam for 1½–2 hours, or cook in the microwave on high setting for 7–9 minutes.

Serve with a sweet flavoured butter (page 14) and a custard sauce (pages 44/45).

MAKES FOUR SIX-PORTION PUDDINGS

BAKED PUDDING OR CAKE-MOULD.

STANDARD PLUM PUDDING

100 g/4 oz plain flour
25 g/1 oz self-raising flour
pinch of salt
100 g/4 oz day-old white breadcrumbs
1 cooking apple, chopped
100 g/4 oz mixed dried fruit
100 g/4 oz soft dark brown sugar
200 g/7 oz shredded suet
150 g/5 oz cut mixed peel
grated rind and juice of 1 lemon
2 eggs
about 125 ml/4½ fl oz milk
1 × 5 ml spoon/1 teaspoon almond essence
1 × 5 ml spoon/1 teaspoon gravy browning
fat for greasing

Grease two 600 ml/1 pint basins or one 1 litre/1¾ pint basin. Sift together the flours and salt into a bowl. Add the breadcrumbs, apple, dried fruit, sugar, suet, peel, lemon rind and juice.

Beat together the eggs, milk and almond essence and stir into the dry ingredients, adding more milk if needed to give a soft dropping consistency. Add the gravy browning to darken the mixture, and mix thoroughly.

Fill the mixture into the basin or basins. Cover with greased paper and a scalded and floured cloth (for boiling) or with greased paper or foil (for steaming), and boil or steam for 5 hours.

To reheat, boil or steam for 1½–2 hours, or cook in the microwave on high setting for 6–10 minutes.

Serve with a sweet flavoured butter (page 14) or a custard sauce (pages 44/45).

MAKES TWO SIX-PORTION OR ONE
TWELVE-PORTION PUDDING

VEGETARIAN
PLUM PUDDING

200 g/7 oz blanched almonds, chopped
25 g/1 oz shelled Brazil nuts, chopped
100 g/4 oz pine kernels
100 g/4 oz cooking apple, chopped
200 g/7 oz dried figs, chopped
100 g/4 oz currants
200 g/7 oz raisins
175 g/6 oz day-old wholemeal breadcrumbs
1 × 5 ml spoon/1 teaspoon mixed spice
100 g/4 oz soft light brown sugar
100 g/4 oz cut mixed peel
pinch of salt
grated rind and juice of 1 lemon
100 g/4 oz butter or margarine
100 g/4 oz honey
3 eggs, beaten
fat for greasing

Grease two 750 ml/1¼ pint basins. Mix together the nuts, apple, dried fruits, breadcrumbs, spice, sugar, peel, salt, lemon rind and juice.

Warm the butter or margarine and honey together until the fat melts, stir in the eggs and stir the mixture into the dry ingredients. Mix all together thoroughly.

Fill into the prepared basins, cover with

COVERING PUDDINGS

Pack the basin with the mixture leaving at least 2.5 cm/1 in headspace, to allow for the pudding to rise.

Cover with greased paper or foil, greased side down, to prevent any steam getting in. Either twist the edge under the rim of the basin or tie tightly with string.

greased paper and a scalded and floured cloth (for boiling) or with greased paper or foil (for steaming). Put into deep boiling water and boil steadily for 3 hours, or half-steam for 3½–4 hours.

Store as for Rich Boiled Christmas Pudding (opposite). To reheat, boil or steam for 1½–2 hours, or cook in the microwave on high setting for 7–9 minutes.

Serve with a sweet flavoured butter (page 14), a custard sauce (pages 44/45), plain yoghurt or soured cream.

MAKES TWO SIX- TO-
EIGHT PORTION PUDDINGS

STEAMING PUDDINGS

If you have a steamer, put the pudding in the perforated top part and keep the water underneath at a gentle, rolling boil.

If you do not have a steamer, stand the pudding basin on an inverted old saucer or plate in a saucepan, with water coming half-way up the sides of the basin. Cover the pan with a tight-fitting lid and simmer gently. This method is known as 'half-steaming'.

With either method, always add more boiling water when the level is reduced by a third.

UNMOULDING PUDDINGS

After removing a pudding from the heat, let it stand for a few minutes to shrink and become firm before turning it out on to a dish. Loosen the sides from the basin with a knife. Put the warmed serving dish upside-down over the basin and turn them over together.

CHRISTMAS PLUM-PUDDING IN MOULD.

PRESSURE COOKING TIMES

Individual: 150 g/5 oz mixture	750 ml/1¼ pints water	10 minutes steaming	50 minutes at HIGH pressure
In one bowl: 400 g/14 oz mixture	1.5 litres/3 pints water	15 minutes steaming	1½ hours at HIGH pressure
In one bowl: 700 g/1½ lb mixture	1.75 litres/3¼ pints water	20 minutes steaming	2½ hours at HIGH pressure
In one bowl: 800 g/1¾ lb mixture	2 litres/3½ pints water	30 minutes steaming	3 hours at HIGH pressure

REHEATING TIMES

Individual	500 ml/18 fl oz water	10 minutes at HIGH pressure
In one bowl	500 ml/18 fl oz water	20–30 minutes at HIGH pressure

TO MAKE PUDDING IN THE ROUND

To make the traditional round ball-shaped Christmas pudding, flour your hands and shape the mixture into a sphere. Place it in the centre of a scalded and well-floured pudding cloth. Tie first two opposite corners, and then the other two corners into knots.

Boil or half-steam the puddings, cool, store and reheat as described on pages 41 and 42.

Turn out the pudding on to a serving dish and, if necessary, refine the shape by smoothing it with the back of a warmed tablespoon.

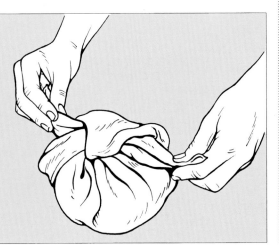

PRESSURE COOKING THE PUDDING

When pressure cooking Christmas and other 'steamed' puddings, a short 'steaming' time must first be allowed, so that the mixture can rise to give an open texture to the pudding. To do this, the valve must be left open and the pudding allowed to steam in the usual way over a low heat for the first part of the cooking; the cooker can then be brought to pressure for the rest of the cooking time.

Leave 2.5 cm/1 in headspace above the mixture in the container. Cook at high pressure and reduce at room temperature.

From: *THE AUTOBIOGRAPHY OF A CHRISTMAS PUDDING,*

A Reminiscence by Letitia Hardy.

❛ It was somewhere about my twelfth Christmas, when I and all our family were assembled in the great dining-room of grandpapa ... there were three Christmas puddings brought to table, and they were every one eaten. . . . The puddings were all large, and the Hardys were all well, and ate as the heroes of Homer might be supposed to do. There was not a vestige of the puddings left, and none was intended to be left, though there were four cooked, the servants having a whole one to themselves. This was, on festive occasions, invariably grandpa's rule. ❜
MRS BEETON'S CHRISTMAS ANNUAL (1868)

Rich boiled Christmas pudding (p.40).

'CHRISTMAS PLUM PUDDING:
— *On Christmas-day a sprig of holly is usually placed in the middle of the pudding, and about a wineglassful of brandy poured round it, which, at the moment of serving, is lighted, and the pudding thus brought to table encircled in flame.*'

MRS BEETON (1861)

★

POURING CUP
CUSTARD

750 ml/1¼ pints milk
1 vanilla pod
3 eggs
2 egg yolks
40 g/1½ oz caster sugar

Warm the milk with the vanilla pod to about 65°C/150°F, and set aside for 30 minutes. Bring it to that temperature again, then remove the vanilla pod, wash and dry it and store it for future use.

Mix the eggs, egg yolks and sugar together thoroughly, and stir in the milk. Strain the custard into a saucepan, a double boiler or a heatproof bowl placed over a pan of simmering water. Make sure the water does not touch the upper pan or bowl.

Cook over a very gentle heat for 15–25 minutes, stirring constantly with a wooden spoon, until the custard thickens to the consistency of single cream. Stir well round the sides as well as the base to prevent lumps forming. Do not let the custard boil. If it shows signs of curdling, put the pan or bowl into cold water, or turn the custard into a clean bowl and whisk rapidly.

As soon as the custard thickens, pour it into a jug to stop further cooking. Keep it warm by standing the jug in hot water. If it is to be served cold, pour the custard into a basin and cover with a piece of moistened greaseproof paper to prevent a skin forming.

MAKES ABOUT 750 ml/1¼ pints

FLAVOURINGS

To vary the flavouring, omit the vanilla pod and infuse strips of lemon or orange rind or a bay leaf in the milk before straining it on to the egg mixture.

For a richer custard, stir 3 × 15 ml spoons/3 tablespoons of double cream into the custard when it is cooling.

★

WHAT'S IN A NAME?

'Cup' or 'boiled' custard is cooked over heat, either directly in a good quality, heavy-based saucepan over a low heat, or in a double boiler or bowl over hot or simmering water. In spite of its name, it should never be boiled but always kept at a temperature below boiling point until all the egg has set evenly and smoothly.

This type of custard was originally called a 'cup' custard because it used to be served cold in individual glass custard cups.

CORNFLOUR
CUSTARD SAUCE

2 × 15 ml spoons/2 tablespoons cornflour
500 ml/18 fl oz milk
2 egg yolks
2 × 15 ml spoons/2 tablespoons sugar
few drops of vanilla essence

Blend the cornflour with a little of the cold milk in a large bowl. Put the remaining milk in a saucepan and heat to boiling point. Stir the milk into the blended mixture. Rinse the pan and return the sauce to it. Bring to the boil, and boil for 3 minutes to cook the cornflour.

Leave to cool, then stir in the yolks and sugar. Cook over a low heat, stirring carefully, until the egg thickens. Do not let it boil. Add a few drops of vanilla essence.

Serve hot or cold.

MAKES ABOUT 500 ml/18 fl oz

 ★

STIR-UP SUNDAY

One of the many traditions associated with Christmas puddings has a strong practical application, since it is well known that rich fruit cakes and puddings improve with keeping. It was customary to have all seasonal puddings and cakes ready by the Sunday before Advent, four weeks before Christmas. This was known as Stir or Stir-up Sunday, and special blessings were given in church.

Generations of families have followed the folkloric tradition of taking it in turns to stir the Christmas pudding, making a silent wish as they do so, and of cooking silver coins or charms in the pudding mixture. Those whose slice of pudding revealed the hidden tokens were considered to be blessed with good fortune for the coming year.

CREAM
CUSTARD SAUCE

4 eggs
100 g/4 oz caster sugar
250 ml/8 fl oz milk
grated rind of 2 oranges
250 ml/8 fl oz single cream

Beat together the eggs, sugar and milk. Add the orange rind and cream.

Pour the mixture into a double boiler or a bowl placed over a pan of simmering water. Cook, stirring constantly, until the sauce thickens. It must not boil, or the sauce will curdle.

Serve hot or cold.

MAKES ABOUT **500 ml/18 fl oz**

CABINET PUDDING.

SWEET
MOUSSELINE SAUCE

4 eggs
2 egg yolks
75 g/3 oz caster sugar
150 ml/¼ pint single cream
2 × 15 ml spoons/2 tablespoons medium-dry sherry

Put all the ingredients in a double boiler or a bowl placed over a pan of simmering water. Cook and whisk until pale and frothy and of a thick, creamy consistency.

Serve immediately.

MAKES ABOUT **600 ml/1 pint**

OTHER PUDDINGS

⭐

A tangy and refreshing lemon sorbet to clear the palate before the customary course of Christmas pudding and mince pies; chilled oranges in a caramel sauce as a colourful alternative dessert; and an ice cream bombe (though not flamed in brandy!) for those in favour of a change.

MINCE PIES

shortcrust pastry using 275 g/10 oz flour or other chosen pastry

flour for rolling out

250 g/9 oz mincemeat (page 12)

25 g/1 oz caster or icing sugar for dredging

Set the oven at 230°C/450°F/gas 8. Roll out the pastry 3 mm/⅛ in thick on a lightly floured surface, and use just over half to line twelve 7 cm/2¾ in patty tins. Cut out twelve lids from the rest of the pastry.

Place a spoonful of mincemeat in each pastry case. Moisten the edges of the pastry lids. Seal the edges well, brush the tops with water and dredge with the sugar. Make two small cuts in the top of each pie.

Reduce the temperature to 200°C/400°F/gas 6. Bake the mince pies for 15–20 minutes.

MAKES TWELVE

OPEN TARTLETS

As an alternative to the traditional double-crust mince pies, make open tartlets. Line the patty tins with pastry and add a spoonful of mincemeat. Cut out small decorative shapes from the pastry trimmings – stars, bells or holly leaves – and place one on each tartlet. Brush the shapes with milk and sprinkle lightly with caster sugar.

SHORTCRUST
PASTRY

275 g/10 oz plain flour

1 × 2.5 ml/½ teaspoon salt

150 g/5 oz fat, eg 50 g/2 oz lard and 75 g/3 oz butter or margarine

4–5 × 15 ml spoons/4–5 tablespoons cold water

flour for rolling out

Sift together the flour and salt into a bowl. Rub the fats into the flour until the mixture resembles fine breadcrumbs. Sprinkle on enough cold water to mix to a stiff dough. Knead the dough very lightly to remove cracks.

Wrap the dough and chill it for at least 15 minutes before using.

Roll out on a lightly floured surface and use as required.

Set the oven at 200°C/400°F/gas 6. Bake the pastry until set. Then reduce the temperature to cook the filling if necessary.

MAKES ABOUT **550 g/1¼ lb**

⭐

Glacé fruit bombe (p.49) and oranges in caramel sauce (p.48).

SWEET PASTE
OR PÂTÉ SUCRÉ

275 g/10 oz plain flour
1 × 2.5 ml spoon/½ teaspoon salt
185 g/6½ oz butter
75 g/3 oz caster sugar
2 small egg yolks
4 × 5 ml spoons/4 teaspoons cold water
flour for rolling out

Sift together the flour and salt into a bowl. Cut the butter in small pieces and rub into the flour until the mixture resembles fine breadcrumbs. Mix in the sugar, then the egg yolks, and enough cold water to make a stiff dough.

Roll out on a lightly floured surface, and use as required. Set the oven at 200°C/400°F/gas 6. Bake the paste until set. Then reduce the heat to cook the filling ingredients, if necessary.

MAKES ABOUT 700 g/1½ lb

★

PUFF PASTRY

200 g/7 oz plain flour
1 × 1.25 ml spoon/¼ teaspoon salt
200 g/7 oz butter
1 × 2.5 ml spoon/½ teaspoon lemon juice
about 100 ml/4 fl oz cold water
flour for rolling out

Sift together the flour and salt into a bowl and rub in 50 g/2 oz of the butter. Add the lemon juice and mix to a smooth dough with cold water. Shape the remaining butter into a rectangle on greaseproof paper.

Roll out the dough on a lightly floured surface into a strip slightly wider than the butter and more than twice its length. Place the butter on one half of the pastry, fold the other half over it, and press the edges together with a rolling pin. Leave in a cool place for 15 minutes to allow the butter to harden. Then roll out into a long strip. Fold the bottom third up and the top third down, press the edges together, and turn the pastry so that the folded edges are on the right and left.

Roll and fold again, cover and leave in a cool place for 15 minutes. Repeat this process until the pastry has been rolled out six times. Finally, roll out as required and leave in a cool place for 20 minutes before cooking.

Set the oven at 220°C/425°F/gas 7. Bake the pastry for 20–25 minutes, or according to recipe. Do not open the door while it is baking.

ORANGES
IN CARAMEL SAUCE

6 oranges
250 ml/8 fl oz water
200 g/7 oz granulated sugar
2–4 × 15 ml spoons/2–4 tablespoons chilled orange juice

Pare the rind carefully from one of the oranges, and cut it into thin strips. Soak in 125 ml/4½ fl oz of the water for 1 hour, then simmer gently for 20 minutes. Drain.

Peel and remove the white pith from all the oranges, and cut the flesh into 5 mm/¼ in thick slices. Put in a glass serving dish.

Put the sugar and the remaining water into a saucepan. Heat gently, stirring until the sugar has dissolved, then boil rapidly until it becomes a golden caramel in colour. Draw off the heat immediately and add enough orange juice to give the consistency of sauce required. Replace

over the heat, stir until just blended, then add the prepared orange rind.

Pour the caramel sauce over the oranges and chill for at least 3 hours before serving.

SERVES FOUR

LEMON SORBET

250 ml/8 fl oz water
2 × 5 ml spoons/2 teaspoons gelatine
150 g/5 oz caster sugar
1 × 2.5 ml spoon/½ teaspoon grated lemon rind
250 ml/8 fl oz lemon juice
2 egg whites

Put the water in a basin and sprinkle the gelatine into the liquid. Stand the basin over a saucepan of hot water and stir the gelatine until it has dissolved completely.

> ❛ ORANGE (*Citrus Aurantium*): — *The principal varieties are the sweet, or China orange, and the bitter, or Seville orange; the Maltese is also worthy of notice, from its red blood-like pulp. The orange is extensively cultivated in the south of Europe, and in Devonshire on walls with a south aspect, it bears an abundance of fruit. So great is the increase in the demand for the orange, and so ample the supply, that it promises to rival the apple in its popularity. The orange-tree is considered young at the age of a hundred years. The pulp of the orange consists of a collection of oblong vesicles filled with a sugary and refreshing juice.* ❜
>
> MRS BEETON (1861)

Boil the remaining water and sugar together for 10 minutes. Stir the dissolved gelatine into the syrup, add the lemon rind and juice, and leave to cool. Pour into a chilled container, cover and freeze for 1 hour.

Whisk the egg whites until they hold stiff peaks, beat the half-frozen ice mixture thoroughly, and fold the egg whites into it. Re-cover and continue freezing for a further 2 hours.

Remove the sorbet to the main part of the refrigerator to soften slightly for about 20 minutes before serving.

Serve in small scoops in stemmed glasses or small dishes. **SERVES SIX TO EIGHT**

Note This sorbet will not freeze hard.

GLACE
FRUIT BOMBE

VANILLA ICE CREAM
500 ml/18 fl oz milk
8 egg yolks
2 eggs
100 g/4 oz granulated sugar
150 ml/¼ pint double cream
1 × 5 ml spoon/1 teaspoon vanilla essence

MOUSSE FILLING
150 ml/¼ pint double cream
25 g/1 oz icing sugar, sifted
2 egg whites
vanilla essence
75 g/3 oz mixed glacé fruits, chopped

Heat the milk until almost boiling. Beat the yolks, eggs and sugar together until thick and white. Then add the hot milk, stirring well. Return the mixture to the saucepan and cook, without boiling, until the custard thickens, stirring constantly. Strain into a bowl and set aside to cool.

Whip the cream until semi-stiff. Add the cold custard and vanilla essence. Turn into a container, cover and freeze for 1 hour. Transfer the semi-frozen mixture to a large bowl and beat to break down the ice particles. Use the mixture to line a bombe mould or bowl, cover and freeze until firm.

To make the mousse filling, whip the cream together with half the sugar. Whisk the egg whites until stiff, and fold in the remaining sugar. Carefully mix the cream and egg whites together, and add the vanilla essence and chopped fruits. Spoon into the centre of the mould, level the top, cover and freeze.

To serve, dip the mould in tepid water for a few moments, remove the cover, and invert the mould over a serving dish. **SERVES EIGHT**

' VENERATION FOR EGGS:—
Many of the most learned philosophers held eggs in a kind of respect, approaching to veneration, because they saw in them the emblem of the world and the four elements. The shell, they said, represented the earth; the white, water; the yolk, fire; and air was found under the shell at one end of the egg. '
MRS BEETON (1861)

TO LINE A BOMBE MOULD

After beating the semi-frozen ice cream, press it against the sides of the mould. Place a small bowl in the centre, cover and freeze.

Remove the inner bowl, fill the cavity with the second mixture, cover and freeze.

Lining a bombe mould.

THE CHEESEBOARD

★

heese, Mrs Beeton declared, was an after-dinner stimulant. This makes it specially appropriate to bring the Christmas meal to a magnificent conclusion. Offer a range of traditional British cheeses, chosen for their variety of colour and texture – the 'portraits' on these pages will help you – with a selection of refreshingly chilled fresh fruits, such as grapes and clementines. Alternatively, follow tradition and offer only one, perfectly ripe, Stilton cheese, with a glass of port or Malmsey Madeira and a dish of walnuts.

BRITISH CHEESES

Cheddar is the best known and most popular British cheese. Like most other British cheeses, it is a full-fat, hard cheese made from cows' milk. Its flavour varies considerably in strength; the highest quality cheese is matured slowly for at least six months, preferably much longer.
Cheshire is more salty than Cheddar, due to the salt in the Cheshire soil where most of it is still made. It is also slightly more acid, and more crumbly. It is naturally white, but a reddish type, dyed with a harmless vegetable dye, is also popular. There is also a fuller-flavoured, creamy-textured *blue Cheshire*, yellow in colour with broad blue streaks. It is especially good with gingerbread, cake or apples.
Derby is a pale honey-coloured, smooth-textured cheese, mild when young but with a certain tang when mature at four to six months old. *Sage Derby* has threads or a broad band of green through it, and the flavour of sage leaves which provide the colouring.
Double Gloucester is straw-coloured or light red, close in texture, and mellow or pungent in flavour when mature.

Lancashire is a semi-hard cheese, white and crumbly, which may be mild or strong.
Leicester, a rich orange-red cheese, is fairly mild, but with a tang when mature. It is soft and crumbly, and may be slightly flaky.
Stilton is considered the king of British cheeses. It is rich and creamy, and slowly matured to let the blue veins develop properly. It is best eaten with bread or plain biscuits, and is an excellent accompaniment to wine, especially Madeira or full-bodied port.

The rind of a stilton is wrinkled and crusty, and the creamy interior is slightly darker near the crust. Top-quality Stilton is still made, as a rule, in cylindrical hoops although jars of Stilton are widely available. It is also sold in film-wrapped or vacuum-packed wedges. Aged Stilton, past its prime, can be potted and used later as a spread (page 19). Once potted, the Stilton will keep in the refrigerator for two to three weeks.

The younger *white Stilton* is crumbly, with a strong aroma and a mild, slightly sour flavour.

Other cheeses include *Red Windsor* which is based on Cheddar and flavoured with red wine. It has a creamier taste and a slightly more acid flavour than mature Cheddar. *Ilchester*, another Cheddar-based cheese, flavoured with beer and garlic, is soft-textured with a full flavour; the garlic is well subdued. *Walton* is a softer cheese based on Cheddar mixed with Stilton, with the addition of walnuts; the taste of Stilton is only mild. *Cotswold* is based on Double Gloucester and flavoured with chives. *Blue Shropshire* has a deep golden taste and clear-cut blue veining. It is lighter in flavour than blue Cheshire or Stilton, but fuller than blue Wensleydale, with its own character. *Lymeswold* is a full fat blue cheese with a white rind while *Melbury* is a mild soft cheese with a white surface mould coat.

Traditional hard cheeses are also available with a reduced fat content. There are also vegetarian hard cheeses, which are made with rennet of microbial origin.

SERVING STILTON

If you buy a whole Stilton, the correct way to care for it is to cut off the top crust in a thin layer; set this aside. When serving the cheese, cut wedges of equal depth from all round the cheese so that the top remains flat. To store the cheese, replace the top crust, wrap in cling film, and keep in a cool place.

'STILTON CHEESE, or *British Parmesan, as it is sometimes called, is generally preferred to all other cheese by those whose authority few will dispute. Those made in May or June are usually served at Christmas; or, to be in prime order, should be kept from 10 to 12 months, or even longer. An additional flavour may also be obtained by scooping out a piece from the top, and pouring therein port, sherry, Madeira, or old ale, and letting the cheese absorb these for 2 or 3 weeks. But that cheese is the finest which is ripened without any artificial aid, is the opinion of those who are judges in these matters. In serving a Stilton cheese, the top of it should be cut off to form a lid, and a napkin or piece of white paper, with a frill at the top, pinned round. When the cheese goes from table, the lid should be replaced.*'

MRS BEETON (1861)

'MODE OF SERVING CHEESE:—*The usual mode of serving cheese at good tables is to cut a small quantity of it into neat square pieces, and to put them into a glass cheese-dish. This dish being handed round. Should the cheese crumble much, of course this method is rather wasteful, and it may then be put on the table in the piece, and the host may cut from it. When served thus, the cheese must always be carefully scraped, and laid on a white d'oyley or napkin, neatly folded.*'

MRS BEETON (1861)

A selection of British cheeses: Stilton, Cheddar, Sage Derby and Leicester.

SWEETMEATS

★

Something sweet to enjoy with coffee and perhaps a liqueur after the meal is irresistible to many people. This selection of quick sweetmeats would look mouth-watering arranged on a stemmed glass dish or in a shallow silver bowl. Think of absent friends, too. The bon-bons would make delightfully personal gifts packed in used wooden date boxes or transparent plastic chocolate boxes lined with stiff white or gold paper doilies.

CHOCOLATE TRUFFLES

50 g/2 oz almonds, chopped
100 g/4 oz plain chocolate
100 g/4 oz ground almonds
2 × 15 ml spoons/2 tablespoons double cream
75 g/3 oz caster sugar
few drops of vanilla essence
grated chocolate or chocolate vermicelli for coating

Brown the chopped almonds lightly under the grill. Break the chocolate into small pieces and melt it in a bowl over a pan of hot water. Remove the bowl from the pan. Add all the other ingredients except the coating chocolate and mix to a stiff paste. Roll into small balls, and toss at once in grated chocolate or chocolate vermicelli.

Put the truffles into paper sweet cases to serve. **MAKES ABOUT TWENTY-FOUR**

★

GLAZED FRUITS

250 g/8 oz grapes or mandarins
50 ml/2 fl oz water
200 g/7 oz lump sugar
few drops of lemon juice
oil for greasing

Remove the pips but do not peel the grapes; peel the mandarins and break into segments. Dry the fruit thoroughly.

Put the water and sugar into a saucepan and dissolve the sugar gently. Add the lemon juice, bring to the boil, and boil to the small crack stage (140°C/275°F). Remove the pan from the heat and place it in cold water for a minute or two to prevent further cooking.

Dip the prepared fruit into the syrup, one piece at a time. Place the glazed fruits on an oiled tray and leave to set.

Put them into paper sweet cases to serve.

MAKES ABOUT 250 g/9 oz

PEPPERMINT CREAMS

400 g/14 oz icing sugar
2 egg whites
2 × 5 ml spoons/2 teaspoons peppermint essence
icing sugar for dusting

Sift the icing sugar into a bowl, and work in the egg whites and peppermint essence. Mix well to a moderately firm paste. Knead thoroughly and roll out, on a board dusted with a little icing sugar, to about 5 mm/¼ in thick. Cut into small rounds or fancy shapes and put on greaseproof paper.

Leave to dry for 12 hours, turning each sweet once. Pack in an airtight container lined with waxed paper.

The sweets may be dipped, or half-dipped, in melted couverture chocolate.

MAKES ABOUT FORTY-EIGHT

★

STUFFED DATES

200 g/7 oz dessert dates

100 g/4 oz whole blanched almonds

25 g/1 oz desiccated coconut

Stone the dates and place an almond in each hollow. Roll them in coconut and put into paper sweet cases. MAKES ABOUT TWENTY-FOUR

Variation Stuff the dates with marzipan (page 58) and roll in caster sugar.

> ' DATES *are imported into Britain, in a dried state, from Barbary and Egypt, and, when in good condition, they are much esteemed . . . They should be chosen large, softish, not much wrinkled, of a reddish-yellow colour on the outside, with a whitish membrane between the fruit and the stone.* '
>
> MRS BEETON (1861)

MARZIPAN
SHAPES

You can either make up your own marzipan/almond paste from the recipe on page 58, or use a packet of the ready-made variety. The latter provides a good base for colouring as it is quite pale. You will need food colouring appropriate to the shapes you are going to make (see below).

If you need marzipan in different colours, eg, for fruit and leaves, or to make a variety of different fruits, first divide up the marzipan according to the number of different colours you need, and colour each piece separately.

To colour the marzipan, dip a cocktail stick into the bottle of colouring, and then dab it onto the mazipan. It is better to start with too little colouring and add a bit more if it is too pale, than to end up with very strongly coloured marzipan. Knead the colouring into the marzipan until it is evenly distributed.

MARZIPAN APPLES

Add green food colouring to the marzipan. Divide it into small pieces and shape each piece into a ball. Paint a little red food colouring on each apple for rosiness. Make a leaf from green marzipan, and use a clove as a stalk.

MARZIPAN BANANAS

Add a little yellow food colouring to the marzipan. Divide it into small pieces and shape each piece into a roll, curving it to the shape of a banana. Brush cocoa powder on for shading.

MARZIPAN CARROTS

Add orange food colouring to the marzipan and shape small pieces into rolls, tapered at one end. Make uneven indentations with the point of a knife and put a small piece of angelica at the top as a stalk. Dust with drinking chocolate powder.

MARZIPAN LEMONS

Add yellow food colouring to the marzipan. Divide it into small pieces and shape each piece into an oval with points at each end. Roll lightly on a grater to make indentations.

MARZIPAN ORANGES

Add orange food colouring to the marzipan. Divide into small pieces and shape each piece into a ball. Roll on a grater to make indentations and toss in caster sugar. Press a clove into the top of each orange.

MARZIPAN SHAPES

Cut the marzipan into 2, 3 or 4 squares and tint each a different colour. Roll out each square to 5 mm (¼ in) thick. Brush each with egg white and place one on top of another. Press lightly together. Brush the top with egg white and sprinkle with caster sugar. Cut through all the layers, making different shapes, such as squares, triangles, rectangles, circles, and diamonds.

MARZIPAN STRAWBERRIES

Add red food colouring to the marzipan. Divide into small pieces and shape each piece into a srawberry shape. Roll each strawberry lightly on a grater to make indentations. Top with a stalk made from a strip of angelica.

DRINKS FOR CHRISTMAS DINNER

★

'A little of what you fancy' may well be the best advice to follow when it comes to choosing wines to serve with the Christmas dinner. Experts may say that you 'must' serve this or that wine with certain foods, and although there are helpful general guidelines, your personal preference should take priority. Wine merchants are always willing to offer advice, so, if in doubt, do ask for guidance. More and more supermarket shelves are marked with tables showing the dryness and flavour of the wines on sale, to make your choice easier.

'Getting into the festive spirit' before the Christmas dinner is certainly traditional, but with possibly a number of wines to accompany the meal, and perhaps a liqueur or spirit to follow, guests – and hosts, too – are increasingly aware that the pre-prandial drinks should be little more than a 'taster'.

A chilled dry sherry of the fino or manzanilla type is a very acceptable way to sharpen the taste buds. These dry fortified wines do not leave a clinging after-taste in the way that sweet ones do. A more unusual choice, and equally delicious, would be a glass of chilled white port.

If you really wish to get the party going, there is nothing to beat a glass of chilled brut (dry) champagne, or a good quality dry, sparkling wine.

WINES TO ACCOMPANY THE MEAL

Some connoisseurs maintain that the cost of the wine should equal that of the food being served – not necessarily a simple equation to calculate, and, for many people, a somewhat heavy strain on the budget. Nevertheless, the message is certainly to spend a little more on wines than usual to complement the time and trouble taken

in preparing, cooking and presenting the meal.

While it is important not to be tied rigidly to rules concerning suitable wines for particular foods, here are some good general guidelines to follow.

With most first courses, and with cold and fish dishes, serve a dry or medium white or rosé wine. Muscadet, Pouilly Blanc Fumé, Chablis, Vouvray and Rosé d'Anjou would all be appropriate. If you are serving smoked salmon or consommé for the first course, you might prefer to serve chilled dry sherry or white port, especially if that was your choice of aperitif.

To accompany the turkey with all the rich trimmings, you could offer either a red or a white wine. Among the reds that would most complement the subtle flavour of the meat are good-quality clarets from Bordeaux, a fruity Rioja from Spain, or Barolo, one of the full-bodied wines from Italy. Among the white wines

which would live up to the occasion are white burgundies or one of the drier, fruitier wines from either the Loire district or Germany.

If the main course is centred around the traditional, delectable and crispy goose, then there can be little argument that a really full-bodied red wine is best to cut the richness of the bird. It is hard to believe that, having eaten such a rich course, inhabitants of Normandy would invite you to join them in 'le trou Normande' (the 'hole' in the meal) – a glass of Calvados, the local apple brandy. Try it, if you will, at your peril!

If you feel the digestive powers of your guests could do well without this 'settler', you could simply follow the main-course wine with just one glass of a fine dessert wine, such as Sauternes, or an Auslese or Spätlese wine from Germany. Any of these would be delicious with the pudding. A more adventurous choice would be Monbazillac from the Bergerac region of France, or the aromatic and fruity Muscat de Beaumes de Venise.

PUNCH-BOWL AND LADLE.

HOW MUCH WINE TO ALLOW

It is usual to allow at least half a 70 cl/1¼ pt bottle (three glasses) of table wine per head. This gives one the chance to serve a glass of white wine with the first course, and two glasses of red (or of a different white wine) with the main course. As it is Christmas, there is every reason to serve a glass of sweet white dessert wine with the pudding.

It is sometimes rather difficult to judge just how much wine will be needed, particularly for a meal which is destined to occupy a large part of the afternoon or evening, and so it is wise to have a bottle or two in reserve, and at the right temperature, in case it is needed.

Once a bottle has been opened, it will keep quite well for several days in a cool place (for red wines) or in a refrigerator (for whites).

TEMPERATURE OF WINES

Nothing does more to destroy good wines than serving them at the wrong temperature: still and sparkling wines that are almost lukewarm, or full-bodied reds that feel and taste as if they have just been brought in from the snow.

As a general rule, dry, white wines and most sparkling wines should be chilled to a lower temperature (10–12°C/50–54°F) than rosé wines

WINE-COOLER.

and the sweeter dessert wines, which are best served at around 14°C/57°F.

Lighter, younger red wines such as Beaujolais and some clarets should be served at a lower scale of 'room temperature', about 15–16°C/59-61°F. Finer clarets and burgundies, and other full-bodied red wines from Italy, Spain and California are served chambré, at a slightly warmer temperature of 16–20°C/61–68°F to complement the myriad flavours and the smoothness of the wines.

FORTIFIED WINES

Fortified wines are produced mainly in Spain and Portugal, and most are strengthened by the addition of grape brandy. The strength is usually between 18 and 25 per cent by volume, compared with 8 to 12 per cent for table wines.

The wines can be classified in two distinct

categories: the dry or medium-dry ones which are usually served chilled, as an aperitif, and the sweeter or very sweet ones which are served with, or more usually after, the dessert course of the meal.

Sherry, port and Madeira are fortified wines, and they all have dry, medium and sweet varieties. Sherries, for example, range from the tinglingly dry fino through medium-dry amontillado to oloroso or cream types. Madeira wines range from Sercial, at the dry end of the scale, through Malmsey to the rich, sweet Bual which is traditionally served as a digestif.

Port spans the dry-to-sweetness scale from white port, which is always served chilled and as an aperitif, to tawny and ruby ports which are enjoyed after the meal.

Vintage port, the finest of all fortified wines, is made from exceptional wine of a single year. It is, alas, always expensive. Much less so are the 'vintage character' or 'late-bottled vintage' ports, which are better than 'standard' port.

Port is traditionally served with the cheese course and guests may continue drinking it with nuts and sweetmeats. Custom has it that port is passed round the table from right to left, and guests pour it for themselves. Sticklers for etiquette will not allow the bottle to be put down on the table until it has completed the round.

The reputation of a certain clerical gentleman prompts people to ask, good-humouredly, of anyone who omits to pass on the bottle or decanter of port, 'Do you know the Bishop of Norwich?'

Sweet fortified wines served as digestifs should be at 'room temperature', no more than 18°C/54°F. Think ahead, and bring the wine from its storage place in good time. On no account should it – or any red wine – be plunged into warm water or artificially heated by standing it on a cooker. Connoisseurs would blanch at the thought! At the very most, wine may be placed in a cool airing cupboard to bring it to the correct temperature.

CHRISTMAS RECIPES

WINE LORE

If serving more than one wine, it is wise to abide by the following rules:

1 White wine before red
2 A light wine before a heavy one
3 A young wine before an old one
4 Dry wine before a sweet one

★

LIQUEURS AND SPIRITS

Fashions in liqueurs are constantly changing, and it would be impossible to offer each guest his or her current favourite. If you are able to provide brandy and a choice of two liqueurs, perhaps one well-known and one more unusual, your hospitality will not be found wanting.

Nearly every country produces one or more liqueurs which are spirit-based, sweetened and flavoured with herbs, spices, fruits, coffee and peppermint or with other spirits such as whisky. Most liqueurs are much less potent than spirits, with an alcohol content ranging from 25 to 35 per cent.

All spirits – the principal ones being brandy, whisky, gin, vodka and rum – are the result of distillation of the basic liquid ingredient: namely, malted barley and water, or wine or cane syrup. The resulting 'raw' spirit is flavoured and matured in oak casks or ceramic-lined tanks, and is skilfully blended to provide a perfectly consistent product. There is no such thing as a vintage year for the distillers of spirits!

On average, spirits have a 40 per cent alcoholic strength, which means that the phrase 'one for the road' has been eliminated from every host's vocabulary. Gone are the days when the worst hazard one might experience on the way home was a wayward horse-drawn carriage.

GLASSES

All drinks seem to taste better when they are served in the correct shape and type of glass and, it has to be said, the finer the glass the greater the enjoyment of the liquor.

Serve sherry in *copitas*, which taper towards the rim, vermouth in small wine glasses, gin and tonic in tumblers or large wine glasses, and whisky in tumblers.

Ideally, wine glasses should be large enough to allow plenty of room to swirl the wine and release its aroma; they should hold a full measure without being filled more than two thirds of capacity. They should be slightly curved inwards – tulip-shaped – at the top, so that the aroma can be concentrated around the nose, and they must be clear, so that one can admire the wine's colour. Many ranges offer a smaller size for white than that for red wine.

Port glasses are small and ideally they, too, should curve slightly inwards at the top to hold the bouquet of the wine.

Aperitif glasses.

SHERRY   WHISKY

Liqueur glasses.

BRANDY   LIQUEUR   PORT

Wine glasses.

PARIS GOBLET   TULIP GLASS

Liqueurs are served in standard liqueur glasses which may be straight-sided or tulip-shaped.

Brandy may be served in special brandy balloon glasses or in small stemmed glasses which curve inwards at the top. Brandy glasses should be warmed very slightly before the spirit is poured in. Cupping the glass in the hand once the brandy has been poured also helps to release the aroma.

All glasses should be cleaned carefully and rinsed thoroughly, as any residual detergent will taint the wine.

DECANTING

Red wines should be uncorked some time (usually about an hour) before being served. Fine old red wines may also need to be decanted.

There are two reasons for decanting: to separate a wine from its sediment – and all good red wines will eventually throw a sediment – and to allow a wine to 'breathe'. It is the act of decanting which lets a wine breathe, rather than the length of time it is done before drinking the wine, so there are no hard-and-fast rules about decanting so many hours before the meal. In most cases, 30 minutes is quite enough.

An older bottle, which has thrown a sediment, should be stood upright for a few hours before decanting it, to allow the sediment to collect low down in the bottle. The bottle's contents should then be poured into a clean, dry decanter or jug in one movement, carefully holding the neck of the bottle in front of a source of light so that one can see when the sediment is beginning to reach

DECANTER.

the neck. Muslin can be used as a sieve for wines with a very heavy sediment, such as port. Filter paper should not be used as it taints wine.

Vintage port often has a wax seal which should be knocked off gently with the end of a corkscrew. Any remains of the wax should be wiped off before removing the cork. Port corks are long, so you will need a long corkscrew to remove them.

To clean a stained decanter, screw up small pellets of newspaper and drop them into the decanter; pour over a little very hot water, and leave for a few minutes, swirling occasionally. The combination of hot water and newsprint will lift the stain. Pour away the water, repeat the process if necessary and rinse thoroughly. A handful of rice poured into the decanter and swirled around with hot water has a similar effect.

SERVING COFFEE

Whichever way you decide to make coffee, it is important that it tastes fresh and has a good aroma.

For roasted, ground coffee of average strength, use about 2 × 15 ml spoons/2 table-

COFFEE-GRINDER.

'THE COFFEE PLANT grows to the height of about twelve or fifteen feet, with leaves not unlike those of the common laurel, although more pointed, and not so dry and thick. The blossoms are white, much like those of jasmine, and issue from the angles of the leaf-stalks. When the flowers fade, they are succeeded by the coffee-bean, or seed, which is inclosed in a berry of a red colour, when ripe resembling a cherry. The coffee-beans are prepared by exposing them to the sun for a few days, that the pulp may ferment and throw off a strange acidulous moisture. They are then gradually dried for about three weeks, and put into a mill to separate the husk from the seed.'

MRS BEETON (1861)

COFFEE.

★

spoons of coffee per 500 ml/18 fl oz water, depending on the flavour of the beans, the fineness of the grind, and the method used to make the drink. Use slightly less Brazilian or Jamaican coffee than Kenyan.

Medium-ground coffee gives the best results when you make coffee in a jug, saucepan or percolator; fine-ground coffee when you use a filter or vacuum-type coffee maker. Always use freshly boiled water and make only enough coffee to serve immediately. Coffee that has 'stood' has a bitter or stewed taste and does nothing to complement any meal.

THE CHRISTMAS CAKE

★

The festival would not be the same, especially for the children, without the snowy-white frosted Christmas cake, the star turn of the matinée. The cake should be made well in advance, so that it has time to mature. But if you possibly can, keep the decorations a secret until the last minute, to preserve the element of surprise.

CHRISTMAS CAKE

fat for greasing the tin
200 g/7 oz plain flour
a large pinch of salt
1–2 × 5 ml spoons/1–2 teaspoons mixed spice
200 g/7 oz butter
200 g/7 oz caster sugar
6 eggs
2–4 × 15 ml spoons/2–4 tablespoons brandy *or* sherry
100 g/4 oz glacé cherries, quartered
50 g/2 oz preserved ginger, chopped
50 g/2 oz shelled walnuts, chopped
200 g/7 oz currants
200 g/7 oz sultanas
150 g/5 oz raisins
75 g/3 oz cut mixed peel

Grease and line a 20 cm/8 in cake tin with double greaseproof paper, and tie a strip of brown paper round the outside of the tin.

Sift together the flour, salt and spice.

Cream the butter and sugar together until light and fluffy. Gradually beat the eggs into the creamed mixture. Fold in the flour, cherries, ginger, walnuts, dried fruits and peel into the creamed mixture. Add the brandy or sherry and mix well. Put into the cake tin and make a slight hollow in the centre.

Bake in a warm oven, 170°C/325°F/gas 3, for 45 minutes. Reduce the heat to 150°C/300°F/gas 2, and bake for a further hour. Reduce the heat again, to 140°C/275°F/gas 1, and continue cooking for another 45 minutes–1 hour, until firm to the touch.

Leave the cake to cool in the tin.

To cover the cake: brush it evenly with apricot glaze, and cover it with almond paste or marzipan. It will then be ready for icing.

APRICOT GLAZE

250 g/9 oz apricot jam
3 × 15 ml spoons/3 tablespoons water

Heat the jam and water gently in a saucepan until smooth.

Sieve the mixture and return to the cleaned saucepan. Bring slowly to the boil and heat gently until thick.

Note The glaze is spread on the cake before applying marzipan, almond paste, or a coating of ground or chopped nuts or crumbs. It is slightly thinner than jam and spreads more easily. It can be stored in a refrigerator for at least 2 weeks.

ALMOND PASTE

300 g/11 oz ground almonds
300–450 g/11 oz–1 lb icing sugar
2 egg yolks *or* 2 egg whites *or* 1 egg
FLAVOURING
3 × 15 ml spoons/3 tablespoons lemon juice *or*
3 × 2.5 ml spoons/1½ teaspoons vanilla *or* almond essence, *or*
1 × 15 ml spoon/1 tablespoon brandy

Work all the ingredients together to make a pliable paste. Handle the paste as little as possible, because the warmth of the hands draws out the oil from the ground almonds.

Makes enough for the top and sides of a 20 cm/8 in cake.

Note You can vary the amount of icing sugar used, within the given limits, according to how sweet you like the paste to be. If you wish, you can use half icing sugar and half caster sugar.

A magnificent Christmas cake using marzipan shapes (p.53) to decorate the smooth royal icing (p.60).

QUANTITIES OF ALMOND PASTE

Keeping the proportions of the ingredients the same, you will need the following amounts to cover cakes of varying sizes:

top only of 18 cm/7¼ in cake –
100 g/4 oz ground almonds, etc;

top only of 20–23 cm/8–9¼ in cake –
150 g/5 oz ground almonds, etc;

top only of 25 cm/10 in cake –
200 g/7 oz ground almonds, etc;

top and sides of 18 cm/7¼ in cake –
200 g/7 oz ground almonds, etc;

top and sides of 20-23 cm/8–9¼ in cake –
300 g/11 oz ground almonds, etc;

top and sides of 25 cm/10 in cake –
400 g/14 oz ground almonds, etc;

ROYAL ICING

2 egg whites
1 × 5 ml spoon/1 teaspoon lemon juice
450 g/1 lb icing sugar, sifted
1 × 5 ml spoon/1 teaspoon glycerine

Put the egg whites and lemon juice into a bowl and, using a wooden spoon, beat just enough to liquefy the whites slightly.

Add half the icing sugar, a little at a time, and beat for 10 minutes. Add the rest of the icing sugar gradually, and beat for another 10 minutes, until the icing is white and forms peaks when the spoon is drawn up from the mixture. Add the glycerine while mixing.

This quantity will be enough to cover the top and sides of a 20 cm/8 in cake; use half this quantity if you want to cover the top only.

For a 25 cm/10 in cake, double the quantities given above to cover the top and sides.

TO COAT A CAKE WITH ALMOND PASTE OR MARZIPAN

Always level the top of the cake first. If it has risen to a peak in the centre, do not cut it off. Cut out a thin strip of paste and put it round the edge to level the top. Roll it flat.

Brush the cake free of any loose crumbs, then brush it with warm apricot glaze (page 58) or warmed apricot jam. Let it cool. If covering only the top of the cake with paste, do not coat the sides unless you want to cover them with chopped nuts.

To cover the top of a cake only On a surface lightly dusted with icing sugar, roll out the almond paste or marzipan into a round or square of the required thickness, and 5 mm/¼ in larger than the top of the cake all round. Invert the cake on to the paste. Hold the cake down with one hand and, using a knife, mould and press the paste into the sides of the cake.

Turn the cake the right way up, and roll the top lightly with a rolling-pin dusted with icing sugar. If not level, make it so by rolling, then invert it again and press the excess paste into place on the sides.

To cover the top and sides of a round cake Roll out the almond paste or marzipan into a circle of the required thickness, and 3–4 cm/1⅛–1¾ in larger than the top of the cake all round. On a cake of average height, this should give an almond paste coating for the sides about half as thick as on top. (If the cake is more than 8 cm/3½ in high, make the circle a little thicker or larger.)

Invert the cake on to the paste, placing it in the centre of the circle. Using the palms of both hands, mould and press the paste on to the sides of the cake, working it upwards to cover them. Press it on firmly and evenly.

Press down on the cake to get a sharp edge between the top and sides. Then roll a straight-sided bottle or jar all round the cake to make the paste on the sides an even thickness. Turn the cake the right way up, and check that it is level.

Moulding the marzipan onto a cake.

TO COVER THE TOP AND SIDES OF A SQUARE CAKE

Cover the sides first. Divide the paste into 2 parts and put 1 aside for the top. Cut the other part into 4 pieces and roll each into a strip to fit one side of the cake. Lay them on a surface lightly dusted with icing sugar. Up-end the cake, and press each side in turn on to a strip of paste. Trim the edges of the paste with a knife if necessary.

Cover the top of the cake exactly as when covering the top only.

Leave the cake for at least 72 hours, or if possible a full week, before icing it, to prevent any risk of almond oil from the paste seeping through the icing and staining it.

Covering a square cake with marzipan.

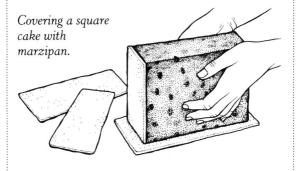

TO ICE A CAKE WITH ROYAL ICING

This classic icing cannot be applied directly to a cake, since it will drag crumbs from the surface of the cake. When it is spread on a cake coated with almond paste or marzipan, it should be the consistency of thick cream.

If an electric mixer is used for beating royal icing, leave the icing to stand for 2–3 hours afterwards, to let any air bubbles escape. Whenever it is left to stand, cover it with a clean, damp cloth to prevent the surface drying out.

First coat Put the cake, covered with well-dried almond paste or marzipan, on an upturned plate or on an icing turntable. Put just under half the icing in the centre of the top of the cake. Smooth it quickly with a spatula that has been dipped into very hot water.

Smooth the rest of the icing over the sides, lifting a little at a time from the bowl, using a hot wetted knife. Have a fine skewer ready to prick any bubbles gently before the surface sets. See that the top edge is sharp and clean. Do not overwork the icing or it will lose its gloss. Allow the cake to dry, away from dust, for 24 hours.

Second coat Once the first coat is completely dry, a second, thinner coat of icing can be poured over the cake if the first coat is not perfectly smooth. This second coat should be thick enough to need a little help with a knife to make it flow gently over the top and sides. Extra egg white can be added to make a coating with a very smooth finish. Alternatively, glacé icing (below) can be used.

Snow scene surface For a 'snow scene', i.e., a coating with peaks and swirls, flick up the icing with a knife, making small peaks. If desired, sprinkle the icing, when dry, with sifted icing sugar to represent newly fallen snow.

GLACE ICING

about 2 × 15 ml spoons/2 tablespoons water
300 g/11 oz icing sugar, sifted
3 × 2.5 ml spoons/1½ teaspoons strained lemon juice *or* orange juice (optional)
colouring (optional)

Put 2 × 15 ml spoons/2 tablespoons water into a small non-stick or enamel saucepan with the icing sugar. Add the lemon or orange juice at this stage, if it is used. Warm very gently.

Beat the mixture well with a wooden spoon. The icing should coat the back of the spoon

thickly. If it is too thick, add 1–2 × 5 ml spoons/1–2 teaspoons water; if too thin, add a very little extra sifted icing sugar. Add colouring, if wanted. Use at once.

Note Icing sugars vary in the amount of liquid they absorb.

TO MAKE A PAPER ICING BAG OR CONE

Use greaseproof paper or vegetable parchment. Cut a square about 25 cm/10 in, and cut it into two triangles.

Take one triangle and fold A over C as shown. Wrap B round to A C and fold in the corners. Cut about 1 cm/½ in off the point and insert the pipe to be used. Repeat the process with the other triangle if a second bag is required.

Greaseproof paper cones can be used only once, but vegetable parchment ones can be wiped out and re-used, as can nylon icing bags.

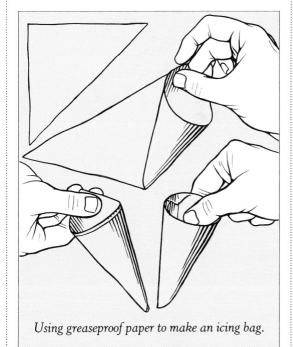

Using greaseproof paper to make an icing bag.

BOXING DAY BUFFET

★

Acold buffet on Boxing Day evening when everyone, including the host and hostess, has time to relax, is one of the joys of the Christmas season. The menu is composed around a traditional boiled ham and a raised pork pie, both of which are cooked in advance, with a selection of salads. The meal ends with Mrs Beeton's special tipsy cake and a clear claret jelly.

BOILED HAM

a raw ham or gammon

GARNISH
raspings (right)
demerara sugar

If the ham or gammon has been hung for a long time, and is very dry and salty, soak it for at least 24 hours, changing the water every 6–8 hours. For most hams, about 12 hours' soaking is sufficient.

Drain, then weigh the ham and calculate the cooking time after soaking the ham. The knuckle end will need less time than the whole joint (see below). Calculate the cooking time for the knuckle end on the thickness of the meat, (usually about three quarters of the total cooking time). Clean and trim off any 'rusty' parts.

Put the ham into a boiling pot big enough to hold it, but keep the knuckle end out of the water. Add enough cold water to cover the joint when it is laid flat in the pan, and cover the pan with a cloth to prevent undue evaporation. Heat to simmering point and simmer gently until tender. Lay the ham flat in the pan to cook the knuckle end at the appropriate time. The ham should always be completely covered with water when it is laid flat while it is cooking. Top up the pot with boiling water as necessary.

When cooked, lift out the ham and remove the rind. Press brown sugar firmly into the surface, all over the joint. Score it in a diamond pattern, and press a clove into the centre of each diamond. Place in a hot oven for 10 minutes. Leave to cool.

CALCULATING THE COOKING TIME

Weigh the joint and measure its thickness – it is the combination of these two factors, not just the weight, that determines the cooking time.

As a guide, allow 30 minutes per 450 g/1 lb meat, plus 30 minutes over for any joint more than 10 cm/4 in thick. For example, cook a 900 g/2 lb joint of ham for 1½ hours.

Do not undercook the meat; and do not cook it in fast-boiling liquid, or the meat will shrink and be tough. To test the joint for tenderness, pierce it close to the bone (if it has one) with a fine skewer.

STUFFED EGGS

4 hard-boiled eggs
25 g/1 oz butter, softened
1 × 15 ml spoon/1 tablespoon mayonnaise
salt and pepper
2 × 5 ml spoons/2 teaspoons Worcestershire sauce (optional)

GARNISH
parsley sprigs
pieces of tomato
sliced gherkin
stuffed olives
radishes

Cut the eggs in half lengthways. Remove the yolks carefully and rub through a fine sieve into a bowl, or mash with a fork. Trim a small slice off the rounded side of each half white so that it stands firmly.

Mix the yolks with the butter, mayonnaise, salt and pepper. Add the Worcestershire sauce, if used. Beat until smooth and creamy, then fill into a piping bag with a 15 mm/¾ in star nozzle and pipe into the egg whites. Garnish with a small parsley sprig, a piece of tomato, a slice of gherkin, a stuffed olive or a radish.

Serve on curled lettuce leaves or watercress sprigs.

RAISED
PORK PIE

about 400 g/14 oz pork bones
1 small onion, chopped
salt and pepper
300 ml/½ pint water or stock
Hot Water Crust Pastry using 250 g/9 oz flour (overleaf)
550 g/1¼ lb lean pork, diced
1 × 1.25 ml spoon/¼ teaspoon dried sage
beaten egg or milk for glazing

Put the pork bones in a saucepan. Add the onion with the salt, pepper, and water or stock. Cover the pan, heat to simmering point and simmer for 2 hours. Leave to cool until jellied.

Line a 1 kg/2¼ lb pie mould with three quarters of the pastry, or use a round cake tin to mould the pie, as described below, keeping the paste about 5 mm/¼ in thick. Reserve the remaining quarter for the lid.

Season the pork with salt, pepper and sage. Put into the prepared pie crust and add 2 × 15 ml spoons/2 tablespoons of the jellied stock. Put on the lid, brush with beaten egg or milk, and make a hole in the centre to allow steam to escape.

Set the oven at 220°C/425°F/gas 7. Bake the pie for 15 minutes. Reduce the heat to 180°C/350°F/gas 4, and cook the pie for a further 1½ hours. Remove the greaseproof paper or mould for the last 30 minutes of the cooking time and glaze the pastry with egg or milk.

When cooked, remove from the oven and leave to cool. Warm the reserved jellied stock and funnel it through the hole in the pastry lid until the pie is full. Leave to cool for 2 hours, or until the stock sets to a jelly.

SERVES SIX TO EIGHT

Garnished boiled ham and red cabbage and apple salad (p.65).

HOT WATER CRUST PASTRY

250 g/9 oz plain flour
1 × 2.5 ml spoon/½ teaspoon salt
90 g/3½ oz lard
125 ml/4½ fl oz milk or water

Sift the flour and salt into a warm bowl, make a well in the centre, and keep the bowl in a warm place. Meanwhile, heat the lard and milk or water together until boiling, then add to the flour, mixing well with a wooden spoon until the pastry is cool enough to knead with the hands. Knead thoroughly and mould as required.

Note Throughout the mixing, kneading, and moulding, the pastry must be kept warm, otherwise moulding will be extremely difficult. If, however, the pastry is too warm, it will be too soft and pliable to retain its shape.

MAKES ABOUT **425 g/15 oz**

TO MOULD A RAISED PIE

Hot Water Crust Pastry using 250 g/9 oz flour (above)
fat for greasing
flour

The pastry must be raised or moulded while still warm.

Reserve one quarter of the pastry for the lid and leave in the bowl in a warm place, covered with a greased polythene bag. Roll out the remainder to about 5 mm/¼ in thick, in a round or oval shape.

Shape the pie gently with your hands. If this proves too difficult, use a jar, round cake tin or similar container, as a mould. Invert it, then

Using a jar to mould a raised pie.

grease and flour the sides and base. Lay the pastry over it and mould round the sides, taking care not to pull the pastry and also making sure that the sides and base are of an even thickness. Leave to cool. When cold, remove the pastry case from the mould and put in the filling.

Roll out the pastry reserved for the lid and cover the filling, pressing the edges of the pastry together firmly. Tie three or four folds of greaseproof paper around the pie to hold it in shape during baking and to prevent it from becoming too brown.

MAKES ONE **15 cm/6 in** PIE

RAISED-PIE MOULD, OPEN.

BEAN SALAD WITH TUNA

550 g/1¼ lb dry flageolet beans
175 g/6 oz tomatoes, peeled, seeds removed and chopped
2 spring onions, chopped
6 × 15 ml spoons/6 tablespoons oil
3 × 15 ml spoons/3 tablespoons white wine vinegar
1 garlic clove, chopped
1 × 15 ml spoon/1 tablespoon chopped parsley
1 (200 g/7 oz) can tuna fish, drained and flaked

Soak the beans in warm water overnight. Drain, put into a saucepan with fresh water, and boil briskly for at least 10 minutes, then cook for about 1 hour, or until tender.

Drain the beans, and mix with the tomatoes and spring onions while still hot.

Mix together the oil, vinegar, garlic and

parsley. Mix the tuna with the hot bean mixture. Pour the cold oil and vinegar dressing over the salad and set aside to cool. **SERVES EIGHT**

RED CABBAGE
& APPLE SALAD

550 g/1¼ lb red cabbage
3 eating apples, preferably with green skins
5 × 15 ml spoons/5 tablespoons French dressing
1 × 5 ml spoon/1 teaspoon prepared mustard
½ box mustard and cress to garnish

Discard any tough stalks or outside leaves of the cabbage and shred finely. Quarter the apples, core and slice thinly. Toss quickly in the dressing to preserve the colour. Add the mustard and mix well, then add the cabbage and toss lightly. Pile into a salad bowl and garnish with cress before serving. **SERVES SIX TO EIGHT**

RICE SALAD

75 g/3 oz long-grain rice
2 × 15 ml spoons/2 tablespoons olive oil
2 × 15 ml spoons/2 tablespoons white wine vinegar
50 g/2 oz peas
1 small green pepper, seeds removed and finely chopped
2–3 gherkins, chopped
snipped chives
salt and pepper
watercress sprigs to garnish

Cook the rice in boiling, salted water for 10–12 minutes. Drain, and stir in the oil and vinegar while the rice is still hot.

Cook the peas in enough salted water to cover until tender; drain thoroughly. Mix all the ingredients together, seasoning well, and pile on to a dish. Garnish with watercress sprigs before serving. **SERVES SIX TO EIGHT**

CLEAR JELLY.

CLEAR
CLARET JELLY

4 lemons
600 ml/1 pint water
175 g/6 oz lump sugar
40 g/1½ oz gelatine
whites and shells of 2 eggs
125 ml/4½ fl oz claret
few drops of red food colouring

Pare the rind from two of the lemons and squeeze the juice from all four. Make up the juice to 125 ml/4½ fl oz with water, if necessary. Put the lemon rind and juice, water, sugar and gelatine into a large saucepan.

Whisk the egg whites lightly and crush the shells; add to the lemon mixture. Whisk over a low heat until just below boiling point. Remove the whisk and allow the liquid to heat until it rises to the top of the pan. Pour in the claret carefully without disturbing the foam 'crust'. Boil again until it rises to the top of the pan.

Remove from the heat, cover and leave for 5 minutes. Strain through a jelly bag. Add the red food colouring and leave to cool. Remove any froth, pour into a wetted mould, and leave for 1–2 hours to set. Cover and store in the refrigerator. **SERVES SIX TO EIGHT**

TIPSY CAKE.

MRS BEETON'S
TIPSY CAKE

1 × 15 cm/6 in sponge cake
red currant jelly (optional)
4–5 × 15 ml spoons/4–5 tablespoons brandy or white wine and brandy
50 g/2 oz whole blanched almonds
375 ml/13 fl oz milk
125 ml/4½ fl oz single cream
8 egg yolks
75 g/3 oz caster sugar

Put the cake in a glass bowl or dish, 16 cm/6½ in in diameter and the same depth as the cake. Spread the cake thinly with jelly, if used. Pour over as much brandy or brandy and wine as the cake can absorb.

Cut the almonds into spikes lengthways, and stick them into the top of the cake all over.

Mix the milk and cream. Beat the egg yolks until liquid, and pour the milk and cream over them. Add the sugar. Cook gently in the top of a double boiler for about 10 minutes, or until the custard thickens, stirring constantly. Let the custard cool slightly, then pour it over and around the cake. Cover and chill. When cold, decorate with small spoonfuls of red currant jelly. **SERVES SIX TO EIGHT**

A CHRISTMAS DRINKS PARTY

⭐

A drinks party is a pleasant way of entertaining a number of guests without a great deal of advance preparation. You may like to offer a full range of drinks, including spirits and fortified wines, or simply table wines. In either case, there should also be non-alcoholic drinks for drivers and teetotallers. Have a quantity of pastry snacks ready in the freezer. Other items, such as dips and crudités, can be made quickly on the day. For a party that lasts 1½–2 hours, allow four or five savouries for each guest, plus nuts, crisps and snack biscuits.

Drinks parties normally take place at midday – when guests may expect to go home to a late lunch – or in the early evening, when they will go home with their appetites whetted for dinner. Experienced party-goers will have left a cold meal ready, or put a casserole in a low oven!

Whether you invite guests to arrive at around noon or six pm, you will want to offer a selection of snack foods like olives, salted nuts and tiny savoury biscuits, and perhaps something a little more substantial such as dips and pastry snacks.

'Something to eat with drinks' will be particularly appreciated by people who have some distance to travel. Drinking even a small quantity of alcohol on an empty stomach is definitely contra-indicated.

For a variety of reasons – the stringent drink-and-drive laws, the ever-rising costs, and the difficulty of serving a wide range of drinks and mixers single-handed – it is becoming less usual for a host or hostess to offer a 'full bar'. A selection of one or two table wines; a dry and a medium sherry; and, if you wish, a choice of beer, lager and cider, as well as some soft drinks, would be appreciated by most guests.

It is worth remembering that however careful your selection of drinks, there will always be some guests who would really prefer iced water.

ARRANGING THE ROOM

The first few moments of a drinks party are the most important for each and every guest. Few people are completely at ease when they arrive, and having a drink – not necessarily an alcoholic one – put in their hand straight away certainly helps to break the ice.

If possible, have someone circulating close to the door with a tray of drinks to offer each newcomer. Afterwards, you may then ask them

SPIRIT STAND

to go to a table where the drinks are served.

Try to plan the drinks table or 'bar' in a position where people can easily reach it, and just as easily move away. An ideal site is in the middle of one long wall in the room, with plenty of space on either side. This is a counsel of perfection, but in any case try to avoid siting the bar in the corner of a room, the ultimate bottle-neck.

Place the food on a separate table or, preferably, on several tables around the room. Serve cold food first, and put hot foods in the oven when most of the guests have arrived so that late-comers are not penalised by lack of choice. Apart from that, it is thoughtful to provide a hot, tasty snack – grilled cocktail sausages, fingers of cheese on toast and so on – just before guests leave.

Allow plenty of space for people to put their drinks down. Cover precious surfaces with a cloth and scatter drinks coasters liberally around the room. Do not forget ash-trays.

Tradition has it that guests circulate around the room at drinks parties, far too busy making conversation to think of sitting down. But do provide a few seats – the sofa pushed into a corner or the dining chairs ranged along a wall – for those who prefer not to stand.

Cocktail vols-au-vent (p.68) and crudités with a soured cream dip (p.69).

CHECK LIST OF DRINKS AND MIXERS

Whisky
Serve with water, lemonade, soda water or ginger ale. The addition of ice is a matter of preference. In very cold weather, 'whisky Mac', mixed with ginger wine, is warming.

Gin
Serve with tonic water, bitter lemon, lime juice, dry vermouth, or 2–3 drops of angostura bitters and iced water. Gin-based drinks are usually served with a thin slice of lemon or a twist of lemon peel and with ice.

Rum
Serve dark or white rum with lime juice, orange juice, lemonade or cola drinks; dark rum can also be mixed with water.

Vodka
Serve with tonic water, lime juice, orange juice, lemonade or cola drinks.

Vermouth, sweet and dry
Serve with tonic water, orange juice or lemonade, and a thin slice of lemon or orange.

White wine
Serve chilled wine half-and-half with soda water – known as a spritzer – or with lemonade or tonic water, for a long and less alcoholic party drink.

SELTZOGENE.

NON-ALCOHOLIC DRINKS

The days when tonic water and orange juice or even orange squash were the only non-alcoholic drinks offered have, happily, long since passed.

Make your selection of chilled soft drinks as interesting and varied as the alcoholic ones. Choose from still, cloudy apple juice served alone or half-and-half with lemonade; sparkling apple juice; still red grape juice or sparkling white grape juice, orange, pineapple, grapefruit, raspberry, peach and almost every other type of fruit juice, including 'orchard' and 'exotic' blends. Most are improved by being served with ice cubes and a twist of lemon or orange.

DRINKS MEASURES

No-one considers it at all mean to measure drinks accurately at a party. Indeed, it is a thoughtful and considerate host who does so. You can fit an optic measure to spirit bottles; otherwise, for each type of drink, work out the correct measure in advance (using water to do so!) and mark a glass accordingly. Use this as a guide when pouring the drinks.

	Glasses per standard bottle
Spirits:	24
Allow 8–10 small bottles of 'mixers' to each bottle of spirit	
Sherry	16
Table wine	6–8
Tomato juice (600 ml/1 pint)	4–6
Fruit juices (600 ml/1 pint)	4
Fruit cordial (allowing 4 litres/ 7 pints water to each bottle)	20–25
Fruit squash (allowing 2.5 litres/ 4 pints water to each bottle)	14–18

How many drinks to allow each guest is the key question. The answer really depends on whether or not your friends have to drive. Three or four 'shorts' was once considered reasonable, but now many people, especially drivers, accept only a couple of alcoholic drinks before going on to soft drinks.

Most wine merchants will allow you to buy drinks on a 'sale or return' basis, so that you can return any unopened bottles without charge – a great help when you are giving a large party. They will also lend you wine and other glasses, often without charge.

COCKTAIL
VOLS-AU-VENT

Puff Pastry, using 200 g/7 oz flour (page 48)
flour for rolling out
beaten egg for glazing

Set the oven at 220°C/425°F/gas 7.

Roll out the pastry about 1 cm/½ in thick on a lightly floured surface, and cut into round or oval shapes. Lay on a baking sheet and brush the top of the pastry with beaten egg.

With a smaller, floured cutter, make a circular or oval cut in each case, to form an inner ring, cutting through about half the depth of the pastry.

Bake until golden brown and crisp. When baked and while the cases are still warm, scoop out any soft paste from the centres.

Cocktail vols-au-vent can be served either hot or cold. If the filling is put into cold pastry cases, make sure it is quite cold. If it is put into hot pastry cases, heat the filling and the pastry separately, and fill the cases at the last minute so that the filling does not make the pastry soft. If soft cheese is used as the basis of a filling, use it cold, mix it with any hot ingredients and fill into hot cases; the heat of the case and the other ingredients should warm it through.

MAKES TWENTY-FOUR 5 cm/2 in SAVOURIES

COCKTAIL
VOL-AU-VENT FILLINGS

WITH WHITE SAUCE BASE

To 250 ml/8 fl oz white sauce made with 175 ml/5½ fl oz milk and 3 × 15 ml spoons/3 tablespoons single cream, add one of the following mixtures.

1 100 g/4 oz cooked flaked haddock, 100 g/4 oz peeled cooked prawns, 1 × 15 ml spoon/1 tablespoon sherry, 1 × 5 ml spoon/1 teaspoon very finely chopped onion, salt and pepper to taste.

2 100 g/4 oz chopped cooked mushrooms, 100 g/4 oz chopped cooked chicken, 1 × 5 ml spoon/1 teaspoon lemon juice, salt and pepper to taste.

WITH SOFT CHEESE BASE

Divide 75 g/3 oz full-fat soft cheese into two equal portions.

1 Mix half the cheese with 100 g/4 oz cooked, chopped streaky bacon rashers; mix the other half with 100 g/4 oz finely chopped cooked mushrooms and a little freshly ground black pepper.

2 Mix half the cheese with a small onion, finely chopped and gently fried; mix the other half with 100 g/4 oz chopped cooked chicken, adding paprika to taste.

THE ANCHOVY.

MRS BEETON'S
CHEESE STRAWS

50 g/2 oz butter
50 g/2 oz plain flour
50 g/2 oz soft white breadcrumbs
50 g/2 oz Cheshire or Lancashire cheese, grated
large pinch of cayenne
salt
flour for rolling out

Rub the butter into the flour, and add the breadcrumbs. Add the cheese with the seasonings. Work thoroughly by hand, to make a smooth dough. Cover and chill for 30 minutes.

Set the oven at 180°C/350°F/gas 4. Roll out the dough 5 mm/¼ in thick on a lightly floured surface. Cut into thin strips about 3 mm × 5 cm/⅛ × 2 in. Bake for 7–10 minutes. Cool on a baking sheet and serve cold.

MAKES FORTY-EIGHT TO SIXTY

CRUDITÉS

These are small raw or blanched vegetables, cut up and served with French dressing or a dip. They are usually arranged in a decorative pattern on a large flat dish or tray, from which people help themselves.

Suitable items to include are: apples, cubed, dipped in lemon juice; black or green olives; carrots, cut into matchsticks; cauliflower florets, blanched; celery, raw or blanched, sliced thinly; courgettes, unpeeled, cut into matchsticks; cucumber, cubed or sliced thickly; fennel, raw or blanched, sliced thinly; green or red peppers, cut into rings or strips; radishes, small, whole, or halved; spring onions, trimmed; tomatoes, thin wedges or slices, or if small, halved.

SAUSAGE ROLLS

400 g/14 oz prepared Puff Pastry (page 48)
flour for rolling out
400 g/14 oz sausagemeat
1 egg yolk, beaten

Roll out the pastry on a lightly floured surface and cut it into sixteen equal-sized squares. Divide the sausagemeat into sixteen equal portions, and form each portion into a roll the same length as a square of pastry. Place one roll of sausagemeat on each pastry square, moisten two edges of the pastry, and fold the pastry over so that they meet. Seal the joined edges and turn the rolls over so the joins are underneath. Leave the ends of the rolls open. Make three diagonal slits in the top of each; brush with egg yolk.

Set the oven at 230°C/450°F/gas 8. Bake the sausage rolls for 10 minutes, or until the pastry is well risen and brown. Reduce to 180°C/350°F/gas 4, and continue baking for 20–25 minutes. Cover loosely with greaseproof paper if the pastry browns too much. MAKES SIXTEEN

SOURED CREAM DIP

½ garlic clove, crushed
1 × 15 ml spoon/1 tablespoon chilli sauce
1 × 5 ml spoon/1 teaspoon creamed horseradish
1 × 15 ml spoon/1 tablespoon Worcestershire sauce
large pinch of mustard powder
pinch of cayenne
1 × 5 ml spoon/1 teaspoon lemon juice
250 ml/8 fl oz soured cream

In a small basin, combine all the ingredients. Cover and chill for 2–3 hours to allow the flavours to develop.

Serve with crudités, savoury biscuits or potato crisps. SERVES EIGHT TO TWELVE

ANCHOVY
TARTLETS

ANCHOVY PASTRY

40 g/1½ oz butter or margarine
75 g/3 oz plain flour
1 egg yolk
few drops of anchovy essence
water
flour for rolling out

ANCHOVY CREAM

1 (50 g/2 oz) can anchovy fillets, drained
yolk of 1 hard-boiled egg
25 g/1 oz butter
pinch of cayenne
3 × 15 ml spoons/3 tablespoons double cream
few drops of red food colouring
paprika
capers to garnish

Set the oven at 200°C/400°F/gas 6. Rub the butter or margarine into the flour, add the egg yolk, anchovy essence, and enough water to mix to a stiff dough. Roll out thinly on a lightly floured surface, and cut into rounds to fit small patty tins. Prick the bases all over. Bake for 6–8 minutes until crisp, then allow to cool.

Pound the anchovies with the yolk of the hard-boiled egg and the butter until smooth; season with a little cayenne. Whip the cream until fairly stiff, and fold it in. Add the red food colouring, drop by drop, until the anchovy cream is pale pink.

Fill the pastry cases with anchovy cream, piling it high in the centre. Sprinkle with paprika and garnish with capers. MAKES TWELVE

A LUNCH PARTY
★

In the middle of the festive season, a lunch menu may be all the more enjoyable for the simplicity of the dishes. Plan the meal around either poached salmon or steak. You could start the meal with consommé, making the soup in advance and leaving only the garnish to prepare on the day, and finish with a choice of two desserts (or just one, and add Clementines in Vodka from the larder) and a varied cheeseboard.

CONSOMME
JARDINIERE

100 g/4 oz shin of beef
125 ml/4½ fl oz water
1 small onion
1 small carrot
1 small celery stick
1.25 litres/2 pints cold brown stock
bouquet garni
salt
4 white peppercorns
white and crushed shell of 1 egg

GARNISH

1 × 15 ml spoon/1 tablespoon finely diced turnip
1 × 15 ml spoon/1 tablespoon finely diced carrot
1 × 15 ml spoon/1 tablespoon small green peas
1 × 15 ml spoon/1 tablespoon tiny cauliflower florets *or* 1 × 15 ml spoon/1 tablespoon finely diced cucumber

Shred the beef finely, trimming off all the fat. Soak the meat in the water for 15 minutes. Then put the meat, water and remaining ingredients into a deep saucepan, adding the egg white and shell last. Heat slowly to simmering point, whisking constantly, until a froth rises to the surface. Remove the whisk, cover, and simmer the consommé very gently for 1½–2 hours. Do not allow to boil or the froth will break up and

cloud the consommé.

Strain slowly into a basin through muslin or a scalded jelly bag. If necesssary, strain the consommé again. Reheat, re-season if required and serve with the vegetable garnish.

To make the garnish, cook the vegetables separately in boiling salted water until just tender. Drain and rinse the vegetables; then put them into a warmed tureen.

Pour the hot consommé over the vegetables and serve. SERVES SIX

PESTLE AND MORTAR.

Left: *Consommé jardiniére.*

Right: *Tweed kettle salmon and petits pois à la Française* (p.72).

TWEED KETTLE
SALMON

800 g/1¾ lb middle cut salmon
500 ml/18 fl oz fish stock or water
250 ml/8 fl oz dry white wine
pinch of ground mace
salt and pepper
25 g/1 oz butter
25 g/1 oz flour
25 g/1 oz shallots or chives
1 × 5 ml spoon/1 teaspoon chopped parsley

Put the salmon in a deep frying pan and add the fish stock or water, wine, mace and seasonings. Poach gently for 10–15 minutes, or until just cooked through. Remove the fish; skin and bone it. Put the flesh in a serving dish and keep hot.

Return the skin and bones to the liquid and simmer gently, uncovered, for 10 minutes, then strain. Return the strained liquid to the pan, and simmer gently, uncovered, until reduced by half. Work the butter and flour together to make a smooth *beurre manié*.

Chop the shallots finely, if used, and add them or the snipped chives with the parsley to the fish liquid. Remove from the heat and gradually add the *beurre manié* in small pieces, stirring constantly. Return to the heat and simmer for another 5 minutes. Season to taste. Pour the sauce over the fish.

Serve with boiled potatoes and peas.

SERVES SIX

STEAKS
WITH MUSTARD SAUCE

6 fillet or sirloin steaks (150-200 g/5-7 oz each)
freshly ground black pepper
40 g/1½ oz unsalted butter
3 × 15 ml spoons/3 tablespoons oil
200 ml/6 fl oz soured cream
4 × 5 ml spoons/4 teaspoons lemon juice
1 × 15 ml spoon/1 tablespoon French mustard
salt

Wipe the steaks and trim off any excess fat. Beat each steak lightly on both sides with a rolling pin. Season with pepper. (Do not salt steaks before frying because this makes the juices run.)

Heat the butter and oil in a heavy-based frying pan. When hot, put in the steaks and fry quickly on both sides for the required cooking time (see below). Transfer the steaks to a warmed serving dish, and keep hot.

Stir the soured cream into the juices in the pan and cook gently, without boiling. Stir in the lemon juice, mustard and salt to taste. Pour the mustard sauce over the steaks and serve at once.

SERVES SIX

STEAK FRYING TIMES

	Fillet	Sirloin
Thickness of meat	2 cm/ 1¾ in	2–2.5 cm/ 1¾–2 in
Cooking times (in minutes)		
Rare	6	5
Medium-rare	7	6–7
Well-done	8	9–10

PETITS POIS
A LA FRANCAISE

50 g/2 oz butter
1 lettuce heart, shredded
bunch of spring onions or 2 shallots, chopped
700 g/1½ lb frozen peas
salt and pepper
pinch of granulated sugar

Melt the butter in a saucepan, and add the remaining ingredients. Cover and simmer gently for 8–10 minutes, or until the peas are very tender. Re-season if required before serving.

SERVES SIX

COFFEE
CHIFFON PIE

PIE SHELL
100 g/4 oz digestive biscuits
50 g/2 oz butter, melted
25 g/1 oz walnuts, finely chopped
25 g/1 oz caster sugar
FILLING
100 g/4 oz caster sugar
2 × 5 ml spoons/2 teaspoons gelatine
2 eggs
250 ml spoon/8 fl oz cold water
1 × 15 ml spoon/1 tablespoon instant coffee
pinch of salt
2 × 5 ml spoons/2 teaspoons lemon juice
DECORATION
whipped cream

To make the pie shell, crush the biscuits with a rolling pin. Mix the butter with the crumbs, nuts and sugar. Line a shallow 18 cm/7½ in pie plate with the mixture; press it firmly and evenly all over the base and sides. Chill to set.

To make the filling, mix 50 g/2 oz of the sugar with the gelatine. Separate the eggs. Heat 3 × 15 ml spoons/3 tablespoons of the water. Dissolve the coffee in the hot water, then add the rest of the water to make the liquid up to 250 ml/8 fl oz. Blend the egg yolks and black coffee in a saucepan or a basin over a pan of hot water or in a double boiler. Add a pinch of salt and stir in the gelatine and sugar mixture. Cook over a gentle heat for about 15 minutes, stirring constantly, until the custard thickens slightly. Do not let it boil. Pour into a cold basin, cover with damp greaseproof paper, and chill until on the point of setting.

Stir the lemon juice into the cooled mixture. Whisk the egg whites until foamy, gradually whisk in the remaining sugar and continue whisking until the mixture is stiff and glossy. Fold the coffee custard into the meringue, pour into the pie shell and chill for at least 1 hour until set. Serve decorated with whipped cream. SERVES FOUR TO SIX

> **HABITAT OF THE SALMON:** —
> *The salmon is styled by Walton the 'king of fresh-water fish,' and is found distributed over the north of Europe and Asia, from Britain to Kamschatka, but is never found in warm latitudes, nor has it ever been caught even so far south as the Mediterranean. It lives in fresh as well as in salt waters, depositing its spawn in the former, hundreds of miles from the mouths of some of those rivers to which it has been known to resort. In 1859, great efforts were made to introduce this fish into the Australian colonies; and it is believed that the attempt, after many difficulties, which were very skilfully overcome, has been successful.*
>
> MRS BEETON (1861)

PEARS WITH WINE

125 g/4½ oz granulated sugar
275 ml/8½ fl oz water
3 × 15 ml spoons/3 tablespoons red currant jelly
2 cm/¾ in cinnamon stick
6 large ripe cooking pears (about 700 g/1½ lb)
275 ml/8½ fl oz red wine
40 g/1½ oz blanched almonds
few drops of red food colouring (optional)

Put the sugar, water, red currant jelly, and cinnamon stick into a saucepan and heat gently until the sugar and jelly have dissolved.

Peel the pears, leaving the stalks in place. Carefully remove as much of the core as possible without breaking the fruit. Add the pears to the sugar mixture, cover, and simmer gently for 15 minutes. Add the wine, and cook, uncovered, for a further 15 minutes. Remove the pears carefully, arrange them on a serving dish and keep warm.

Remove the cinnamon stick. Shred the almonds and add to the pan. Boil the liquid rapidly until it is reduced to a thin syrup. Add a few drops of red food colouring if the colour is not deep enough. Pour the syrup over the pears and serve warm, with fresh single or double cream.

This dessert can also be served cold. Pour the hot syrup over the pears, leave to cool, then chill before serving.

Note Alternatively, the pears can be baked at 120°C/250°F/gas ½ for 4–5 hours. SERVES SIX

STEWED PEARS.

LOYSEL'S HYDROSTATIC URN.

> **A VERY SIMPLE METHOD OF MAKING COFFEE.**
> **INGREDIENTS:** — *Allow ½ oz, or 1 tablespoonful, of coffee to each person; to every oz. allow ½ pint water.*
>
> *Have a small iron ring made to fit the top of the coffee-pot inside, and to this ring sew a small muslin bag (the muslin for the purpose must not be too thin). Fit the bag into the pot, pour some boiling water in it, and when the pot is well warmed, put the ground coffee into the bag; pour over as much boiling water as is required, close the lid, and, when all the water has filtered through, remove the bag and send the coffee to the table. Making it in this manner prevents the necessity of pouring the coffee from one vessel to another, which cools and spoils it. The water should be poured on the coffee gradually, so that the infusion may be stronger; and the bag must be well made, that none of the grounds may escape through the seams, and so make the coffee thick and muddy.*
>
> MRS BEETON (1861)

A DINNER PARTY

★

Roast pheasant with ham stuffing, the main dish of this suggested menu for a formal dinner party, would also make a delicious alternative to poultry or beef for Christmas dinner. The meal could start with a choice of two fish and seafood dishes – you could also serve a vegetable soup if you wished – and draw to a spectacular climax with two highly decorative and complementary desserts, a choux pastry ring and a fresh fruit salad basket, and Irish coffee.

POTTED SHRIMPS
OR PRAWNS

250 g/9 oz unsalted butter
450 g/1 lb peeled cooked shrimps or prawns
large pinch of ground white pepper
large pinch of ground mace
large pinch of ground cloves
melted Clarified Butter (page 17)
lemon wedges

Melt the unsalted butter in a pan and heat the shellfish very gently, without boiling, with the pepper, mace and cloves. Turn into small pots with a little of the butter. Leave the remaining butter until the residue has settled, then pour the butter over the shellfish.

Chill until firm, then cover with clarified butter. Store in a refrigerator for not more than 48 hours before use.

Serve with lemon wedges and very thin slices of brown bread and butter.   SERVES SIX

★

THE SHRIMP.

SMOKED
MACKEREL PÂTÉ

40 g/1½ oz Clarified Butter (page 17)
3 shallots, very finely chopped
75 g/3 oz concentrated tomato purée
1 × 5 ml spoon/1 teaspoon soft light brown sugar
juice of ½ lemon
8 crushed peppercorns
1 × 5 ml spoon/1 teaspoon chopped fresh basil, or large pinch of dried basil
large pinch of dried tarragon
few drops of Tabasco sauce
550 g/1¼ lb skinned smoked mackerel fillets
100 ml/4 fl oz double cream
additional melted clarified butter for sealing
parsley sprigs to garnish

Melt the clarified butter in a saucepan and cook the shallots gently until softened. Add the tomato purée, sugar, lemon juice, peppercorns and herbs, and cook gently for 4–5 minutes to make a sauce. Add the Tabasco sauce, remove from the heat and leave to cool.

Purée the sauce, mackerel and cream in a blender or pound to a smooth paste. Turn into a suitable dish or mould, or into individual dishes, and leave to cool. Cover with clarified butter.

‘ THE HEIGHT OF EXCELLENCE IN A PHEASANT: — *Kept . . . a proper length of time . . . then it becomes a highly-flavoured dish, occupying, so to speak, the middle distance between chicken and venison. It is difficult to define the exact time to "hang" a pheasant; but any one possessed of the instincts of gastronomical science, can at once detect the right moment when a pheasant should be taken down, in the same way as a good cook knows whether a bird should be removed from the spit, or have a turn or two more. ’

MRS BEETON (1861)

THE PHEASANT.

Leave until the butter is firm.

Garnish with parsley, and serve with hot dry toast.   SERVES SIX

ROAST PHEASANT
WITH HAM STUFFING

2 pheasants
½ onion, sliced
50 g/2 oz butter

STUFFING

25 g/1 oz butter or margarine
100 g/4 oz onion, chopped
100 g/4 oz mushrooms, chopped
50 g/2 oz lean ham, chopped
75 g/3 oz soft white breadcrumbs
1 × 15 ml spoon/1 tablespoon stock or red wine
salt and pepper
watercress sprigs to garnish

Wash the giblets, cover them with water, add the onion and simmer gently for 40 minutes. Strain and reserve the liquid.

Make the stuffing. Melt the butter in a small saucepan and cook the onion until soft. Stir in the mushrooms, ham, breadcrumbs, stock or wine and seasoning. Divide the stuffing between the body cavities of the birds. Truss the birds neatly and put them in a roasting tin. Spread with the butter.

Set the oven at 190°C/375°F/gas 5. Roast the birds for 45 minutes–1 hour, depending on size, basting occasionally. Transfer the birds to a heated serving dish and remove the trussing strings. Garnish with the watercress.

Pour off all but 2 × 15 ml spoons/2 table-spoons of the fat in the pan and use the reserved stock to make gravy. Serve with Fried Bread-crumbs (below). SERVES SIX

FRIED BREADCRUMBS

Heat a little butter in a frying pan, add some soft white breadcrumbs, season to taste with salt and pepper, and fry until well browned. Drain well on absorbent kitchen paper. Serve hot.

Fruit salad in a melon basket (p.76).

DUCHESSE
POTATOES

700 g/1½ lb old potatoes
40 g/1½ oz butter or margarine
1 egg plus 1 yolk, or 3 egg yolks
salt and pepper
grated nutmeg (optional)
butter or margarine for greasing
beaten egg for brushing

Boil or steam the potatoes. Drain thoroughly, and sieve. Beat in the butter or margarine and egg and egg yolks. Season to taste with salt and pepper and add a little grated nutmeg, if used.

Spoon the mixture into a piping bag fitted with a large rose nozzle and pipe rounds of potato on to a greased baking tray. Brush with a little beaten egg.

Set the oven at 200°C/400°F/gas 6. Bake the potatoes for about 15 minutes, or until they are a good golden brown.

Note The potatoes can be piped on to the baking tray and then baked when required. If a piping bag is not available, shape the potato into diamonds, rounds or triangles. Criss-cross the tops with a knife, brush with the egg, and bake as above. SERVES SIX

MANGE-TOUT
PEAS

These flat pea pods are widely available both fresh and frozen throughout the year. The word literally meats 'eat all' which is what you do.

To buy: Allow 50–75 g/2–3 oz per person. If buying the vegetables fresh, choose mange-tout peas that are a good green colour and appear bright.

To store: They should be eaten as fresh as possible, but can be kept for a day or two in the bottom of a refrigerator.

To prepare: Remove the tops and tails of the mange-tout peas and any strings from the sides of older pods.

To boil: Cook fresh mange-tout peas in the very minimum of boiling salted water for about 2–3 minutes, or until just tender. Drain thoroughly, turn into a serving dish, and season with pepper, preferably freshly ground. Spoon plenty of melted butter over them and serve as soon as possible.

To steam: Season the mange-tout peas with salt and cook in the top of a steamer over a pan of boiling water for 5 minutes. Drain and serve as for boiled mange-tout peas.

Cook frozen mange-tout peas according to the directions on the packet.

GLAZED CARROTS

550 g/1¼ lb young carrots
50 g/2 oz butter
3 sugar lumps
large pinch of salt
beef stock
1 × 15 ml spoon/1 tablespoon chopped parsley

Prepare the carrots but leave them whole. Melt the butter in a saucepan. Add the carrots, sugar, salt and enough stock to half-cover the carrots. Cook gently, without a lid, for 15–20 minutes, or until the carrots are tender, shaking the pan occasionally.

Remove the carrots with a perforated spoon and keep warm. Boil the stock rapidly in the pan until it is reduced to a rich glaze. Replace the carrots, two or three at a time, and turn them in the glaze until they are thoroughly coated. Put in a serving dish and garnish with parsley before serving. SERVES SIX

FRUIT SALAD
IN A MELON BASKET

1 large green melon
100 g/4 oz black grapes
100 g/4 oz green grapes
4 mandarins or satsumas
2 kiwi fruit
1 small can black stoned cherries, drained
SYRUP
pared rind and juice of 1 lemon
500 ml/18 fl oz water
75 g/3 oz granulated sugar

To make the syrup, put the lemon rind and juice into a saucepan with the water and sugar. Heat gently until the sugar has dissolved, then bring to the boil, and continue boiling until the syrup has been reduced by about half. Remove from the heat, strain, and leave to cool.

To prepare the melon basket, remove the top third of the fruit crossways, leaving a narrow strip for the handle. Keeping the case intact, scoop out the flesh from the rest of the fruit, leaving about a 1 cm/½ in rim. Cut all the melon flesh into small cubes, or into balls, using a small fruit baller.

Prepare the other fruits according to type. Cut black and white grapes in half and remove the pips. Divide the mandarins or satsumas into segments, discarding the pips and white stringy fibres. Peel and slice the kiwi fruit and halve the slices.

Put the melon and other fruits into a bowl. Pour the syrup over the fruit and mix gently, taking care not to break up the fruit. Cover and chill for at least 2 hours to allow the flavours to blend.

Cut a thin slice from the base of the melon so that it will stand upright. Stand the melon basket on a serving dish. Use a perforated spoon to transfer the fruit salad to the melon container, piling it up into a high mound. Spoon in some of the syrup, and serve the rest separately.

Serve with chilled single or double cream.

SERVES SIX

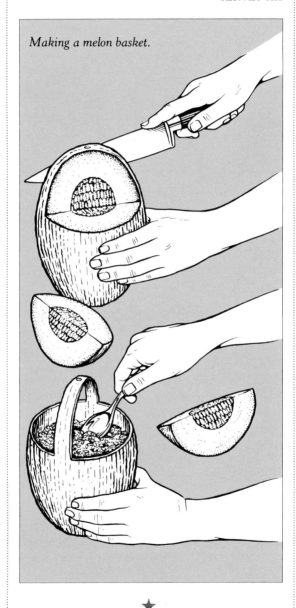

Making a melon basket.

★

PARIS-BREST
(Ring Gâteau with Praline-flavoured Cream)

butter for greasing
350 g/12 oz freshly prepared Choux Pastry (right)
1 egg yolk, beaten with a little milk
25 g/1 oz flaked almonds
icing sugar for dusting

PRALINE CREAM

50 g/2 oz unblanched hazelnuts
125 g/4½ oz granulated sugar
2 × 15 ml spoons/2 tablespoons water
125 ml/4½ fl oz double cream
125 ml/4½ fl oz single cream

Grease a baking sheet lightly with butter. Spoon the choux pastry into a piping bag with a 1 cm/½ in nozzle and pipe an 18 cm/7½ in ring of paste on the sheet. Alternatively, pipe it into a lightly greased 18 cm/7½ in flan ring. Brush the top of the ring with egg wash, then sprinkle liberally with the flaked almonds.

Set the oven at 190°C/375°F/gas 5. Bake the ring for 30 minutes. Cool on the sheet or in the flan ring, if used.

To make the praline cream, rub off any loose skins from the hazelnuts. Heat the sugar and water until the sugar is a light golden brown. Stir in the nuts. Turn the mixture on to an oiled marble or metal surface and leave to harden. Crush the cooled praline finely. Whisk the double cream until very stiff, gradually whisk in the single cream, then fold in the praline.

Split the choux ring into two layers, remove any soft pastry from the inside, and fill with the praline-flavoured cream. The cream will stand up above the pastry casing. Join the two halves together carefully so that the gâteau is like a sandwich with a very thick filling. Dust the almond-topped surface of the gâteau with icing sugar. Serve immediately.   **SERVES SIX**

CHOUX PASTRY

200 ml/6 fl oz water
40 g/1½ oz butter or margarine
pinch of salt
75 g/3 oz plain flour, sifted
1 egg yolk
2 eggs

Put the water, fat and salt into a saucepan, and bring to the boil. Remove from the heat and add the flour all at once. Return to the heat and beat well with a wooden spoon until the mixture forms a smooth paste, which leaves the sides of the pan clean. Remove from the heat, cool slightly, then add the egg yolk and beat well. Add the whole eggs, one at a time, beating thoroughly between each addition.

Note This pastry rises better if used while still warm, but raw pastry or baked shells can be frozen successfully.

MAKES ABOUT 350 g/12 oz

IRISH COFFEE

2 × 15 ml spoons/2 tablespoons Irish whiskey
1 × 5 ml spoon/1 teaspoon brown sugar
125 ml/4½ fl oz hot, strong black coffee
4 × 5 ml spoons/4 teaspoons double cream, lightly whipped

Warm a 200 ml/6 fl oz glass, pour in the whiskey and add the brown sugar. Top up to within 2 cm/¾ in of the rim with hot, strong black coffee and stir to dissolve the sugar. Pour the cream into the glass slowly over the back of a rounded spoon held close to the surface, so that it floats on the top of the coffee. Do not stir after the cream has been added. Serve immediately.

FILLS ONE GLASS

☆ 77

A HOT BUFFET

★

When planning a hot buffet party, your first thought is likely to be, 'What can we have for a change?' A selection of mildly spiced curry dishes is the perfect answer. The main dish, using minced meat, is not expensive. All the spiced dishes, and the two desserts, can be made in advance and frozen, so you have only to cook the rice on the day. Offer a selection of fruit chutneys, grilled poppadoms and, if you wish, a cool, crisp green salad.

KEEMA
(Minced Meat Curry)

150 ml/¼ pint vegetable oil

2 large onions, sliced

4 garlic cloves, crushed

small piece of ginger root, peeled and grated

5 × 5 ml spoons/5 teaspoons ground coriander

2 × 5 ml spoons/2 teaspoons turmeric

1 × 2.5 ml spoon/½ teaspoon chilli powder

1 × 5 ml spoon/1 teaspoon ground cumin

1 × 5 ml spoon/1 teaspoon cumin seeds

4 black peppercorns

3 bay leaves

2 cloves

1 whole cardamom

small piece of cinnamon stick

2 green chillies

450 g/1 lb lamb bones

1 kg/2¼ lb minced beef or lamb

350 ml/12 fl oz water

Heat the oil in a saucepan, and fry the onions until they begin to colour. Add the garlic, spices and whole chillies, stirring constantly. Cook rapidly for about 2 minutes. Add the meat bones, and fry quickly until brown. Add the minced meat, and stir for about 10–12 minutes, or until all the lumps are broken up and it is evenly fried. Add the water, bring to the boil, reduce the heat, cover and simmer for 1 hour, adding a little more water if necessary. Discard the bones and whole chillies before serving.
Serve hot.   SERVES TEN

★

INDIAN COOKS

PULAO RICE
(Fried Rice)

400 g/14 oz Basmati rice

2 × 15 ml spoons/2 tablespoons vegetable oil

1 onion, very thinly sliced

1 × 2 cm/¾ in piece cinnamon stick

2 whole cardamoms

2 bay leaves

4 black peppercorns

1 × 2.5 ml spoon/½ teaspoon cumin seeds

900 ml/1½ pints water

2 × 5 ml spoons/2 teaspoons salt

Wash the rice in a colander under warm running water, rubbing it between your hands until the water runs clear. Drain and put to one side.

Heat the oil in a deep saucepan, and fry the onion until transparent. Add all the spices and fry over a medium heat for 2–3 minutes, or until they give off a fragrant aroma. Add the water and salt. When the water begins to boil, add the rice. Bring back to the boil, then reduce the heat as low as possible. Cover the pan with a tight-fitting lid. Cook for 15 minutes, or until the rice is dry.   SERVES TEN

★

From top left in a clockwise direction: *Aloo (p.80), pulao Rice, puris (p.80), dal and keema.*

ALOO
(Fried Spiced Potatoes)

1 kg/2¼ lb potatoes
1 green chilli
5 × 15 ml spoons/5 tablespoons vegetable oil
1 large onion, diced
2 × 5 ml spoons/2 teaspoons mustard seeds
2 × 5 ml spoons/2 teaspoons turmeric
1 × 5 ml spoon/1 teaspoon chilli powder
1 × 5 ml spoon/1 teaspoon salt
100 ml/4 fl oz water
3 × 15 ml spoons/3 tablespoons fresh lemon juice (optional)

Parboil the potatoes and cut them into pieces. Chop the green chilli finely and discard the seeds.

Heat the oil in a saucepan and fry the onion until soft and transparent. Add the mustard seeds and fry for 1 minute. Add all the other spices, the salt and chopped green chilli, and fry for 1 minute. Add the parboiled potatoes, and stir until well coated with the spicy mixture. Add the water. Cover with a lid, reduce the heat, and cook gently for 15–20 minutes, or until the potatoes are completely cooked.

Sprinkle with lemon juice, if liked, and serve hot.   SERVES TEN

DAL
(Indian Spiced Lentils)

1 large onion, thinly sliced
2 tomatoes, roughly chopped
small piece of ginger root, peeled and grated
400 g/14 oz red lentils
750 ml/1¼ pints water
2 green chillies
2 × 5 ml spoons/2 teaspoons turmeric
2 × 5 ml spoons/2 teaspoons ground coriander
1 × 2.5 ml spoon/½ teaspoon chilli powder
1 × 2.5 ml spoon/½ teaspoon ground cumin
1 × 5 ml spoon/1 teaspoon salt
SAUCE
3 × 15 ml spoons/3 tablespoons vegetable oil
3 garlic cloves, finely chopped
1 × 5 ml spoon/1 teaspoon cumin seeds
1 × 10 cm/4 in piece cinnamon stick
6 dried red chillies

Put all the ingredients into a saucepan, bring to the boil, reduce the heat, and simmer until the lentils are tender.

For the sauce, heat the oil and fry the garlic until golden. Add the spices and fry for 2 minutes. Stir this sauce into the lentils and cook for 10 minutes. The lentils will absorb the fragrance of the spices.

Serve hot.   SERVES TEN

PURIS
(Deep-fried Unleavened Wholemeal Bread)

450 g/1 lb wholemeal flour
1 × 5 ml spoon/1 teaspoon salt
flour for kneading
vegetable oil for deep frying

Mix the flour and salt in a bowl. Gradually add enough water to make a soft pliable dough. Turn on to a floured surface and knead until firm. Cover with a damp cloth and leave for 30 minutes. Divide the dough into twenty-four equal portions. Shape into balls and roll out each one into a thin round pancake about 10 cm/4 in in diameter.

Heat the oil in a deep frying pan. When it begins to sizzle, drop in a puri. Press it gently with a spoon. It should puff up immediately. Cook for about 10 minutes until golden brown on both sides, turning once. Remove and drain thoroughly. Keep hot while frying the remaining puris in the same way.

Serve hot.   MAKES TWENTY-FOUR

'INDIAN CURRY-POWDER, *founded on Dr. Kitchener's Recipe* INGREDIENTS: — ¼ lb of coriander-seed, ¼ lb of turmeric, 2 oz of cinnamon seed, ½ oz of cayenne, 1 oz of mustard, 1 oz of ground ginger, ½ oz of allspice, 2 oz of fenugreek-seed.

Mode: — *Put all the ingredients in a cool oven, where they should remain one night; then pound them in a mortar, rub them through a sieve, and mix thoroughly together; keep the powder in a bottle, from which the air should be completely excluded.*

Note: — *We have given this recipe for curry-powder, as some persons prefer to make it at home; but that purchased at any respectable shop is, generally speaking, far superior, and, taking all things into consideration, very frequently more economical.* '

MRS BEETON (1861)

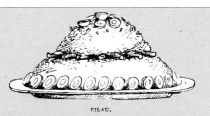

PILAU.

APPLE SNOW

8 large cooking apples
pared rind and juice of 2 lemons
about 200 g/7 oz granulated sugar
500 ml/18 fl oz milk
4–5 eggs
100 g/4 oz caster sugar
2 × 5 ml spoons/2 teaspoons cornflour or arrowroot
8 individual sponge cakes
glacé cherries to decorate

Cook the apples, then purée in a blender. Add the lemon juice to the purée, sweeten to taste and leave to cool.

Put the lemon rind into a small saucepan with the milk and heat gently for 15 minutes, then strain. Separate the eggs and blend the yolks and caster sugar together with the cornflour or arrowroot. Add the lemon-infused milk. Cook, stirring constantly, in a pan for 20–30 minutes, or until the custard coats the back of the spoon. Cool.

Split the sponge cakes in half and arrange them in the bottom of a glass dish. Pour the custard over them. Whisk the egg whites until they form stiff peaks, then fold into the apple purée. Pile the mixture on top of the custard and decorate with the glacé cherries. Chill.

SERVES TEN

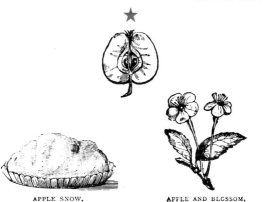

APPLE SNOW.　　APPLE AND BLOSSOM.

SCANDINAVIAN
FRUIT FOOL

1 kg/2¼ lb mixed soft fruit, frozen, eg raspberries, red currants, blackberries
300 ml/½ pint water
about 200 g/7 oz granulated sugar
50 g/2 oz ground sago or 2 × 15 ml spoons/2 tablespoons cornflour
caster sugar for sprinkling
50 g/2 oz flaked almonds to decorate

Put the fruit into a saucepan with the water and simmer gently for 5 minutes. Sieve the fruit, or purée in a blender and then sieve to remove all the pips; return to the pan. Add sugar to taste. Blend the sago or cornflour with a little of the purée and bring the remaining purée to the boil. Add the sago or cornflour and bring back to the boil, stirring constantly until the fool thickens.

Remove from the heat and turn into two large or ten small dishes. Sprinkle with a little extra caster sugar to prevent a skin forming, and then sprinkle on the flaked almonds. Chill well and serve with whipped cream and boudoir biscuits.

SERVES TEN

A CHILDREN'S PARTY

★

Younger people – almost however young – have very strong views on the kind of party they want to have, and the food they want to enjoy with their friends. Savoury foods are firm favourites. Do not fall into the trap of making a large selection of cakes and other sweet things more to satisfy your own need to 'put on a good spread' than to please the young hosts and guests.

The success of a children's party depends on really careful planning and organisation. Decide how many children you can cope with, invite them in good time and be specific about when the party starts and when the children should be collected.

Tea itself will take a surprisingly short time. The food should be chosen to please the children rather than their mothers. Children's tastes are relatively unsophisticated – sausages and fish fingers could be their idea of a good party. Choose savoury rather than sweet things; they tend to be more popular and healthier. Serve orange and lemon squash to drink. Remember to cover the carpet around the tea-table, and think about using disposable table-ware.

TWIRL THE TRENCHER.

The mothers or fathers of some of the children may stay for part or all of the afternoon, in which case you will need to provide plenty of tea to drink and some extra sandwiches and cakes.

VICTORIA SANDWICH CAKE

fat for greasing
175 g/6 oz butter or margarine
175 g/6 oz caster sugar
3 eggs
175 g/6 oz self-raising flour or plain flour and 1 × 5 ml spoon/1 teaspoon baking powder
pinch of salt
raspberry or other jam for filling
caster sugar for dredging

Grease and line two 18 cm/7½ in sandwich tins. Cream the butter or margarine and sugar together until light and fluffy. Beat the eggs until they become liquid, and add them to the butter mixture gradually, beating well after each addition. Sift together the flour, salt and baking powder, if used. Stir into the mixture, lightly but thoroughly, until evenly mixed. Alternatively, use an electric mixer to make the mixture by the one-step method.

Set the oven at 180°C/350°F/gas 4. Divide the mixture between the tins and bake for 25–30 minutes. Cool on a wire rack. When cold, sandwich together with jam. Sprinkle the top with caster sugar, or cover it with glacé icing (page 61) in a feather or other decorative pattern.

MAKES ONE **18 cm/7½ in** SANDWICH CAKE

VARIATION

To make a chocolate sandwich cake, use 150 g/5 oz self-raising flour and 25 g/1 oz cocoa powder, and add a few drops of vanilla essence with the eggs. Fill with chocolate butter icing.

CAKE BASKET.

A Victoria sandwich cake decorated with feather icing (p.84) and chopped nuts.

FEATHER ICING

Make up some white glacé icing (page 61) using 175 g/6 oz icing sugar. Remove 2 × 15 ml spoons/2 tablespoons and tint it with a few drops of food colouring. Brown and red are the colours usually chosen, as they show up well.

Coat the top of the cake with the white icing. Spoon the tinted icing into a piping bag fitted with a fine writing pipe, and pipe parallel lines over the white icing; do this quickly before the coating sets. Then run a cocktail stick or fine skewer lightly across the cake in parallel lines, backwards and forwards at right angles to the piping. Leave to set firmly before cutting.

COVERS TOP OF ONE **18 cm/7½ in** CAKE

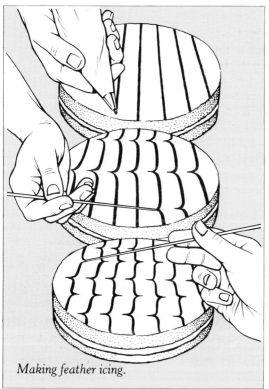

Making feather icing.

CRUNCHIES

100 g/4 oz margarine
125 g/4½ oz rolled oats
75 g/3 oz demerara sugar
fat for greasing

Set the oven at 190°C/375°F/gas 5.

Melt the margarine and stir in the oats and sugar. Press into a greased 28 × 18 cm/ 11 × 7½ in tin and bake for 15 minutes. Cut into squares or strips while warm, and leave in the tin until cool.   MAKES ABOUT TWENTY

FRUIT PUNCH

about 175 g/6 oz caster sugar
1.25 litres/2 pints water
5 × 15 ml spoons/5 tablespoons strong tea without milk
juice of 6 lemons
juice of 6 oranges
500 ml/18 fl oz grape juice
1 (225 g/8 oz) can crushed pineapple
about 1 litre/1¾ pints ginger ale
ice cubes
DECORATION
slices of lemon
slices of orange
1 (175 g/6 oz) bottle maraschino cherries

Boil the sugar and water together for 6 minutes. Add the tea, leave to cool, then chill. When cold, add the fruit juices and pineapple. Chill for about 2 hours.

Just before serving, pour in the ginger ale to taste. Add ice cubes and decorate with the sliced fruit and cherries. Older children will feel very grown-up to be offered this fizzy, fruity punch.
FILLS TWENTY-FIVE SMALL GLASSES

COCKTAIL
SAUSAGES

Children love sausages, and their very own party is the ideal time to indulge that universal craving.

Bite-sized sausages are best – avoiding the need for knives and forks. If you cannot buy cocktail sausages, use chipolatas instead. Make each into two small sausages by squeezing the middle and pushing the meat to each end. Give the casing a good twist, and cut through the twist.

Grill, bake or fry the sausages, whichever is most convenient. Serve them piping hot, speared on cocktail sticks and accompanied by a bar-becue-style dip. They look specially good if you push the sticks into a large scrubbed potato. If you wish, alternate the speared sausages with pineapple chunks or cubes of Cheddar cheese.

Allow four cocktail sausages, or two chipolatas for each guest.

PARTY
SANDWICHES

Sandwiches are an important part of any children's party spread. It is best not to be too adventurous with the fillings – the youngest members of the family are notorious for being creatures of habit – but you and the children can have fun with the shapes. Mix and match white and wholemeal breads sliced into fingers, rolled into spirals and cut out with biscuit cutters.

RIBBON SANDWICHES

Use a white and a brown loaf. Cut off all the crusts and cut thin slices lengthways from both

loaves. Spread the filling evenly. Assemble a striped loaf by alternating white and brown slices in layers. Press the slices together firmly, wrap in cling film, and chill. To serve, cut the bread through the layers.

CHEQUERBOARD SANDWICHES

Prepare a ribbon sandwich (above) cutting all the bread slices 1 cm/½ in thick. Cut only four slices from each loaf, and spread the filling evenly. Make up the slices into a loaf. Cut this ribbon loaf into 1 cm/½ in thick slices and spread each slice with butter and filling.

Pile four slices one above the other with strips of bread all running in the same direction, but with brown strips over white strips and vice versa, making a design of squares when seen from the side. Place the top slice buttered side down. Press the stack firmly together, wrap in cling film, and chill well. Repeat this process with all the remaining slices.

To serve, cut each stack into slices with a chequerboard design.

Making chequerboard sandwiches.

ROLLED SANDWICHES

Use 1 thin white or 1 thin brown slice of bread, cut lengthways from a loaf. Cut off the crusts. Spread thinly with filling, and roll up like a Swiss roll. If necessary, secure with a cocktail stick.

Wrap in foil, and chill. To serve, cut in thin rounds from the roll.

Making rolled sandwiches.

CHRISTMAS SANDWICH SHAPES

Use thinly sliced white or wholemeal bread, or a mixture of both. (Fancy sandwiches are an easy way to introduce reluctant children to the benefits of wholemeal bread.) Place two pieces of bread together and cut through them with a large biscuit cutter – a bell, Christmas tree, Santa Claus or any other shape you have – cutting out two or more shapes per slice if possible.

Save the off-cut pieces of bread. You can process them in a blender or food processor to make crumbs for a stuffing or topping. By buttering and filling the sandwiches after cutting out the shapes, you do not waste the costly ingredients.

Spread the shapes with softened butter or margarine on one side, then with the filling. Assemble the sandwiches and arrange them on a serving plate so that the shapes can be clearly seen.

SANDWICH
FILLINGS

Easily spread fillings and those comprising finely chopped ingredients are most suitable to serve at children's parties. Fillings such as whole slices of meat are more difficult to handle, and the sandwich may disintegrate in the excitement of the moment. And of course for fancy-shaped sandwiches, easily spread fillings are essential.

SAVOURY FILLINGS

Mix grated hard cheese or soft easily spread cheese with:
* chopped or sliced salad vegetables such as cucumber or celery;
* chopped olives, gherkins or chives;
* chutney or sweet pickles;
* chopped nuts such as walnuts or peanuts;
* crisply cooked, crumbled bacon.

Mix chopped hard-boiled or scrambled eggs with:
* finely chopped ham or frankfurters;
* mashed sardines;
* chopped or sliced fresh salad vegetables (eg celery, tomato, green pepper) and soured cream;
* chopped fresh herbs such as green spring onion, mint, chives, parsley.

Mix chopped nuts with:
* finely chopped or grated salad vegetables (eg grated carrot), flavoured with lemon juice;
* mashed avocado pear, flavoured with lemon juice to prevent discoloration.

SANDWICH TRAY.

Mix minced cooked chicken and ham or tongue with:
* melted butter to moisten and mayonnaise to bind.

Mix minced cooked turkey or chicken with:
* peanut butter and ordinary butter mixed together.

SWEET FILLINGS

Mix fresh fruit (chopped, mashed or grated), with:
* chopped dried fruit;
* chopped nuts;
* a well-flavoured jam, eg apricot or plum, or honey.

Always include a few drops of lemon or orange juice to prevent discoloration and to sharpen the flavour. Full-fat soft cheese or cream cheese make an interesting mixture, especially with chopped dried dates.

PEANUT BUTTER
SLICES

400 g/14 oz self-raising flour
pinch of salt
175 g/6 oz crunchy peanut butter
125 g/4½ oz sugar
1 egg
250 ml/8 fl oz milk
fat for greasing

Set the oven at 190°C/375°F/gas 5.

Sift together the flour and salt. Cream the peanut butter and sugar. Add the egg and milk and stir in the flour. Turn the mixture into a greased 23 × 12 × 7 cm/9 × 5 × 3 in loaf tin and bake for 1–1¼ hours until golden brown. Cool on a wire rack.   MAKES ABOUT TWELVE

A TEENAGE PARTY

⭐

ood may have to take second place to music at a teenage party, but it must be interesting – without being too unusual – and there must be plenty of it. You could provide a selection of Greek dishes and a simple meat loaf, to serve with hot garlic bread, jacket potatoes and a green salad, and, for dessert, a choice of a lightly spiced cake and a fruit fondue. For older guests, there is a cider and a wine cup, pleasant alternatives to cola drinks.

HUMMUS
(Chick-pea Dip)

450 g/1 lb cooked chick-peas
225 ml/7 fl oz tahini (sesame seed paste)
150 ml/¼ pint lemon juice
80 ml/3 fl oz cooking liquid from chick-peas, if required
1 garlic clove, chopped
salt
2 × 15 ml spoons/2 tablespoons olive oil
chopped parsley

Grind the chick-peas in a nut-mill, or crush in a pestle and mortar to make a smooth paste. Alternatively, purée the chick-peas in a blender.

In a mixing bowl, blend the tahini and lemon juice. The mixture should have the consistency of thick cream. If it is too stiff, thin with some of the liquid from cooking the chick-peas. Add the ground chick-peas and garlic. Stir briskly until well blended. Season with salt. Place the hummus in a shallow bowl, trickle the olive oil over it, and sprinkle with chopped parsley.

Serve as a first course with French bread, crispbread or pitta bread.   SERVES TWELVE

⭐

MOUSSAKA

3 aubergines
salt
4 × 15 ml spoons/4 tablespoons olive oil
2 large onions, chopped
2 garlic cloves, grated
1 kg/2¼ lb uncooked lamb or beef, minced
pepper
1 × 15 ml spoon/1 tablespoon chopped parsley
4 tomatoes, peeled, seeds removed and chopped
300 ml/½ pint dry white wine
300 ml/½ pint milk
2 eggs
3 egg yolks
generous pinch of grated nutmeg
125 g/4½ oz kefalotiri or Parmesan cheese, grated
fat for greasing

Cut the aubergines into 1 cm/½ in slices, sprinkle them with salt and set aside to drain on a large platter.

Heat the olive oil in a frying pan, add the onion and garlic, and sauté gently until the onion is soft. Add the minced lamb or beef, and continue cooking, stirring with a fork to break up any lumps in the meat. When the meat is thoroughly browned, add salt, pepper, the pars-

ley and tomatoes. Mix well, and add the white wine. Simmer the mixture for a few minutes to blend the flavours, then remove from the heat.

In a basin, beat together the milk, eggs, egg yolks, salt and grated nutmeg. Add about half the cheese to the egg mixture, and beat again briefly.

Grease a large oven-to-table baking dish. Drain the aubergine slices and pat dry with absorbent kitchen paper. Place half in the bottom of the casserole and cover with the meat mixture. Lay the remaining aubergine slices on the meat and pour the milk and egg mixture over them. Sprinkle the remaining cheese on top.

Set the oven at 180°C/350°F/gas 4. Bake the moussaka for 30–40 minutes, until the custard is set and the top is light golden brown. Serve from the dish.

Note Moussaka is best made a day ahead, then reheated, covered, in a warm oven.

SERVES TWELVE

⭐

Chocolate and butterscotch fruit fondues (p.89).

BLACK PEPPER.

SOUVLAKIA
(Lamb Kebabs)

100 ml/4 fl oz olive oil
juice of 1 lemon
salt and freshly ground pepper
1 kg/2¼ lb boneless lamb
450 g/1 lb small onions or shallots
salt
dried crushed oregano

Mix the olive oil, lemon juice, salt and pepper in a basin. Cut the lamb into 2 cm/¾ in square pieces, about 5 mm/¼ in thick. Put the meat in the olive oil mixture. Stir to coat all the pieces with the marinade, and leave to stand for 1 hour, stirring once or twice.

Blanch the onions or shallots in boiling, salted water for 3 minutes. Drain thoroughly.

Drain the meat, reserving the marinade. Thread the meat and onions on skewers (about 20 cm/8 in long), starting and ending with a piece of meat.

Put the skewers under a moderately high grill for 15–20 minutes, or until the meat is cooked, turning several times. Dip into the marinade again, then sprinkle liberally with oregano.

Note In Greece, where this dish originates, the skewers are usually made of wood, soaked in water before use, so that they will not char when grilling. Metal skewers are perfectly acceptable.

SERVES TWELVE

TURKEY LOAF

75 g/3 oz long-grain rice
350 g/12 oz cooked turkey meat
6 streaky bacon rashers, rinds removed
salt and pepper
2 eggs
40 g/1½ oz thyme and parsley stuffing mix
grated rind of 1 lemon
2 × 5 ml spoons/2 teaspoons paprika
fat for greasing

Cook the rice in boiling salted water for 10 minutes. Mince the turkey and bacon, and mix with the salt, pepper and eggs. Drain the rice and add to the turkey mixture. Mix thoroughly.

Make up the stuffing according to the directions on the packet. Add the lemon rind and paprika, and mix well. Put half the turkey mixture in a greased tin, and spread with stuffing; cover with the remaining turkey mixture.

Set the oven at 190°C/375°F/gas 5. Cook the loaf for 35 minutes. Serve hot or cold.

SERVES TEN TO TWELVE

CARROT CAKE

5 eggs, separated
275 g/10 oz caster sugar
grated rind of ½ lemon
275 g/10 oz ground almonds
275 g/10 oz grated carrots (weight after grating)
1 × 2.5 ml spoon/½ teaspoon ground cinnamon
pinch of ground cloves
3 × 15 ml spoons/3 tablespoons plain flour and 1 × 5 ml spoon/1 teaspoon baking powder or 3 × 15 ml spoons/3 tablespoons self-raising flour
pinch of salt
4 × 5 ml spoons/4 teaspoons lemon juice
fat or oil for greasing
ICING
175 g/6 oz icing sugar
1 × 15 ml spoon/1 tablespoon egg white
4 × 5 ml spoons/4 teaspoons lemon juice
apricot glaze (page 58)

Beat the egg yolks until they become liquid, add the sugar and beat together until pale and creamy. Add the lemon rind. Beat the almonds into the creamed mixture and stir in the grated carrots. Sift together the spices, flour and salt, and stir into the mixture. Add the lemon juice.

Whisk the egg whites until stiff but not dry. Stir 2 × 15 ml spoons/2 tablespoons into the carrot mixture, then fold in the rest lightly with a metal spoon. Turn the mixture gently into a greased shallow 25 cm/10 in cake tin or pie dish.

Set the oven at 190°C/375°F/gas 5. Bake the cake for 1¼–1½ hours, or until a thin hot skewer inserted in the centre comes out clean.

Meanwhile, make the icing. Mix together the sugar, egg white and lemon juice to make a fairly stiff icing. Warm the apricot glaze and spread it on the warm cake. Spoon the icing into a piping bag with a 5 mm/¼ in plain nozzle, and pipe a pattern of concentric rings on the cake. Leave to cool.

MAKES ONE **25 cm/10 in** CAKE

CHOCOLATE
FRUIT FONDUE

450 g/1 lb sponge sandwich cake or Madeira cake
apricot or other jam
4 large bananas
3 large eating apples
2 × 15 ml spoons/2 tablespoons lemon juice
1 (450 g/1 lb) can sliced peaches, drained
1 (450 g/1 lb) can pineapple cubes, drained

CHOCOLATE SAUCE

400 g/14 oz plain dessert chocolate, broken into pieces
300 ml/½ pint whipping cream
6 × 15 ml spoons/6 tablespoons sweet sherry or pineapple juice
50 g/2 oz unsalted butter

BUTTERSCOTCH SAUCE

50 g/2 oz butter or margarine
75 g/3 oz soft light brown sugar
50 g/2 oz granulated sugar
150 g/5 oz golden syrup
150 ml/¼ pint double cream
2–3 drops of vanilla essence

To prepare the 'dippers', slice the cake horizontally, spread one layer with jam and sandwich the two halves together again. Cut into cubes about 2.5 cm/1 in. Slice the bananas thickly, slice the apples, and toss the fruits in lemon juice to prevent discoloration.

To make the chocolate sauce, put the pieces of chocolate into a double boiler or a basin over a bowl of simmering water. Stir in the cream and sherry or pineapple juice, and continue stirring. When the mixture is smooth, stir in the butter a little at a time. Serve hot.

To make the butterscotch sauce, heat the butter or margarine, the sugars and syrup in a heavy-based saucepan. When the sugar has melted, stir, then heat gently for a further 5 minutes. Remove from the heat. Stir in the cream and vanilla essence and, still away from the heat, stir until the sauce is smooth. Serve hot or cold.

Put both sauces in bowls and arrange the cubes of cake and the fresh and canned fruits on serving plates. Provide long split-wood kebab sticks for guests to spear the dippers and twirl them in one of the sauces.

Note A washable tablecloth is a wise safety precaution!   SERVES TWELVE

' CHOCOLATE AND COCOA:—
Both these preparations are made from the seeds or beans of the cacao-tree, which grows in the West Indies and South America. The Spanish, and the proper name, is cacao, not cocoa, as it is generally spelt...., The cocoa tree [Theobroma cacao] was cultivated by the aboriginal inhabitants of South America, particularly in Mexico, where, according to Humboldt, it was reared by Montezuma. It was transplanted thence into other dependencies of the Spanish monarchy in 1520; and it was so highly esteemed by Linnaeus as to receive from him the name now conferred upon it, of Theombra, a term derived from the Greek, and signifying 'food for gods'. '
MRS BEETON (1861)

COCOA-BEAN.

CIDER CUP

1 litre/1¾ pints cider
500 ml/18 fl oz soda water
thin strips of cucumber rind
thin strips of lemon rind
2 × 5 ml spoons/2 teaspoons lemon juice
2 × 5 ml spoons/2 teaspoons caster sugar

Chill the cider and soda water for 30 minutes.

Put the rest of the ingredients into a large jug, and stir in the chilled cider and soda water. Serve at once.   FILLS TWELVE WINE GLASSES

SANGRIA

75 g/3 oz granulated sugar
75 ml/3 fl oz water
1 orange, sliced
1 lime or lemon, sliced
1 litre/1¾ pints red or white wine
12 ice cubes

Put the sugar and water into a saucepan and stir over a gentle heat until the sugar has dissolved. Pour the syrup over the sliced fruit and leave to cool.

Pour the fruit and the syrup into a jug, and add the wine and ice cubes. Stir well, and serve at once. Put two or three slices of fruit into each glass.   FILLS TWELVE WINE GLASSES

A HOUSE FULL OF GUESTS

★

If you have family and friends staying for three or four days over the holiday, you will be grateful for your larder and freezer stocks. Guests will not expect every meal to be a banquet, so here are some homely and quick-to-prepare dishes to serve when you all get in from a bracing walk, or want a cosy evening round the fire. Some recipes use the principal Christmas left-overs of ham and turkey. And – just for your house guests – there's a traditional Christmas log.

TURKEY SOUP

| carcass and trimmings of 1 turkey |
| 25 g/1 oz lean back bacon rashers, rinds removed |
| 25 g/1 oz butter or margarine |
| 1 onion, sliced |
| 1 large carrot, sliced |
| ½ parsnip, sliced |
| 1 celery stick, sliced |
| 25 g/1 oz plain flour |
| 1 litre/1¾ pints water for each 400 g/14 oz cooked turkey remains |
| bouquet garni |
| 1 clove |
| 25–50 g/1–2 oz breast of turkey |
| salt and pepper |

Weigh the carcass and trimmings, and break the carcass into pieces. Dice the bacon. Melt the butter or margarine in a large saucepan. Add the carcass pieces, meat trimmings and bacon and fry until browned. Remove them and reserve the fat in the pan. Put the vegetables into the pan and fry gently until golden brown. Add the flour and fry gently until golden brown. Stir in the water and heat to boiling point. Add the bouquet garni and clove. Return the turkey carcass, trimmings and bacon to the pan. Cover, and simmer for 1½–2 hours.

Meanwhile, cut the pieces of breast meat into 5 mm/¼ in dice. Strain the soup, add the diced meat and reheat. Season to taste.

Note Leftover pieces of stuffing improve the flavour and help to thicken the soup.

SERVES FOUR

FISH & CORN CHOWDER

| 325 g/11 oz sweetcorn kernels, canned or frozen |
| 250 g/9 oz potatoes |
| 550 g/1¼ lb white fish |
| 2 × 15 ml spoons/2 tablespoons salt |
| large pinch of ground white pepper |
| 3 streaky bacon rashers, rinds removed and finely chopped |
| 1 onion, thinly sliced |
| 3 celery sticks, thinly sliced |
| 25 g/1 oz plain flour |
| 500 ml/18 fl oz milk |
| 50 g/2 oz butter |
| 1 × 15 ml spoon/1 tablespoon chopped parsley |

Drain the canned corn, or thaw the frozen corn, and set aside. Cut the potatoes into 2 cm/¾ in cubes, then boil for 5 minutes in enough salted water to cover. Cut the fish into 6 cm/2¼ in pieces and add to the potatoes with the salt and pepper. Simmer, covered, for 12 minutes.

Meanwhile, fry the bacon separately until just crisp, then remove from the pan. Cook the onion and celery together in the bacon fat until the onion is golden. Remove the onion and celery with a perforated spoon and add to the fish mixture with the bacon. Reserve the fat in the pan.

Add the flour to the bacon fat and mix well. Cook gently for 2–3 minutes without colouring, then add the milk gradually, stirring all the time until thick. Add to the fish mixture. Stir in the corn and butter, and cook for a further 5 minutes. Garnish with the parsley and serve hot.

SERVES SIX

THE JOHN DORY.

Bûche de Noël (p.93).

SWEET & SOUR
PRAWNS

550 g/1¼ lb peeled cooked prawns

2 × 15 ml spoons/2 tablespoons medium-dry sherry

salt and pepper

3 × 15 ml spoons/3 tablespoons oil

2 onions, cut into rings

2 green peppers, seeds removed and cut into rings

150 ml/¼ pint chicken stock

1 (400 g/14 oz) can pineapple pieces, drained

4 × 5 ml spoons/4 teaspoons cornflour

2 × 15 ml spoons/2 tablespoons soy sauce

150 ml/¼ pint white wine vinegar

75 g/3 oz sugar

400 g/14 oz whole cooked prawns to garnish

Marinate the prawns in the sherry and seasoning for 30 minutes. Heat the oil and fry the onions and peppers gently until tender. Add the stock and pineapple pieces. Cover and cook for 3–5 minutes. Blend the cornflour, soy sauce, vinegar and sugar, and stir into the mixture until thickened. Add the prawns and cook for 1 minute. Garnish with whole prawns and serve with rice.   SERVES SIX

' THE PRAWN: — *This little fish bears a striking resemblance to the shrimp, but is neither so common nor so small. It is to be found on most of the sandy shores of Europe. The Isle of Wight is famous for shrimps, where they are potted; but both the prawns and the shrimps vended in London, are too much salted for the excellence of their natural flavour to be preserved. They are extremely lively little animals, as seen in their native retreats.* '

MRS BEETON (1861)

HAM SLICES
WITH APPLE

6 large ham or gammon slices or steaks,
about 1 cm/½ in thick

150 g/5 oz soft light brown sugar

75 g/3 oz soft white breadcrumbs

200 ml/6 fl oz pineapple juice

GARNISH

3 cooking apples

75 g/3 oz margarine

Remove the rind from the ham or gammon and snip the fat at intervals to prevent it curling. Put the slices or steaks in a frying pan with a very little water, heat to simmering point and simmer for 10 minutes, turning them once. Drain. Lay the slices or steaks overlapping each other slightly in a large, shallow, ovenproof baking dish.

Mix together the sugar and breadcrumbs, and spread the mixture over the slices or steaks, then trickle the pineapple juice over them.

Set the oven at 180°C/350°F/gas 4. Cook the slices or steaks, uncovered, for 25 minutes.

Meanwhile, cut the apples into rings, 2 cm/¾ in thick. Melt the margarine in a frying pan, and fry the apple rings until tender but not soft. Garnish the slices or steaks with the apple rings and serve immediately. SERVES SIX

BOILED HAM.

DEVILLED
TURKEY

550 g/1¼ lb cold roast turkey

DEVILLING BUTTER

50 g/2 oz butter

large pinch of cayenne

large pinch of ground black pepper

1 × 5 ml spoon/1 teaspoon curry paste

pinch of ground ginger

Mix together all the ingredients for the devilling butter.

Divide the turkey into convenient portions for serving, remove the skin and score the flesh deeply. Spread lightly with the prepared butter and leave for 1 hour (or longer if a highly seasoned dish is required). Grill the turkey for about 8 minutes, turning once, until crisp and brown.

Serve with a barbecue sauce. SERVES SIX

CAULIFLOWER
WITH MUSHROOM SAUCE

1 kg/2¼ lb cauliflower

50 g/2 oz butter

25 g/1 oz flour

375 ml/13 fl oz vegetable stock or milk

175 g/6 oz button mushrooms, finely chopped

4 egg yolks

1 × 15 ml spoon/1 tablespoon lemon juice

salt and black pepper

pinch of grated nutmeg

6 slices of bread

butter

Break the cauliflower into medium florets and boil or steam them until just tender. Drain thoroughly and keep hot.

Melt the butter in a saucepan, stir in the flour and cook for 1 minute. Draw off the heat and stir in the stock or milk gradually. Return to the heat, bring to the boil, stirring constantly, and cook until the sauce thickens. Add the mushrooms to the sauce, and simmer gently for 5 minutes.

Beat the egg yolks lightly, beat in the lemon juice and 2 × 15 ml spoons/2 tablespoons of the hot sauce, then stir into the remaining sauce. Heat gently, but do not allow the sauce to boil after the egg yolks have been added or it will curdle. Season to taste and add the nutmeg.

Toast the bread, stamp out rounds with a plain cutter, and butter each one. Arrange the cauliflower neatly on the toast and pour the sauce over. Serve as soon as possible.

SERVES SIX

IRISH
SODA BREAD

700 g/1½ lb plain flour

1 × 5 ml spoon/1 teaspoon bicarbonate of soda

1 × 5 ml spoon/1 teaspoon salt

1 × 5 ml spoon/1 teaspoon cream of tartar
(if using fresh milk)

about 250 ml/8 fl oz buttermilk or soured cream
or fresh milk

flour for dusting

fat for greasing

Mix all the dry ingredients together in a bowl and make a well in the centre. Add enough buttermilk, soured cream or fresh milk to make a fairly slack dough, pouring it in almost all at once, not spoonful by spoonful. Mix with a wooden spoon, lightly and quickly.

With floured hands, put the mixture on a lightly floured surface and flatten the dough into a circle about 3 cm/1¼ in thick. Turn on to a greased baking sheet, and make a large cross in the surface with a floured knife to make the bread cook through thoroughly.

Set the oven at 190–200°C/375–400°F/gas 5–6. Bake the bread for about 40 minutes. Pierce the centre with a thin skewer to test for readiness; it should come out clean. Wrap the loaf in a clean tea-towel to keep it soft until required.   MAKES ONE **700 g/1½ lb** LOAF

BANANAS
IN RUM

6 large bananas

4 × 15 ml spoons/4 tablespoons soft brown sugar

1 × 5 ml spoon/1 teaspoon ground cinnamon

25 g/1 oz butter

5–6 × 15 ml spoons/5–6 tablespoons rum

Cut the bananas in half lengthways, and lay them flat on a plate. If this is done some time before the dish is cooked, sprinkle the bananas with a little lemon juice to prevent the fruit turning brown.

Mix together the sugar and cinnamon, and sprinkle the bananas with the mixture. Melt the butter in a frying pan and fry the bananas flat-side down for 1–2 minutes until lightly browned underneath. Turn them over carefully, sprinkle with any remaining sugar and cinnamon, and continue frying.

When the bananas are soft but not mushy, pour the rum over them. Tilt and baste, then light the rum; baste again. Scrape any cara-melised sugar from the base of the pan and stir it into the rum. Shake the pan gently until the flames die down.

Arrange the bananas on warmed serving plates, pour the rum sauce over them and serve with double cream.   SERVES SIX

BÛCHE DE NÖEL
(Chestnut Christmas Log)

SPONGE

butter for greasing

100 g/4 oz icing sugar

3 eggs

4 × 5 ml spoons/4 teaspoons rum

65 g/2½ oz self-raising flour

icing sugar for dusting

FILLING

2 × 440 g/15 oz cans unsweetened chestnut purée

275 g/10 oz butter, softened

125 g/4½ oz caster sugar

2 × 15 ml spoons/2 tablespoons rum

DECORATION

marrons glacés or glacé cherries and angelica

Grease a 35 × 25 cm/14 × 10 in Swiss roll tin and line it with greased paper. Set the oven at 220°C/425°F/gas 7.

Warm a mixing bowl with hot water, then dry it. Sift the icing sugar into the bowl, and break in the eggs. Beat or whisk vigorously for 5–10 minutes until the mixture is very light and fluffy, adding the rum while beating. When the mixture is like meringue, fold in the flour gently. Turn the mixture into the prepared tin, and bake for 7 minutes. Meanwhile, prepare a 40 × 30 cm/16 × 12 in sheet of greaseproof paper and dust it with icing sugar. Remove the sponge from the oven, loosen the sides from the tin if necessary, and turn it on to the greaseproof paper. Peel off the lining paper. Trim the edges of the sponge if they are crisp. Roll it up tightly with the greaseproof paper, beginning at one long side to make a long thin roll, or at one short end for a shorter roll. Cool.

Meanwhile, prepare the chestnut butter cream for the filling. Turn the purée into a bowl and beat in the butter, then add the sugar and rum.

When the sponge is cold, unroll it carefully.

Cover the underside of the sponge with just over half the butter cream, laying it on thickly at the further edge. Then re-roll the sponge, and place it on a sheet of greaseproof paper, with the cut edge underneath. Cover the sponge with the remaining butter cream, either spreading with a knife or using a piping bag with a ribbon nozzle, and imitating the knots and grain of wood. Chill and serve decorated with glacé fruits.

SERVES SIX TO EIGHT

ATHOLL BROSE
DESSERT

ATHOLL BROSE

275 g/10 oz medium oatmeal

about 200 ml/6 fl oz water

4 × 15 ml spoons/4 tablespoons heather honey

1 bottle whisky

DESSERT

250 ml/8 fl oz double cream

3 egg whites

roasted almonds to decorate

To make the Atholl Brose, put the oatmeal into a small basin and add enough water to make a paste. Leave for 30 minutes, then drain, reserv-ing the liquid. Press the oatmeal well into the sieve, to squeeze out as much cloudy liquid as possible. Add the honey to the liquid and stir in thoroughly. Pour into a large bottle, add the whisky and shake well. Store, and use as required. Always shake well before use.

To make the dessert, pour 1 × 15 ml spoon/1 tablespoon Atholl Brose into each of six individual glass dishes. Whip the cream until stiff and whisk in 6 × 15 ml spoons/6 tablespoons Atholl Brose. Whisk the egg whites until stiff and fold lightly into the cream mixture. Spoon into the six glass dishes on top of the Atholl Brose, then chill. Decorate with almonds.   SERVES SIX

DECORATIONS

★

There are many different ways to make your Christmas a truly sparkling occasion. Not least of these are the decorations you choose for your home. Your theme could be all white or traditional holly green and berry red. You could add lavish touches of silver and gold. This is easy and inexpensive to achieve with chain-store baubles, paint-sprayed twigs and shiny ribbons. Or you could choose a less traditional but equally effective colour theme to carry through your decorations, such as dark blue and brilliant orange, or purple and gold.

Colour plays a very important part in Christmas decorations, and can be as restrained or as flamboyant as you wish. Consider the colours, textures and patterns of the decor in each room you intend to trim (not forgetting the kitchen and even the bedrooms) and see if one linking colour theme could be appropriate and attractive for the decorations right through your home.

The tradition of decorating the home with evergreens predates the Christmas festival itself. Whether you have the opportunity to cut armfuls of holly and ivy for yourself, or you simply add a bunch of mixed greenery to your shopping list in the weeks before Christmas, you will find foliage the most versatile and varied decoration of all. Gather or buy as many different types of evergreens as you can. Those with glistening, shiny leaves will reflect every shaft of candle- and firelight, and sprays of matt-surfaced foliage will, by their very contrast, flatter the holly and ivy.

Give all the boughs of greenery a good, long drink in tepid water as soon as you bring them indoors and then, even if you arrange them with no source of moisture at all, they will stay fresh-looking and bright for the twelve days of Christmas and more. Candles have a special part to play in the joy and sparkle of Christmas, and can be the inspiration for a kaleidoscope of ideas for table decorations.

Your Christmas tree could be decorated in a variety of ways: all in white, in brilliant red, or in a dazzling array of colours. Children especially like to make tree decorations – it keeps them busy and has a practical application.

Christmas is a time for giving and there are many imaginative ideas that can be developed for decorative stockings and presents to fill them, and for parcel wrappings and trims. They will all fulfil the old adage: 'it's the thought that counts'.

VASE OF TINTED GLASS.

THE CHRISTMAS TREE

★

here is nothing so enchanting as bringing home the Christmas tree, frostily green, prickly and smelling delightfully of pine, hanging on the tiny decorations one by one, and switching on the lights for the first, joyous, time. The tradition of decorating our homes with a Christmas tree seems to belong to the distant past, though it was, in fact, introduced to Great Britain only in Victorian times. With modifications to suit changing circumstances, such as everlasting and even wallhanging trees, the tradition is as evocative as ever.

THE FIRST
CHRISTMAS TREE

Legends surrounding the Christmas tree abound, and have become part of the fabric of the Christmas story.

One of the earliest relates to St Boniface, who went as a missionary to Germany in the eighth century. There, he is said to have come across a sacred oak which was used as a sacrificial altar. According to the legend, he cut down the tree and, by so doing, saved a young boy's life.

Miraculously, a young fir tree sprang up between the gnarled roots of the oak, and St Boniface saw this new tree as symbolic of his Christian faith.

The first record of a fir tree brought indoors relates to one which Martin Luther illuminated with candles, to remind children of the light which Jesus Christ brought to the world. Still in Germany, there are later references, in the seventeenth century, to fir trees decorated with fruits, nuts, sweets and paper flowers.

It was this custom that Queen Victoria's Consort, Prince Albert, brought to Britain in 1841, when he had a lighted tree set up in

Windsor Castle, introducing his family to the joy he remembered from his own German childhood.

Bringing home the Christmas tree was a

special part of the excitement, as Victorian paintings and drawings show us. The picture of children trundling home through the snow with the all-important tree in tow on a sled is a familiar theme for Christmas cards.

By tradition, the lights on the Christmas tree should not be switched on until Christmas Eve, in celebration of the birth of the Infant Jesus. But in practice few families, especially where there are children, can resist the temptation of setting an illuminated tree in their windows several days, even weeks, in anticipation of the festival.

SPRUCING UP
YOUR TREE

The traditional Christmas tree is the Norway spruce, *Picea abies*, a member of the Pinaceae family of evergreen conifers. The tree is a native of the mountainous regions of Scandinavia, and grows throughout northern and central Europe and the eastern United States.

The single needle-like leaves grow spirally around the shoots, which later bear tiny, pale green peg-like projections where once there were leaves.

Both male and female flowers, which open in May, are borne on the same tree. The male flowers, about 1 cm/½ in long, are clustered at the tips of the shoots and turn yellow when they start to shed pollen. The female flowers turn from pink to green.

The fruits are hard, woody cones about 12.5–15 cm/5–6 in long, which turn from green to a warm brown as they ripen in autumn.

The trees can grow to a height of 36 m/120 ft or even larger, and the timber, a softwood known as deal, is used for housebuilding and paper pulp. Turpentine is extracted from the stem, and in Germany the bark is used as a dye, for tanning.

TEN WAYS TO TIE UP YOUR TREE

Ribbon bows make some of the prettiest and quickest of tree decorations, and find favour with people of all ages. Here are ten quick tips to give your tree a party look. Jumble sales and 'bits and pieces' boxes become treasure troves at a time like this.

1. For a country look, plait several thicknesses of raffia, then tie them into bows around the tree shoots.

2. Make up random-coloured skeins of thick yarn – quick-knit wool or rug yarn for example – plait the strips (which keeps them from unwinding) and tie them into large bows with long trailing ends.

3. Hunt for bargains on the ribbon counters and choose the brightest 'end of lines' you can find. Tartan ribbons, red and white checked gingham,

polka-dot patterns, would all be attractive and unusual.

4. Save narrow lace edging or hunt for jumble-stall bargains. Frosty white lace bows are lovely.

5. Cut strips of brightly coloured crêpe paper, tie it into bows and fix them to the tree with a wire through the back of the loop.

6. Tissue paper makes crisp and crackly bows, but is not very easy to tie. Shape the two side loops, then stick a bar loop through the centre.

7. Buy a roll of rainbow-coloured paper-chain paper and tie it into bows instead.

8. Thinly pare oranges – use the fruit in a salad – or lemons and trim the rind into even strips. Tie them into bows, then dry them in a cool oven for an hour or so. They will keep their shape and deepen in colour.

9. Tie a huge, generously full bow on top of the tree in place of a fairy. White ribbon threaded with gold or silver looks suitably festive.

10. 'Finish off' the tree trunk with a large bow tied just below the lower branches, with the ends trailing over the rim of the container.

To decorate the container, tie a bow with a wide piece of ribbon and fix it in place with wire.

CARING FOR YOUR TREE

If you buy a fresh tree 'straight from the forest', try to select one which still has its roots. You could then, if you have a garden, keep alive the spirit of Christmas by planting the tree outside once again immdiately after the festivities are over for another year.

In any case, a tree with roots will stay fresh longer when it is planted in soil in a container, especially if it is watered regularly.

Trim the tree roots to fit into the waterproof trough or pot, and pack the soil firmly around them.

Keep the soil moist throughout the holiday, but not permanently wet. Spruce trees are not at all happy standing with their feet constantly in water.

If you care for the tree in this way, you should be able to avert that annual problem of the needles dropping and becoming enmeshed in the carpet pile.

A NINETEENTH-CENTURY TRADITION

❛ *A young fir is generally selected and little presents of various kinds are bound on the branches, crochet-purses, bon-bons, preserved fruits, alum-baskets, charms, dolls, toys in endless variety etc., distributed over the tree according to fancy. The whole is illuminated by numerous little wax tapers which are lighted just before the guests are admitted to inspect the tree.* ❜

Extract from 'The Dictionary of Daily Wants' of 1858.

TEN TIPS FOR
CONTAINERS

1. If the most convenient waterproof container – a bucket or old enamel bread bin for example – is not very attractive to look at, do not resort to covering it with coloured tissue or crêpe paper. Any water spilt when watering a rooted tree could have disastrous consequences for the floorcovering or tabletop. The paper dyes are notoriously non-fast.

2. One way of disguising the container is by standing it in a 'planter's' basket. Charity and ethnic shops sell attractive and inexpensive ones.

3. Disguise round or rectangular containers by covering them with a strip of flexible split bamboo matting, the kind used for sunblinds.

4. Make a rustic-look outer covering for a rectangular container by nailing together thin branches to make a four-sided 'box'.

5. Bind thick string or cord round and round an unsightly container to give it an interesting but unobtrusive, texture. 'Paint' the container with glue first.

6. Plant a table-top tree in an earthenware flower pot – there is nothing wrong with that for looks. Do not forget to place a non-porous saucer or dish under it.

7. Cover the soil on top of a planted tree with pulled-out pieces of cotton wool, or spray-on designer snow for an authentic wintry look.

8. Or sprinkle a thin layer of pot pourri over the soil. This is a specially pretty idea for a table-top tree.

9. If you choose a tree with a sawn-off trunk and no roots, you can buy a criss-cross metal stem holder. A thumb-screw bolt holds the trunk securely upright.

10. If you are not happy about the metallic look of this utilitarian device pile mock presents (wrapped boxes that are not meant for opening) over and around the base.

EVERGREEN
CONE TREE

A table-top tree to decorate a party table, to stand on a pedestal in a room corner, or on a deep windowsill where it will delight passers-by.

YOU WILL NEED

* a suitable container, such as a wide, shallow basket
* ballast to steady the container, such as a few clean, dry, smooth stones
* a piece of chicken wire with 5 cm/2 in mesh
* wire cutters
* stout wire or stub wires
* cuttings of evergreens, such as holly, ivy, juniper, yew, cypress or silvery artemisia – all one species, or a mixture
* trimmings – see suggestions

Cut the wire netting and wrap it to make a cone shape. Crunch the cone to minimise the size of the holes, taking care to retain the general shape. The circumference of the finished cone base should be almost the same as that of the container rim.

Place the ballast stones in the basket. Stand the wire cone on top and fix the shape to the basket, tying it on with a few short lengths of wire.

Cut the evergreens into short lengths and push them into the wire cone. Turn the container around and work from all sides, making sure to keep a neat shape. Trim off any stray or unruly stems.

Decorate the evergreen tree with wrapped sweets, small dried flower posies, small ribbon bows, miniature baubles, foil stars, cinnamon quills, nuts, what you will.

Tie a full bow of wide satin ribbon or silver or gold parcel ribbon and fix it with a piece of wire to the front of the basket.

CHRISTMAS CARD
TREE

A straggly indoor tree, its frosty-white branches laden with colourful greetings cards, can be a decorative focal point. It is practical too, solving the eternal problem of displaying the Christmas cards where they will not get blown or knocked over.

YOU WILL NEED

* a tree stem with many well-spaced side shoots – hazelnut is ideal
* spray paint – white, silver or red are most effective
* a suitable container, such as an earthenware flower pot or a china or pottery plant holder
* soil, quick-setting florist's clay or plaster of Paris, to 'plant' the tree
* a packet of wire tree-bauble hangers
* baubles or ribbon bows to trim the tree

Spray the tree branches with your chosen paint. This is a task best undertaken outdoors on a calm day. If it has to be done indoors, cover every surface within nozzle range with news-

A Christmas card tree.

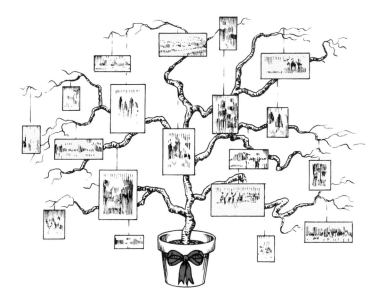

paper, and spray the branches and shoots a little at a time, from close range. Turn the tree over and spray the reverse side, making sure that it is evenly covered. Leave it to dry.

Plant the tree firmly and securely in the container, using whatever means of fixing you choose.

Decide where the tree is to stand. It makes a difference whether it will be viewed from all angles or (if it is to be placed against a wall) just from the front.

Hang the Christmas cards accordingly, arranging them to make the tree equally colourful from all sides, or having them all facing forward. Hang the largest ones towards the centre and base of the tree, and the smallest ones at the top and the tips of the shoots.

When you have opened your presents, you can add more colour and warmth by hanging the gift tags on the tree, too.

If the tree is packed with the blossom of greetings cards it will need little if any extra adornment. If not, adding a few baubles and tying on a few ribbon bows – one at the tip and a larger, matching one around the container – is a good idea.

WALL-MOUNTED EVERGREEN TREE

The comings and goings of a busy family Christmas and the extra pressure on room space if you plan to give a party, can make a free-standing Christmas tree, even a table-top model, something of a luxury in volume terms.

But no room is ever too small, nor too crowded with the trappings of the festive season, to find space for a wall-mounted tree.

Evergreen branches festooned with baubles, bows and beads are a very pretty way to decorate a plain wall in the hall or sitting room, and seem tailor-made for the 'picture area' over a fireplace. Do not think of them just as alternative Christmas trees, but as attractive and highly decorative optional extras.

Take stock of the wall area to be decorated by the branch tree, and judge what size and shape will look best – whether the branches should have a natural upward curve, should sweep gracefully down in a shallow arc or (less likely) should be straight.

With this requirement in mind, select just the branch or branches you need. You may be able to use an off-cut from a Christmas tree, yours or someone else's, which has been trimmed off to give the tree a more even shape, or find a long, flat branch of yew, juniper or laurel.

More attractive still, if you have access to a garden, gather two or three branches of different species, perhaps a long gnarled shoot pruned from the apple tree, and a couple of evergreens such as yew and shiny ivy, complete with clusters of fruits.

Tie the branches together and fix them to the wall as unobtrusively as possible. To avoid damage to the wall, it may be best to knock some tacks into a picture rail and suspend the greenery on lengths of colourless thread.

Trim the branches with baubles, bonbons, tinsel, strings of beads and so on, and tie a large ribbon bow, bouquet style, around the lower stem.

If the wall tree is hung over a lighted fireplace, be sure to keep the branches and any decorations well away from the fire.

A wall-mounted evergreen tree.

PAPER
CHRISTMAS TREE

For the ultimate in space-saving trees, make a paper or card tree, complete with its own decorations, to hang on a wall or door. This design is specially suited to decorate a narrow hall or passage, where there is rarely room to be expansive, and will prove specially popular for children's rooms, where the trees can act as a festive version of a pegboard, a vehicle for all manner of Christmassy cut-outs.

Paper trees flourish in all sizes, from small saplings to hang above a fireplace or cupboard to sturdy, full-grown pines that reach from the skirting board to the ceiling. The only limits are imposed by your own available wall space, and the size of the materials you have to hand.

Decide what size your tree is to be, scale up the template and draw it on to newspaper, and cut out the shape. Trace the tree shape on to a piece of card or stiff paper. If you cannot find a piece of card large enough for your requirements, stick several pieces together – cereal packets are ideal – with sticky parcel tape. Then cover the card with parcel wrapping paper, sticking it neatly down all over and cutting and folding over the edges of the shape.

For an unusual and attractive finish, cover the card with a collage of patterned wrapping papers (a good way to use up saved paper from last year) in toning or contrasting colours.

Fix a loop or a brass curtain ring to the top and to the lowest branches of the tree, and hang it on the wall. Transparent threads suspended from a picture rail may be the neatest fixing method.

Cut out motif shapes from coloured card, shiny papers, heavy-quality foil, or felt, and fix them to the tree. Blue tacky clay or press-on sticky fixing pads will do this neatly and easily.

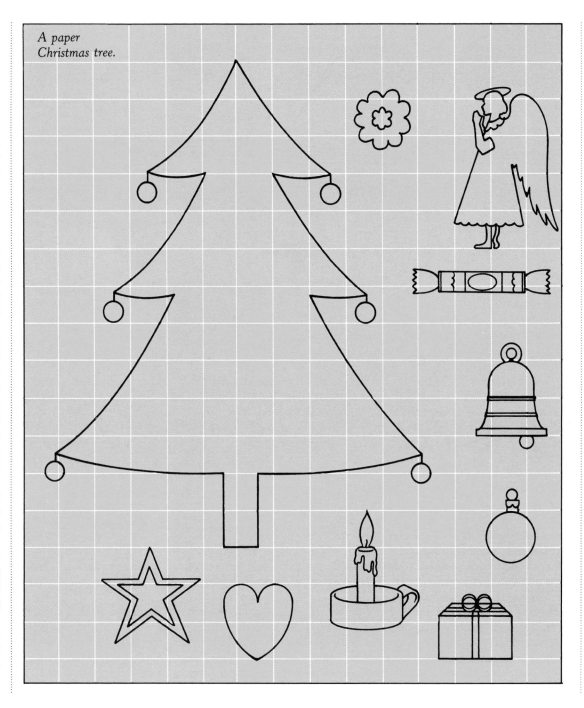

A paper Christmas tree.

EDIBLE TREE DECORATIONS

Follow the charming Victorian tradition of decorating the Christmas tree with tempting goodies. They make delightful take-home presents for young visitors, and delicious stay-at-home extras for the family.

★ Make multi-coloured ribbons of Smarties to drape from branch to branch. Thread the sweets on to thick cotton, using a sharp, fine needle and knot the yarn behind the first and last sweet. Leave long ends to tie to the shoots.

★ Or tie the sweetie-strings into circles and loop them over the tips of branches.

★ Buy tiny baskets from a charity shop and fill them with sweets wrapped in coloured foil. You can even colour-match your choice to your decorative theme.

★ Buy a packet of large pretzels, the salty, savoury snacks to enjoy with drinks, and hang them on the tree. The shapes are fascinating, and the salt crystals glisten like frost.

★ Fill mini baskets with a mixture of nuts and tiny tree baubles – a decorative way to use any that are without loops.

★ Cut bunches of black or green grapes into small clusters. Paint them all over with lightly-beaten egg white and toss them in caster sugar. Leave them to dry, then hang them, sparkling with 'frost', on the tree.

★ Make gingerbread men, bells, stars, trees, boots, sacks – any shape you can cut with your biscuit cutters or devise for yourself. The basic recipe is given below. Children love decorating the biscuits with coloured glacé icing, silver confectionery balls and coloured dragées. And they love eating them!

For a collection of inedible play-dough decorations, see page 102.

GINGERBREAD DECORATIONS

225 g/8 oz self-raising flour
1 × 2.5 ml spoon/½ teaspoon salt
1 × 5 ml spoon/1 teaspoon mixed spice
2 × 5 ml spoons/2 teaspoons ground ginger
100 g/4 oz margarine
75 g/3 oz soft light brown sugar
3 × 15 ml spoons/3 tablespoons milk, plus extra for brushing

Sift the flour, salt and spices into a mixing bowl. Rub in the margarine until it is evenly mixed. Stir in the sugar and milk and mix to a fairly stiff dough.

Roll out the dough on a lightly-floured board. Cut into decorative shapes. Gather up the trimmings, shape them into a ball, roll out the dough and cut out more biscuits. Place the biscuit shapes on a greased baking sheet and brush them lightly with milk.

Bake in the oven at 200°C/400°F/gas 6 for 15 minutes, or until the biscuits are golden brown. Transfer them to a wire rack and leave them to cool.

DECORATING THE BISCUITS

Make up glacé icing (see page 61) and colour it as you wish.

'Dress' gingerbread men and women in brightly coloured clothes, with confectionery balls or Smarties for buttons and features. Ice gingerbread bells and stars in white and spangle them with silver or gold balls. Outline tree shapes with pale green icing and sprinkle on coloured hundreds and thousands before the coating dries.

Cover Santa's boots or toy sack bright red, with a snow-white trim. The sack could be brimming over with tiny coloured sweets, or piped with toy shapes in glacé icing.

DRIED FLOWER DECORATIONS

Dried flowers, with their crisp and crackly petals and bright and shiny looks, make natural looking tree decorations which are especially pretty on green or silver everlasting trees.

★ Fill tiny baskets with dried flowerheads in any colours to suit your theme. Strawflowers (*Helichrysum bracteatum*) that have separated from their stalks take on a new lease of decorative life.

★ Make tiny posies of mixed flowers – white pearl everlasting, short sprays of statice and so on – and tie them with ribbon bows.

★ Thread the zingy orange seedpods of Chinese lanterns on to thick cotton to make bright flower-chains.

★ On a larger scale, a similar idea makes an attractive alternative to a fairy on top of the tree.

★ Buy the cheapest miniature crackers you can find (or make your own; see page 130). Stick single strawflower heads or tiny dried flower posies in the centre as a prettier-than-usual motif.

★ Spray shapely seedheads, such as poppy and love-in-a-mist, silver, gold or red, tie them into bunches and hang them on the tree.

★ Spray teasels, those spiky, egg-shaped seed carriers, in your chosen colour and tie each short stem with a ribbon bow.

★ Restore jaded tree baubles (or even cracked ones) by sticking on flat dried flower heads such as helipterum, xeranthemum or strawflowers.

★ Lightly spray faded dried flower stems such as snippings of clarkia, larkspur, statice or delphinium, or clusters of hydrangea florets with shiny or coloured paints. Leave them to dry, then compose them into posies for the tree.

PLAY-DOUGH DECORATIONS

★

No matter how frenzied the activity in the kitchen and the household in general, however many cards there are to write and presents to wrap, time can tick slowly by for children impatient for Christmas Day to dawn.
Every wise parent is well prepared for the inevitable statement, even at this time of year, from young children who exclaim, 'I'm bored. What shall I do next?'
Making play-dough shapes is a suggestion that is sure to meet with approval, and will bear decorative fruit for years to come.

The art of making play-dough decorations has all the creative satisfaction of mixing, kneading and rolling pastry; the difference is that you cannot eat the end results. You hang them on the Christmas tree, on doors, walls and in windows. You can make personalized shapes for your friends (perhaps using their initials), create tiny decorations to hang on parcels or fill a Christmas stocking, or even mould small items to furnish a doll's house or a play shop.

The shapes can be as simple as the young designer pleases. A plain ring twisted and baked to a toasty-brown dangling from a bright red ribbon looks just as enchanting as a complicated plait or a flower with multi-coloured petals.

Do not allow children to get so carried away with the excitement of the craft that they expect to be able to eat the decorations after all. They are unbearably salty – the mixture is called salt dough in the United States – and in any case they are baked to an unpalatable degree of hardness. They have to be. Any residual moisture would encourage the growth of mould, and the decorations would lose one of their major advantages, that they really are virtually ever-lasting.

THE BASIC DOUGH

★ 450 g/1 lb plain flour
★ 150 g/6 oz salt
★ 2 × 5 ml spoons/2 teaspoons glycerine
★ water (see method)

YOU MAY ALSO NEED

★ pastry board
★ rolling pin
★ tracing paper
★ cardboard for templates
★ glue
★ craft knife
★ 1 egg yolk
★ 1 × 15 ml spoon/1 tablespoon milk
★ pastry brush
★ red, green or other food colourings
★ a toothpick
★ clear varnish
★ parcel ribbon for hanging directions

Mix together the flour, salt and glycerine. Pour on enough water to make a fairly stiff dough. Shape the dough into a ball and put it in a plastic bag. Leave it in the refrigerator for several hours, or overnight.

If you wish to make cut-out shapes and do not have suitable biscuit cutters, draw round shapes from Christmas cards or colouring books. Draw the shapes on greaseproof paper, roughly cut round the outlines and stick them on to cardboard, such as used cereal packets. Accurately cut out the shapes.

The next day, knead the dough by hand, or in an electric mixture, until it is smooth. If you want to colour the dough, then this is the time to do it.

Tear off small pieces of the dough, put them into bowls and sprinkle on one or two drops of food colouring, red for berries, flowers and some fruits, green for leaves and other fruits. If you would like to make a Holy Family, you might like to use blue for Mary's cloak and the Baby's shawl, red for Joseph's and green for the shepherds' garments.

Sprinkle a little flour on a board and roll out the dough to an even thickness of about

6 mm/³⁄₁₆ in. Do not make tree decorations too thick or they will hang heavily on the branches. Cut out the shapes you wish, or mould the dough to make fruit, 'mince pies' and so on.

To make plaits, one of the traditional salt-dough decorations, cut three strips about 18 mm/¾ in wide. Roll the strips to make sausage shapes. Press one end of each of the strips together and plait them in the usual way. Cut off the dough at the ends, shape the plait into a circle and press the joined ends together. Cut out bow or leaf shapes to cover the join, or cover it with a ribbon bow once baked.

Use a toothpick to press a hole into solid shapes, for the hanging ribbon. Mark on any texture details, such as leaf veins.

Brush uncoloured dough with a glaze of beaten egg and milk and place the shapes well apart on a baking sheet. Leave them in a warm room for at least 24 hours so that they dry thoroughly before baking.

Bake the dough in the oven at 160°C/325°F/gas 3 for 1–1½ hours or until the shapes are completely dry. Remove them from the oven and leave them to dry.

If you wish, paint the cool dough shapes with clear varnish, to make sure that they catch every sparkle from the tree lights.

Thread ribbon through hanging decorations.

WAYS TO USE PLAY-DOUGH SHAPES

Use gingerbread men cutters to make dough-boy shapes, and stand them, hands linked, around an indoor flower pot. It is a lovely way to disguise and embellish a plain container for a table-top Christmas tree or a dried flower model. Stand the pot on a plate or dish, stand the dough-boy shapes around the pot, facing outwards, and attach them to the pot with small dabs of blue tacky clay. Sprigs of holly and ivy around their feet complete an unusual decoration.

Make a collection of simple fruit shapes such as apples and pears and pile them in a pottery dish. Plain brown glazed or realistically coloured, they will be equally effective.

Take a design tip from Finland. Make a large play-dough heart and hang it on a red ribbon in the window. A single candle burning nearby celebrates the light that Christ's coming brought to the world.

Make the play-dough into twisted candle shapes to fit small Christmas tree holders. You can colour the candles red, the flames orange – or not, as you wish. They will symbolize the light in a safe, unusual and decorative way.

Children can have a great deal of fun making and decorating pretend food such as a plate of tasty-looking mince pies or jam tarts. Make sure that everyone realises the 'food' is not for real.

Make a nativity scene of play-dough figures and stand them in a group on a board covered with hay or straw.

Make a nativity tree, with the play-dough shapes as the only decorations. Use a small table-top Christmas tree or a twig tree to display cutouts of the Holy Family, the Three Wise Men and the stable animals.

Make a Nativity tree, with the play-dough square or oblong boxes for example – and tie them around with ribbon. They look almost as enticing as real parcels on the tree.

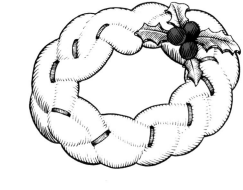

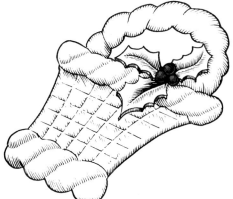

Play-dough decorations and fruit

BRINGING IN THE HOLLY

An evergreen welcome wreath on the front door, a mistletoe kissing ring in the hall, sprigs of holly over the picture frames, trails of ivy leaves looped above the fireplace – when did the custom of decorating our homes with evergreens begin? We take a look at ancient customs and beliefs, and how they have gradually been adapted for our own celebrations.

Ancient peoples in many parts of the world believed evergreens to have magical powers, perhaps because their dark and lustrous leaves remained on the branches when other trees all around (the deciduous ones) were bare. And so they brought evergreen branches indoors to pay homage to their gods, to brighten their homes and rejoice in the natural world during the dark days of winter.

The ancient Scandinavians particularly, in a land of almost constant winter darkness, had a magnificent festival in honour of the god Thor and Mother Night, and evergreen branches and the Yule log were an important part of these celebrations, which marked the beginning of the winter solstice.

The Romans considered evergreens to be a symbol of good luck, and brought them indoors to bestow good fortune on the household for the coming year. They also exchanged presents during the festival of Kalends, on January 1st, and high-ranking officials were expected to present gifts to the Emperor. At first the most joyous gifts they could imagine were evergreen, mainly laurel, branches, because of their symbolism. Later the gifts became more symbolic still, and the Romans gave honey and cakes to ensure that the new year would be full of sweetness, and gold, so that prosperity could be guaranteed.

It was not until Victorian times that the practice of decking the home with evergreens reached its peak, and whole families shared in the joy of gathering in the greenery and looping it into garlands to outline stairways, doorways and windows.

There is a special joy still today in 'bringing in the holly'. Anyone who has a garden or the chance to take a walk in the country, taking a trug and secateurs, will find the sojourn both rewarding and therapeutic – a pleasant interlude from the rush and crush of Christmas shopping!

Even in the heart of cities, the harshness of winter is softened by the fronds of ivy clinging to walls and colonizing waste ground, and market stalls are decked with bunches of holly and mistletoe to buy.

Imitation evergreens are becoming more flattering every year, and it is now possible to buy sprigs of fir and spruce, garlands of holly and ivy and bunches of mistletoe almost indistinguishable from the natural plants.

TRADITIONS
& BELIEFS

Throughout history evergreens have been endowed with both mystical and medicinal properties. Many of these traditional beliefs linger on in the customs we follow today.

Bay Since ancient times the bay tree was associated with valour and glory, and bay leaves signified good cheer, and continuity of esteem and affection.

Cedar The tree signified strength and fortitude, and the leaves incorruptibility.

Cypress In Victorian times cypress was said to convey death, grief and mourning.

Holly This most symbolic of evergreens has long been used to signify eternal life. In ancient times it was thought to be a deterrent to witches and, as such, considered a sign of good luck.

Custom decreed that it was unlucky to bring holly indoors before Christmas Eve, or to discard it before Twelfth Night; throwing away a symbol of good fortune was considered to be asking for trouble.

In the Middle Ages it was thought that if the first bough of holly brought into the house in winter had prickly leaves, the master would rule the household throughout the coming year. If on the other hand, the holly leaves were smooth and without prickles, it would be a year of petticoat rule. In general, holly was thought to represent the male.

The Christian church accepted some of the ancient symbolism of the plant. The sharp, prickly leaves became associated with the Crown of Thorns worn by Jesus at Calvary, and the red berries with His blood. Because of these associations holly is known in Scandinavia as 'the Christ-Thorn'.

Ivy In the Victorian language of flowers, ivy was thought to signify friendship, fidelity and marriage. Long before that, perhaps because of its clinging properties, ivy was understood to represent the female of the species, and it was thought that, just by bringing it indoors, the plant used to bestow the gift of fertility on a household.

Like holly, ivy was considered a symbol of good luck and, if it grew up the walls of a house, to protect the occupants from harm and the evil spirits. If this most tenuous and hardy of evergreens withered and died, then that was bad news indeed, and disaster was expected.

In Roman times ivy had strong associations with Bacchus, the god of wine – a sore point with the early Christians. Their misgivings were eventually overcome because of the many supposed medicinal uses of the plant. A vinegar made from the berries was taken against disease, a remedy that was resorted to at the time of the Great Plague. Cups were shaped from ivy wood and these vessels, too were credited with healing powers. For example, children suffering from whooping cough were told to drink from them.

Laurel The fleshy, shiny leaves of laurel have a long association with victory, honour and glory. Garlands made from them were awarded to the victors in the Olympic Games, and to people attaining distinction in all kinds of walks of life in Ancient Rome. The phrase 'resting on your laurels' and the current practice of giving a laurel wreath to victors in motor-races both emanate from those times.

Laurel branches were among the first to be used to decorate Christian churches at Christmas time.

Mistletoe According to the Victorians, the giving of a sprig of mistletoe signified the surmounting of all difficulties, and the overcoming of all obstacles. Its symbolism extends way back to the time of the Druids, and of course sprigs of mistletoe form a traditional part of our Christmas festivities even today. For more details, see page 110.

Pine Bunches of pine were hung indoors in Medieval times to mask the smell of dampness, and were specially valued in sickrooms for their sweet fresh smell and supposed disinfectant properties.

Yew Branches of yew were once understood to convey sadness and sorrow, probably because the trees were so frequently planted in churchyards.

THE HOLLY AND THE IVY

The holly and the ivy,
When they are both full grown,
Of all the trees that are in the wood,
The holly bears the crown:

★

CHORUS: The rising of the sun
and the running of the deer,
The playing of the merry organ
Sweet singing in the choir, -

★

The holly bears a blossom,
As white as the lily flower,
And Mary bore sweet Jesus Christ
To be our Saviour:

★

The holly bears a berry
As red as any blood,
And Mary bore sweet Jesus Christ
To do poor sinners good:

★

The holly and the ivy,
When they are both full grown,
Of all the trees that are in the wood,
The holly bears the crown:

EVERGREEN
IDEAS

* Fill a shallow basket with pine cones and tuck in a few sprigs of evergreens for a lovely contrast of texture and colour.
* Make the most of a few precious fresh flowers, such as lilies or mophead chrysanthemums. Fill a jug with sprays of ivy and high points of twigs, spruce or yew and arrange just three flowers against this lustrous background.
* Arrange three or four chubby candles on a flat dish, cover the surface with sphagnum moss and tuck in a few evergreen sprays for an Advent ring with a difference.
* For a bright and shiny table centre, fill a large glass storage jar with baubles (loopless ones will do). Stick a thin trail of ivy leaves to spiral round the outside, and tuck a thick sprig of ivy into the neck.
* If there really is no space on the Christmas dinner table for a formal decoration it is a charming idea to scatter small sprays of holly or other evergreens on the table among the dishes.
* For a door or wall wreath that looks good enough to eat, wire tiny clementines or russet apples on to a preformed foam ring. Press in evergreen sprays such as ivy, cypress, juniper, to fill in the spaces.
* Hang a shaggy, verdant ball of evergreens in the hall or a room corner. Cut short sprays of greenery and press them into a large potato,

which will yield moisture and keep the sprays fresh-looking. Add tiny baubles or ribbon trails for extra glitter.
* Make a buffet table the focus of attention by pinning or tacking trails and loops of ivy to outline the front edge of a cloth. Tiny posies of dried flowers are a naturally pretty extra trim.
* Bring a straw shoulder-bag into the festivities. Fill a shopping bag brim-full of evergreens, Chinese lanterns, honesty, spindle berries, whatever, and hang it on the wall. It is a lovely idea for a hallway.
* Make a decorative version of a carved wooden swag. Ask a greengrocer to save the plaited base of a garlic string, cover it with nuts, dried flowers and evergreens. Wire on the natural materials and finish it off with a flourish – a raffia bow is appropriate.

KNOW YOUR
HOLLIES

The familiar holly which decorates our homes at Christmas is *Ilex aquifolium*, known as Common Holly or English Holly. The evergreen tree, which can grow to a height of 25 m/80 ft, is a native of Europe, North America and West Asia. The leaves are shiny, wavy and, on all except the oldest of trees, sharply prickled.

The tree bears both male and female flowers which are creamy white, and ripen to bright red, four-seeded berries in November.

Holly wood is hard and finely grained, and much valued in decorative wood work.

Other distinctive varieties of holly are:
Ilex aquifolium bacciflora which offers quite different decorative properties, since it carries bright yellow berries.

'Hedgehog Holly', *I. aquifolium* 'Ferox', is a male clone and as such, does not bear fruits. The

leaves, much smaller than those of Common Holly, are covered with prickles on the upper surface and deeply and minutely wavy. You can always cheat, and bind clusters of false berries on to the branches.

The variegated leaves of the Golden King holly (*I. × altaclarensis*), a hybrid between Common Holly and Canary Holly, are the main decorative feature. Most are dark green edged with yellow, though they can be completely and attractively all-yellow. The fruits, in striking contrast, are the familiar red.

ADVENT
WREATHS

Advent wreaths are not only decorative, they are versatile too. You can compose a table-top wreath quickly and easily on a preformed foam ring, which you can buy from florists, or improvise and build up the design on a flat dish or cake tin lid. Traditional red and green, luxurious gold, frosty white, or the natural look, you can interpret the basic idea in any way you please.

BASIC TABLE-TOP
WREATH

YOU WILL NEED

* one 22.5 cm/9 in polystyrene foam-filled ring, from florists
* four 22.5 cm/9 in non-drip candles, red, white, green, silver or gold
* a selection of short sprays of evergreens such as holly, ivy, juniper, cypress, yew, spruce

* a selection of dried flowers, seedheads, nuts, false berries, miniature baubles or other trims
* about 50 cm/20 in of 2.5 cm/1 in wide ribbon for bow
* a short length of thin wire.

Step 1 Place the ring on a flat surface. Press one candle firmly into the foam, then position the other three at equal distances around the ring.

Step 2 Insert short sprays of evergreens around the ring. Take care that the leaves hang low over both the inside and outside of the ring to conceal the utilitarian but not attractive plastic ring casing.

Step 3 Continue to fill in the ring, clustering short leaf sprays around the base of the candles. Turn the ring around to check that it is equally attractive from every angle.

Step 4 Add any colourful trimmings of your choice. You can group them around all four candles, concentrate the visual interest around one candle – if, for example, the wreath is to be placed on a side table and viewed from one side – or distribute the trimmings evenly, tucking them in among the leaves to give an all-round effect.

Step 5 Tie the ribbon into a bow and trim the ends. Thread the wire through the back of the loop and twist the ends. Press the wire into the foam to position the bow on the side of the design.

CANDLE-POWER

Make design variations of the Advent wreath. Press a single candle into the foam ring and design the wreath so that attention is focussed around it. Or fix one or more candles into short, unobtrusive holders and stand them in the centre of the ring.

IMAGINATIVE IMPROVIZATION

If you have no time to rush to the florist's to buy a foam ring, cut out blocks of stem-holding foam and arrange them in a ring around the outside of a flat dish or upturned cake tin lid. Push the candles through the foam and anchor them firmly to the base with a dab of tacky clay. Complete the design with evergreens and trimmings which spill well over into the centre of the ring, hiding all of the foam.

Note Never leave lighted candles unattended in a room, especially in a household where there are young children or pets.

ADAPTING THE
BASIC IDEA

ALL THAT GLISTERS

For a glittering gold Advent wreath, choose gold candles – spiral-twisted ones are attractive – mini gold baubles and gold ribbon trims.

Position the candles and arrange the evergreens. Spatter them with gold spray paint so that they look as if they have been speckled with golden raindrops.

To do this, hold the paint nozzle about 10 cm/ 4 in away, and press the top in short, sharp bursts.

Position the baubles – or use golden strawflowers instead – and finish the design with one or four golden ribbon bows.

FROSTY WHITE

Team up a quartet of white candles and tiny sprays of white dried flowers, such as pearl everlasting and daisy-type helipterum, and include natural or pretend mistletoe among the evergreens.

BERRY RED

Choose holly with the most generous berry-to-leaf ratio you can find, or cheat and add clusters of false berries. Add to the visual impact by wiring together clusters of miniature red baubles and arrange them at the base of bright scarlet candles. Finish off the wreath with eye-catching bows of red and white checked gingham ribbon or a dazzling polka-dot design.

THE NATURAL LOOK

Choose dark green candles for a wreath with an air of the country. Intersperse the evergreen sprays with stems of wheat, barley or oats, poppy and love-in-a-mist seedheads, and nuts. To attach these, press a dab of blue tacky clay on to each nut, push in a hair pin or a loop of wire, and insert the end in the foam.

WELCOME WREATHS

The idea of hanging a welcome wreath of evergreens on the door dates back to Roman times, when a garland of leaves signified good luck and good fortune. The Victorians took up the basic theme and, in their own special way, embellished it by adding bonbons and baubles, tokens and treats.

The basic design is infinitely variable, based on a preformed polystyrene foam-filled ring and decorated with your own choice of materials such as holly, ivy, cypress, nuts, cones, dried flowers and ribbon bows. Having made a welcome wreath for the front door you can then carry through the idea, in any of the variations, as an indoor decoration.

A door wreath of holly and cypress.

BASIC
DOOR WREATH

YOU WILL NEED

* a 22.5 cm/9 in polystyrene foam-filled ring, from florists'
* a roll of medium-gauge wire for hanging, and wiring cones etc
* a selection of short sprays of evergreens such as holly, ivy, juniper, cypress, yew, spruce
* a selection of nuts, cones, false berries, miniature baubles, dried flowers or other trims.
* about 60 cm/24 in of 4 cm/1½ in wide satin ribbon for bow

Step 1 Bind the wire round and round the plastic ring and twist the ends into a loop.

Wiring the ring for hanging.

Step 2 Select any cones or nuts you want to include in the design. These will need to be twisted on to wires, to make them secure enough for a vertical-hanging design.

Cut lengths of wire about 12.5 cm/5 in. To wire cones, press the wire between one layer of 'petals', bring together the two ends and twist them to form a stem. Wrap the wire around each nut and twist the ends.

Wiring cones and nuts.

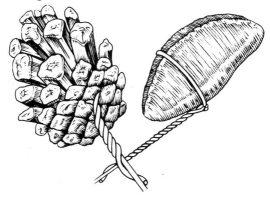

Step 3 Cover the ring generously with short sprays of evergreens of your choice. You can use only holly or a blend of several species.

Step 4 Add to the basic design as you wish, arranging cones, nuts, false holly berries or baubles. Dried flowers are not suitable trimmings for a wreath in a windy or exposed outdoor position.

Step 5 Tie the ribbon into a full bow or a double bow and wire to the top or base of the design. Hang the wreath on a hook on the door, or wire it to the door knocker.

A spruce ring.

VARIATIONS
ON THE THEME

SPRUCE RING

Use off-cuts from the Christmas tree – the shaggy ends that need trimming – to make a spruce ring for a door or fireplace wall. Longer sprays at the top, breaking the neat circular look, make the design unusual and interesting.

A dried flower ring.

DRIED FLOWER RING

For a front door protected by a storm porch, or a design to display inside, the basic wreath can be made very attractive with small posies of dried flowers (wire the stems to make miniature bunches) and seedheads.

THE WILD LOOK

For an unconventional and effective design that is sparing in its use of evergreens, make a ring that features bare branches. Position the short woody stems first (apple is ideal) and then fill in with cones and evergreens.

A lucky horseshoe – a variation on the traditional wreath.

LUCKY HORSESHOE

Make a 'lucky horseshoe' design in the usual way. Cut a one-third segment from the polystyrene ring, using a sharp kitchen knife. (You can use this section to make a crescent-shaped table decoration). Bind a wire round the top of the horseshoe to form a hanging loop, and fill in the shape with evergreens. Arrange spiky, trailing ends to emphasise the effect.

EVERGREEN POSY

A design with all the freedom you could wish – a shaggy 'posy' of apple twigs, spruce, ivy, laurel and holly. Bind a few cones to the twigs. Bind the stems firmly, and be generous with the ribbon bow.

An evergreen posy using twigs and cones.

O THE MISTLETOE BOUGH (BOW).—*Old Song New Sung.*

MISTLETOE

Throughout the ages mistletoe has been shrouded in an aura of mystery. Perhaps this is because it is a parasite, growing on the branches of trees, and was therefore thought to be strange.

The plant played an important part in Druid rituals, a fact that has weighed heavily against it in the eyes of the Christian church, where, in many instances, it is still not allowed to take its place alongside the holly and the ivy in the Christmas decorations.

One exception to this prohibition was York Minster, where a bunch of mistletoe was carried in procession to the high altar as a sign of amnesty to all criminals. The temporary pardon came to an end with the removal of the mistletoe on Twelfth Night.

The Druids gathered their branches of mistletoe in November, ceremoniously cutting it down from the trees with a golden instrument and catching it – without its being allowed to touch the ground – on a white sheet.

The evergreen branches were divided among the community and hung over doorways to symbolize peace and hospitality, and were be-

lieved to offer protection against thunder, lightning and evil spirits, and to banish poisons.

The Druids also used mistletoe as a symbol of fertility, believing it to have magical powers. The plant's innocent association with kissing games at Christmas probably stems from this belief.

In Victorian times, mistletoe was shaped into a ball – to represent the form in which it grows – or bound on to a frame to make a kissing ring. Each time a gallant beau captured a shy maiden beneath the mistletoe and claimed a kiss, the act was recorded by the removal of a berry. When the branches were bare, the kissing had to stop.

> ' *Pick a berry off the mistletoe*
> *For ev'ry kiss that's given.*
> *When the berries have all gone,*
> *There's an end to kissing.* '
>
> Traditional rhyme

PLANT PORTRAIT

Mistletoe is a shrubby parasite, *Viscum album*, which forms in tight round clusters on the branches of apple, poplar and other trees. It is found in the south and east of England, but is a much more familiar sight in France.

The mistletoe balls grow to about 60 cm/2 ft across and are yellowish green in colour. The leaves are a pale lime green and the flowers, which are mostly unisexual, are yellow. The fruit takes the form of small, round milky-white berries.

MISTLETOE DECORATIONS

A sprig of mistletoe hanging in the porch, the hall or some unexpected and shady room corner is all that is needed for the traditional Christmas kiss. But a Victorian-style mistletoe ball or kissing ring, both simple to make on wire frames, are romantic and decorative features in their own right.

TO MAKE A
MISTLETOE BALL

YOU WILL NEED

* ★ 2 wire coat hangers
* ★ a roll of medium-gauge binding wire
* ★ about 500 g/1 lb of sphagnum or other moss
* ★ a selection of evergreens, including mistletoe
* ★ about 40 cm/16 in of 4 cm/1½ in wide ribbon for bow

Step 1 Bend each coathanger to form a circle. Use wire cutters to cut off one of the hooks. Put the two circles together so that the frames cross over, to make the outline of a sphere. Bind the two circles together with wire at the top and bottom.

Step 2 Pack handfuls of the moss around the frame, binding it on with roll wire taken round and round the moss.

Step 3 Compose short sprays of evergreens into small posies, and bind them to the frame, placing them so tht the leaves of each bunch cover the stems of the one before. Make sure that the mistletoe sprays are given due prominence. Continue binding on evergreens until the frame is completely covered.

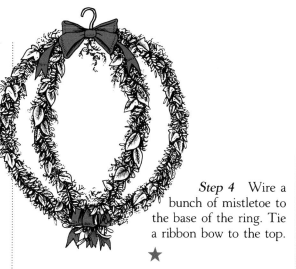

Step 4 Wire a bunch of mistletoe to the base of the ring. Tie a ribbon bow to the top.

★

TO MAKE A
MISTLETOE RING

YOU WILL NEED

* ★ one 25 cm/10 in wire frame, from florists'
* ★ a few handfuls of sphagnum or other moss
* ★ a roll of medium-gauge binding wire
* ★ a selection of evergreens including mistletoe
* ★ about 2.5 m/2½ yd, 4 cm/1½ in wide satin ribbon
* ★ about 1 m/1 yd matching 2.5 cm/1 in wide satin ribbon

Step 1 Pack the sphagnum moss on both sides of the wire frame and bind it over and over with the wire until it is evenly covered.

Step 2 Cut four lengths of wire about 20 cm/8 in long. Wrap one round the ring, twist the two ends together close to the ring and shape the remaining length into a loop. Repeat with the other three wires, making hanging loops at equal distances around the frame.

Step 3 Make up bunches of evergreens – holly, ivy, whatever you have – and bind them on to

the frame to pack it closely. When the frame is covered, push in the mistletoe sprigs to give them pride of place.

Step 4 Cut the wide ribbon into five equal lengths. Tie one end of each of four of the ribbons to a wire loop. Bring the other ends together neatly – it may be necessary to adjust the length, according to the height of the ceiling. Staple the ends together, and fix a wire loop for hanging.
  Cut the narrower ribbon into four equal lengths and tie bows to the loops around the ring.

Step 5 Wire a bunch of mistletoe to the top loop, and tie on a bow with the remaining length of wide ribbon.

A kissing ring

111

MISTLETOE POSY

With all its romantic associations, mistletoe makes a charming decoration for a bedroom.

Since mistletoe is normally less easy to come by than other evergreens, it is a good idea to make a generous bunch of ivy (the variegated form gives a lighter look to the design) and bind on short sprays of mistletoe. If the milky-white berries are somewhat sparse, compromise and add a few clusters of false ones.

A smaller version of the posy on the pillow and another to decorate a gift make Christmas morning memorable and special.

Shiny satin ribbon bows to tone with your furnishings, or lace ribbon bows to capture the mood of the occasion, add to the glamour.

EVERGREEN GARLANDS

There is something so exuberant and luxurious about ribbons or swags of evergreens, and yet they are simple, if somewhat time-consuming, to make.

The ribbons are built up on thick cord packed with moss and bound round and round to form a flexible, natural-looking rope. If traces of the moss base do show through in the finished design, all is not lost.

Gather together a selection of evergreens or, if you prefer, amass a single type such as ivy, or spruce branches. Give the greenery a good long drink of water, all day or overnight before you begin your decoration.

TO MAKE A SWAG

YOU WILL NEED

* a piece of thick cord
* sphagnum or other moss
* a roll of medium-gauge wire
* a selection of evergreens
* a selection of trimmings, such as nuts, cones, small fruits, dried flowers and seedheads, baubles, ribbon bows
* ribbon for large decorative bows

Step 1 Measure the cord for the space allocated, allowing for graceful drapes. Cut the cord and, if the garland is to be looped in the centre, mark that point.

Step 2 Pack handfuls of moss round the cord and bind it on, taking the wire round and round.

Step 2

Step 3 Cut the evergreens into short, even sprays and gather them into bunches.

Step 4

Step 4 Work from one end towards the centre of the rope. Place the first bunch, stem ends towards the centre, against the end of the rope. Arrange the stems so that the foliage completely covers the front of the rope and bind on the stems. Place the next bunch so that the foliage covers the stems of the first, and bind that in place. Continue until you reach the centre of the rope. Repeat the design on the other side.

Step 5 Bind on more foliage to cover the stem overlap in the centre of the design.

Step 6 Add the decorations you have chosen. Nuts and cones and small fruits will need to be wired. Stand back and assess the design to check that the colours and textures are evenly distributed.

Step 6

Step 7 Hang the garland in place. Tie ribbon bows – perhaps one in the centre and one at each end – and wire them in place.

DESIGN
NOTEBOOK

There are several ways to vary the colour, texture and personality of the decoration.

SILVER BALLS

Wire chestnuts, spray them with silver paint and leave them to dry. Decorate the garland with the nuts, silver baubles, sprays of honesty, clusters of white everlasting flowers and silver ribbons.

THE SCANDINAVIAN LOOK

Make the garland with spiky shoots cut from a Christmas tree. Decorate it with tiny red and white ribbon bows wired to the branches and long trailing bows in matching ribbons at the hanging points.

FRUIT AND NUT DESIGN

Trim the garland with tiny clementines, apples and nuts, including a few pecans if possible, for their unusual and warm colour. Twine thin strands of dried orange peel among the evergreens. For a light-weight alternative, substitute Chinese lanterns for the fruits.

LAZY RIBBON

If your fireplace wall is not made to take a hanging decoration, make a garland to rest on the mantelpiece and trail over the ends. Or place one along a wide windowsill or on top of a low cupboard or bookcase.

A finished swag on a mantelpiece. An attractive variation is to hang swathes of swags along the banisters of the staircase.

DECORATIONS

THE TABLE
★

aying the table for Christmas dinner is like setting the stage for a special production. You will need to attend to every detail from placing the cutlery and wine glasses to arranging fruit and flower decorations.

THE DRESS
REHEARSAL

Christmas comes but once a year – and so does the Christmas dinner. In most households the festive meal is the most expansive and the most formal one in the annual calendar.

It may be the only occasion when the extra leaf is put into the dining table; when all the chairs are put around it, and when every last vegetable dish and sauceboat is in use. And if this is to be your first at-home Christmas, or the first one in a new home, it may well be your first opportunity to see how the whole scene comes together.

The occasion is too important, and Christmas Day itself too packed with activity, to leave any detail to chance. It might be a good idea to stage a dress rehearsal a few days in advance, just to check that everything will run smoothly.

Extend the table if necessary and place the chairs around it. Set out the heat-resisting place mats if the surface requires them. Position the extra mats that will be needed for all the vegetable dishes and sauceboats, and for the poultry and meat if you plan to carve them at the table.

Set a large dinner plate and a small side plate at each place setting, then arrange the cutlery and a wine glass for each wine you plan to serve throughout the meal. Position the vegetable

dishes, sauceboats, butter dishes, pepper and salt pots and everything else that is to go on the table, and position them and reposition them until you have a workable and elegant arrangement.

Christmas dinner is meant to be a friendly occasion and the table is expected to resemble a 'groaning board'. But it should not be so cramped that it looks untidy, nor so over-crowded that guests can scarcely find space to rest a glass in safety.

If this dress rehearsal confirms your worst fears, and there is just not space for everything, consider carving the meat at a side table and passing the vegetables round for guests to help

The Christmas dinner table
perfectly laid out.

themselves from a large serving plate – the way it used to be done.

If placing the cutlery and all the glasses poses space problems, consider setting out the dessert spoons and forks, the fruit knives, and the dessert wine and liqueur glasses once the main course has been cleared away.

If not only the table but the geography of the room looks cramped, sit at the table and check on the elbow room. It may be necessary to extend the table in another way, or to rearrange the seating, placing two chairs instead of one at the end of the table perhaps.

FLOWERS
FOR THE TABLE

Flowers have a very special role to play on the Christmas dinner table. A somewhat delicate role, since they should provide the pretty finishing touches without at any time detracting by either sight or smell from the food.

Tall containers such as candlesticks, wine carafes converted to elegant table pedestals, and long, narrow specimen-bloom vases are economical with table space. You can compose a cascade of evergreen leaves and berries, a crescent of freesias and spray carnations, or a shower of gypsophila and rosebuds in a container that takes up no more of the table surface than a coffee cup or wine glass.

If you choose a design of this kind, in a tall container, plan the arrangement so that the flowers and foliage curve naturally downwards without over-extending the overall height. Remember the rule that guests facing each other across the table must be able to see and talk to each other comfortably.

By complete contrast, and if there is space, you can design a long, narrow arrangement to follow the lines of a rectangular table, or an all-round one for a circular table, or flatter guests with designs in miniature, a personal flower arrangement at each place setting. There are designs and ideas for combining flowers and candles on pages 116 and 117.

CRISP,
WHITE LINEN

Once you have sized up the table for space and layout, bring the table coverings into the rehearsal and check the cloth, place mats and napkins. A crisp white cotton or linen cloth, still the most traditional and most flattering background for food, looks wonderful, but only if it is crisp, and sparkling white.

A cloth that looks slightly jaded can be transformed by having brightly coloured place mats arranged on top, at each setting. A lace cloth looks more festive if it is placed over a colourful undercloth. A length of cotton from the market, or a roll of coloured paper, will do.

If your table surface is a special feature you can use place mats instead of a cloth but they should be crisp to the point of being stiff and starchy. Try to launder them just before the day and store them where they will not become crushed or creased.

Napkins, whether you choose linen or good-quality paper ones, can be simply utilitarian or they can become a decorative feature. See pages 120 and 121 for ideas for folding napkins into butterfly, fan, tulip, the bishop's mitre and other shapes.

As you arrange the cutlery and glasses (see below for details of the layout) take a leaf from the footman's book (see panel) and polish each piece with a dry, clean cloth until it gleams.

PLACING
THE CUTLERY

The general rule is that cutlery should be set in the order in which it is to be used, working from the outside inwards, towards the plate. In this way, guests should be able to tell at a glance how many courses are to be served.

Lay the knives, blades pointing inwards, with spoons on the right side of the plate, and forks on the left. This layout should always be followed, even for a left-handed guest.

If there is to be soup, a fish course, a meat course, a dessert, cheese and fresh fruit, the layout on the right of the plate would be (from the outside) soup spoon, fish knife, meat knife, dessert spoon, cheese knife and fruit knife. To the left of the plate (again from the outside) there would be the fish fork, main-course fork, dessert fork and (if one is used) fruit fork.

To save space from the sides of the place settings an alternative layout is to place the cheese knife on the side plate and the dessert spoon and fork (with handles pointing right and left respectively) above the plate.

PLACING THE
WINE GLASSES

Sparkling, shining glass glinting in candlelight is one of the most attractive elements of a formal dinner table.

Place the glasses in a straight line across the top of the right-hand cutlery, in the order of use. This may be a tumbler for water on the right, then a glass for white wine, then one for red wine and lastly a glass for port or liqueur, on the left of the row.

LUNCHEON TABLE LAID FOR EIGHT PERSONS.

CHRISTMAS
POSIES

Make a charming gift for each guest around the table, a posy of evergreens and flowers composed, Victorian style, in a paper doily.

Cut a hole in the centre of a small white or gold paper doily. Compose a tiny posy of cypress leaves, gypsophila, mistletoe sprigs, spray carnations, or shiny pretend berries, and bind the stems.

Push the posy stems through the doily centre and sticky-tape the doily to hold it in place. Tie a ribbon bow around the posy stem.

FLOWERS
& CANDLES

Christmas is a wonderful time for turning back the clock and appreciating the gentle and flattering light of candles; no longer a necessity of modern life but now a special joy.

Where there is no room for a Christmas tree, a lighted candle could be placed in a window. A dish of nightlights or stubby candles could decorate a hearth that may not now be in use. An elegant candlestick could be arranged with a cascade of flowers and foliage. A long, low design of dried flowers and flickering candles

could be made in advance as a special dinner-party table centre. Even the children could make a safe and simple composition of berries and candles. Candles and flowers have a natural and delightful affinity.

A DESIGN FOR THE CHILDREN

The combination of berry-bright evergreens and brilliantly-coloured nightlights makes an exciting group to delight the children. And the candles, on a flat, broad plate, are perfectly safe. The bird choralling its approval is a special Christmas species, a pottery pie funnel.

ELEGANT CANDELABRA

A three-pronged candle-holder in silver-plate, wrought iron, brass or wood, can easily be converted into a delightful floral centrepiece. Resplendent in all its glory, it has a single central candle and two cascades of flowers.

YOU WILL NEED

★ a suitable candelabrum
★ two metal or plastic candlecup holders, from florists'
★ florists' extra-tacky fixing clay
★ pre-soaked moisture-holding florists' foam
★ florists' self-adhesive tape
★ a selection of evergreens and seasonal flowers such as cypress, ivy, spray carnations, chrysanthemums, carnations and alstroemeria
★ a 25 cm/10 in candle, or size according to scale of design

Step 1 Press a thin strip of clay around the base of each holder. Press one 'cup' into each of the two outer candle cavities.

Step 2 Place a piece of pre-soaked foam into each holder. Secure it with two pieces of tape criss-crossed over the foam and on to the holder.

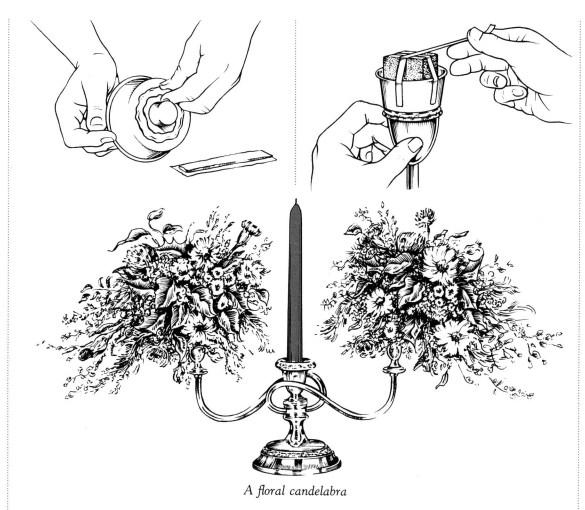

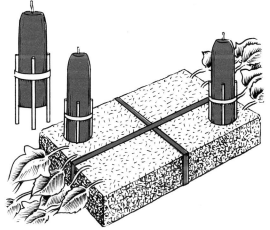

YOU WILL NEED

- ★ a shallow container
- ★ dry florists' foam
- ★ florists' self-adhesive tape
- ★ two candles
- ★ eight matchsticks
- ★ a selection of slender evergreen leaves such as cypress and ivy
- ★ a selection of dried seedheads such as honesty, wheat and barley
- ★ a selection of dried flowers such as straw-flowers, helipterum, ammobium, rosebuds

Step 1 Position the foam in the container and tape it in place.

Step 2 Tape four matchsticks to each candle (see below) and position them in the foam.

Step 3 Define the length of the design by inserting long trails of evergreens and cereals. Conceal the foam with short sprays of evergreens pushed close against it.

Step 4 Build up the design with the dried flowers, alternating colours and textures. Insert a few small sprays of evergreens for contrast.

A floral candelabra

Step 3 Arrange the foliage and long, slender stems of buds and flowers so that they slant outwards and downwards at each side. Cut short sprays of evergreen leaves and press them into the foam so that the leaves cover and conceal it.

Step 4 Arrange larger, round and fully-opened flowers in the centre of the design to make a gentle, domed curve.

Keep the foam topped up with water so that it is permanently moist.

A GRACEFUL TABLE CENTRE

A long, narrow design, a ribbon of dried or fresh flowers and candles, is sparing of space on a crowded table and would look equally at home on a sidetable or sideboard. Dried flowers have one distinct advantage over fresh ones, you can compose the design well in advance of the day.

THE BUFFET TABLE

★

Boxing day buffet set with a traditional cold collation; the drinks table at a neighbourly get-together; a table set aside with help-yourself snacks for an informal 'at home' gathering – there is space on all these occasions for a floral arrangement that catches the eye from across a crowded room, and remains to decorate the table stylishly when the party is almost over.

Whenever you are planning a buffet, it is natural that the menu will to a large extent dictate the table layout, and thus determine what prominence the flower arrangements are to have.

It may be that a dressed ham or a brace of cold roast ducks will occupy the centre ground, indicating that a floral design on either side is called for. It may be that on a drinks table crowded with bottles, glasses and snacks and likely to be the focus of lively activity, a small, squat and utterly unshakeable design is all that could be accommodated. On the other hand a table set with low-profile items like dips and plates of savouries might be rescued from obscurity by an eye-catching design lifted way above table height.

As always, there are the twin considerations of design and practicality to take into account. And where practicality is concerned, arrangements for a buffet table are almost the reverse of those for a dining table. No-one has to crane their neck to catch a glimpse of their opposite neighbour through a haze of flowers and foliage. Buffet tables give more scope for originality and flamboyance, in the use of both containers and materials.

Miniature trees, like balls of flowers on a chunky stem, cascades of flowers and twigs on a pedestal and low arrangements like jewels in a box take time and care to arrange.

When time is short and instant effect is needed, let imagination have free rein. For an informal lunch or supper a collection of glass storage jars with, variously, tiny baubles, shells, dried flower heads, small cones, pot pourri and red kidney beans, and just one with a few long-stemmed flowers such as lilies or gerberas. On a similar theme, use a long, slender pasta jar elongated still further with a handful of twigs and showy chrysanthemums, or with honesty and Chinese lanterns.

Everyday containers like glass jars can be decorated by tying flouncy ribbon bows or decorators' beads around the neck. Pearlised beads lift an ordinary jar way above its humble origins.

Scatter short sprays of holly, ivy or dried flowers or clusters of cones and baubles over the tablecloth. Pin slender ribbons of evergreens, such as natural stems of climbing ivy, to the front of a cloth, or tack on random posies of dried flowers to give the vertical drape visual interest.

A BASKET OF FLOWERS

A flat, steady and sturdy design that will come to no harm, no matter how frenzied the activity around the table. The container is a lidded basket-weave box. An old sewing box, a wooden 'deed' box or a child's pencil case would all be suitable. The flowers are sturdy, too, long-lasting spray chrysanthemums partnered with trails of silver-green eucalyptus.

YOU WILL NEED

* a suitable lidded container
* polythene or foil to line it
* pre-soaked florists' foam
* florists' self-adhesive tape
* a selection of foliage and flowers such as eucalyptus, ivy and spray chrysanthemums
* two cocktail sticks

Step 1 Line the box with polythene or foil so that the moisture does not harm it, or seep through. Cut a piece of foam that will extend about 2.5 cm/1in above the rim, so that stems may be angled downwards, below the container rim. Tape the foam in place.

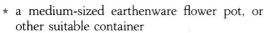

Step 2 Arrange long trails of foliage such as eucalyptus and ivy to slant below the container rim. Cut short sprays and place them to slant forwards.

Step 3 Fill in the design, placing long stems of buds to blend with the side trails and short stems of the fuller flowers to give weight at the centre of the design.

Partly close the container lid and fix it in place with two cocktail sticks.

If you do not have a lidded container of any kind, follow the long, low and sturdy theme by using a shallow container such as a baking dish or butter dish.

★

PEDESTAL
CENTREPIECE

A glass or china cakestand or ham dish makes a perfect pedestal for the centre of a buffet table. Make the shape as straggly and wild as you like, and as space permits. Knarled, bare apple or larch branches and, if you can find them, some covered in moss or lichen contrast strikingly with the cool elegance of exotic flowers such as lilies or gerberas.

YOU WILL NEED

* a suitable pedestal base
* a four-pronged plastic foam holder, from florists'
* florists' extra-tacky adhesive clay
* pre-soaked florists' foam
* florists' self-adhesive tape
* a few thick, gnarled branches
* sprays of evergreen such as fir and pine
* a few large pine cones, mounted on wires (see page 108–9)
* a selection of flowers such as chincherinchee, alstroemeria, lilies and carnations

A pedestal centrepiece.

Step 1 Press a strip of adhesive clay around the base of the pronged foam holder. Press it into place in the centre of the stand. Position the pre-soaked foam in place, for extra security, taking the tape out to the sides and under the plate.

Step 2 Place the branches to outline the height and width of the design. Position long stems of evergreens between the branches, and short stems to cover the foam. Position the cones in clusters around the base.

Step 3 Position long flower stems to follow the height and width of the design. Chincherinchee and alstroemeria both make dramatic pointed shapes.

Step 4 Fill in the centre of the design with round and showy flowers such as lilies and carnations.

FLOWER-BALL
TREE

Not so much an alternative to a Christmas tree, more an alternative flower arrangement – a flower-ball that would look marvellous in the centre of a large buffet table.

Made of dried flowers and foliage, the tree is a good investment in terms of time. If it eventually looks a little lack-lustre and starts to fade, a handful of crisp papery flowers is all it needs for a refresher course.

YOU WILL NEED

* a medium-sized earthenware flower pot, or other suitable container
* plaster of Paris or other material to hold the stem (see page 98)
* a stout twig for the stem, about 30 cm/12 in long
* a ball of florists' foam, 12 cm/5 in diameter
* florists' self-adhesive tape
* dried lepidium, sea lavender or grasses for the background material
* a roll of medium-gauge wire
* a selection of dried flowers such as strawflowers, helipterum and immortella for the colour accents
* moss or pot pourri to cover the fixing material

Step 1 Fix the stem in the pot by your chosen method. See the notes on page 98. Press the foam ball on to the stick and tape it in place.

Step 2 Cut the background material into short even lengths. Form them into small bunches and twist wire around the stems. Press them into the foam ball, taking care to keep an accurate, if somewhat straggly, spherical shape.

Step 3 Compose the dried flowers into small bunches and bind the stems with wire. Press them into the foam, taking care to distribute the colour and visual interest evenly around the tree.

Cover the fixing material in the pot with a layer of moss or pot pourri.

A flower-ball tree.

FOLDED NAPKINS

★

It is tempting to think that folding crisply-starched snow-white linen napkins into imaginative shapes such as a butterfly or bishop's mitre belongs to the distant, more leisurely past. It really is no more difficult than creating simple paper shapes. So easy, in fact, that children can do it. Practise first on paper napkins, then surprise your guests on Christmas Day with attractive shapes created from napkins in red, green, white or gold.

THE FAN

A pleated fan shape of crisp white linen or bright red cotton is held firmly in the neck of a wine glass. This design is useful if you wish to set out the first course ready on individual plates, and to place a decoration – a tiny gift or a berry and flower posy – on the side plates.

1. Fold the napkin in half lengthways and fold it into equal pleats.

2. Fold the concertina pleats. Run your fingers down each crease to set it.

3. Fold the pleated napkin in half lengthways.

4. Place the folded end in the neck of a glass and open out the fan.

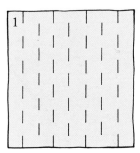

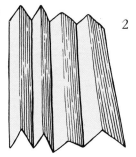

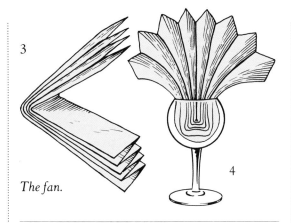

3

The fan.

4

THE CANDLE

This design, a tight spiral to stand on a plate, is a good choice if you wish to add a little personal touch. Tuck a sprig of holly in the top of the napkin for the men and a rosebud for ladies.

1. Fold the lower right-hand point of the napkin diagonally towards, but not meeting, the opposite corner.

2. Starting from one corner, roll the napkin tightly along the fold.

3. Ease the base of the candle shape into a napkin ring and stand it on a plate.

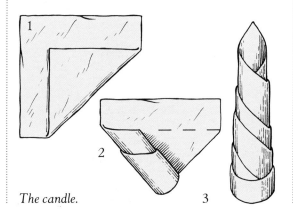

The candle.

3

THE LILY

A design with all the exuberance of the festive season, the lily shape flows gracefully from a wine glass.

1. Fold the napkin into four.

2. Fold it diagonally across.

3. Turn back two loose sections on either side.

4. Pleat and pull down two loose leaves from either side of the centre.

5. Stand the base in a glass and ease out the pleats.

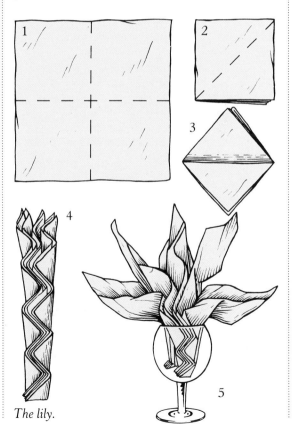

The lily.

The Bishop's mitre.

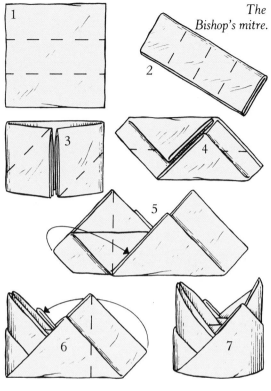

THE BISHOP'S MITRE

One of the best-known and most impressive-looking napkin designs, the mitre makes a convenient container for a small bread roll, a tiny gift or a flower nosegay.

1. Fold the napkin into three.

2. Fold ends, A, and A, over to centre line, B.

3. Fold the corners, C, and C, to the centre.

4. Fold the back across at the dotted line, D.

5. Tuck point E into pleat F.

6. Tuck point G into pleat H on the reverse side.

7. Neaten the finished design.

THE BUTTERFLY

A light and airy shape that looks just as attractive in a pastel colour as it does in sparkling white. A small leaf or flower spray may be tucked into one side.

1. Fold the two edges to the centre, making a long rectangle. Fold the nearest section over again to make a thin rectangle.

2. Form an inverted double fold on both sides, so that the folded ends meet in the centre.

3. Hold the napkin firmly with one hand. Fully open out the right-hand edge to form a triangle. Flatten the shape. Take the left corner back to the right-hand side, to form two wings.

4. Gently open out the wings to form the butterfly shape.

The butterfly.

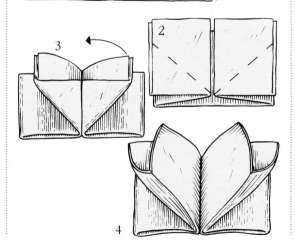

CHRISTMAS STOCKINGS

★

The children have posted their letters to Santa Claus or whispered in his ear in the local store, hung up their stockings on Christmas Eve and put out a mince pie and a mug of cocoa to greet Santa on his rounds. This scene, and so many variations of it, are the very fabric of many a child's (and even many an adult's) joy of Christmas. You can make it extra special by creating your own stockings and exciting fillers.

The idea of hanging up stockings brimming over with presents is such a delightful one that it can happily be extended beyond the traditional situations of the fireplace and the bedpost.

There is such a special excitement to opening a collection of tiny packages that it is an idea well worth carrying through other gift situations too. Children may want to wrap up their own special gifts and put them in a stocking to take to grandparents. If a school friend or young neighbour is ill or in hospital, children may contribute a present for a get-well stocking, and if a group of children want to say thank you, to a teacher or child minder – well, no-one is too old to enter into the spirit of the gift.

MAKING
THE STOCKING

The good thing about Christmas stockings is that they come in all shapes and sizes and offer hope to people of all skill levels, even those who cannot thread a needle.

If knitting is your forte, take a standard sock pattern, the largest available size, and knit it in a progression of colourful stripes, in traditional bright red with white ribbing, in green with a white mock fur trim; whatever takes your fancy. Appliqué small knitted squares to represent parcels, Santa's beard cut from combed white felt, a Christmas tree shape in looped wool – stockings are fun to make as well as to receive.

If sewing (or even cheating with double sticky tape) is your preference, make up the basic shape from the template and go to town on the decorations. Cut out felt bells, crackers, stars, candles and angels by sizing-up the design shapes on page 100, embroider the recipient's name in thick yarn, hang tassels of multi-coloured yarns from the top, sew on mini baubles, stick on paper snow-flakes – the choice is almost infinite.

STOCKING
FILLERS

FOR FLOWER ARRANGERS

As you can see from other pages, some small items of equipment can be useful in many different floral designs.

★ a spray of evergreens and dried flowers to trim the stocking
★ florists' adhesive tape
★ florists' extra-tacky clay
★ packet of marbles, for stem holding
★ four-pronged plastic foam holders
★ floral secateurs
★ roll of fine or medium-gauge wire
★ can of gold or silver spray paint
★ packets of cut-flower feed crystals
★ flower drying desiccant such as silica gel crystals
★ false holly or mistletoe berries
★ small, slender candles
★ small fir cones
★ silk flowers
★ coloured ribbons
★ water sprayer

FOR DAUGHTERS AND AUNTS

Girls and women of all ages enjoy glamorous presents and can be delighted by anything with a hint of humour: a clown brooch or an up-to-the-minute hair clip. Trim the stocking with a floppy silk flower.

* guest soaps
* lavender sachets
* lamp-bulb ring and essential flower oil
* pot pourri
* scented drawer sachets
* scented nightlights and candles
* fun or glamour tights
* fun ceramic brooch
* special tree decoration
* scented wooden apple or pear
* herbal tea sachets
* butterfly-shape hair clip
* earrings
* orange cloved pomander
* colourful scarf

THE TWELVE DAYS OF CHRISTMAS

‘ *On the twelfth day of Christmas my*
true love sent to me
Twelve ladies dancing,
Eleven lords a-leaping,
Ten drummers drumming,
Nine pipers piping,
Eight maids a-milking
Seven swans a-swimming,
Six geese a-laying,
Five gold rings,
Four calling birds,
Three French hens,
Two turtle doves,
And a partridge in a pear tree ’

Anon

FOR SONS AND NEPHEWS

Boys and men, people say, are impossible to buy presents for. Pack a stocking with these surprises, and trim it with a bag of gold-foil covered chocolate coins.

* puzzle key ring
* tin of fruit drops or peppermints
* cassette cleaning kit
* paper or model-making glue
* coloured felt pens
* polishing cloth
* packet of coloured drawing pins
* favourite chocolate bars
* plastic tweezers
* T-shirt transfer

FOR DEDICATED COOKS

Busy cooks can never have too many of the good things they use in the kitchen. Decorate the top of a stocking with sprays of bay leaves and holly, a cinnamon quill and a couple of heads of garlic.

* jars of herbs and spices
* bouquets garnis
* stock cubes
* miniature bottles of spirit or liqueur
* vanilla pods
* cinnamon quills
* preserve-jar labels
* freezer tape
* freezer ball-point pen
* biscuit cutters
* packet of edible gold-leaf
* neck-chain pinger-timer

FOR BUSY EXECUTIVES

People who are busy being upwardly mobile would appreciate all the help you can give to aid efficiency. Decorate the stocking with a huge coloured plastic paperclip and a tartan ribbon bow.

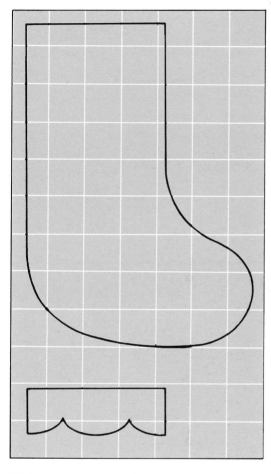

Christmas stocking template.

* coloured stick-on memo pads
* packet of coloured paperclips
* bottle of typing or manuscript eraser
* scented wooden balls as ‘comforters’
* ball-point pens of all kinds
* coloured highlighter pens
* paper knife
* small pocket notebook
* mini stapler
* coloured plastic paper pegs

GIFT WRAPPING

★

An attractively wrapped gift can give almost as much pleasure as the gift itself. It could be a small square box wrapped in silver paper, covered with gold sequin trim and tied around with a gold metallic bow, or an intriguing cracker-shape decorated with a holly berry spray or a cardboard cone speckled with cut-out paper snowflakes. There are numerous variations. One thing is certain, however modest the gift, if it is wrapped with care and style, every fold neatly executed and every bow deftly tied, the recipient's appreciation will be increased many-fold.

Whether you plan to give a friend a pearl necklace or a pair of gardening gloves, a bottle of the most expensive cologne or a chain-store equivalent, it makes no difference. The wrapping should be as neat and attractive as you can make it.

Can anyone really pretend to experience just as much pleasure when being handed an awkwardly-shaped parcel hurriedly wrapped around in ill-meeting paper, and one that is carefully and thoughtfully wrapped, tied, trimmed and presented with style? Few, except for the most impatient-fingered of children, one suspects.

On the minus side, it does take more time to wrap parcels carefully. And trimming them does call for a little more variety in the bits and pieces drawer than a sheet of last year's paper and a roll of sticky tape.

The good thing is that gift wrapping is superbly satisfying. It must be. What could possibly give more pleasure than presenting a gift beautifully? All the folding, cutting, joining, sticking, matching, wrapping, trimming and tying is wonderfully soothing after the hurly-burly of actually buying the presents.

Another important plus factor is that gift wrapping can involve the whole family, and does not call on any special skills, except perhaps a

little patience. Anyone can cover a box neatly with paper or foil. Anyone can tie it around with ribbon and stick, if not tie, a neat and tidy bow. And anyone can start looking around for trimmings, colour combinations, pattern partnerships and other decorative themes that will make gift wrapping the fun it should be.

Experienced hands at the task begin to see the presentation possibilities before they buy the present – that octagonal-shaped candle could go inside a cardboard tube and be disguised as a Christmas cracker. The less nimble-fingered may start, at least, by matching their gifts to boxes of all shapes and sizes.

PLANNING
AHEAD

Think about parcel wrapping well in advance, and start saving everything and anything that might be useful. Boxes are high on the list, and it is worth while keeping as many as you can, stored one inside the other to minimise space. Plastic boxes that are sold with gold-wrapped chocolates, wooden date boxes (which may need

washing and drying), shoeboxes and ones in which small pieces of kitchen equipment were packed, they will all make the parcel-wrapping task easier.

Boxes that loudly proclaim their former contents or dull brown cardboard ones will need to be covered. See the diagrams overleaf.

Scraps and off-cuts from hobby materials make attractive and personalised parcel trims. Material scraps can replace paper to wrap small parcels – a box covered in red and white check gingham cotton and tied with a red ribbon bow looks as smart as any wrapped in paper. Scraps of ribbon, braid, fringing, lace edging and bias binding can be used for tying or to make fancy bows or flowers, so save them all.

Snippings of dried flowers – side shoots from large arrangements or flowerheads that have separated from their stems – can be gathered into posy trims or stuck on to plain wrappings; so much prettier than any printed label.

Odd-shaped corners and strips of coloured paper and thick card left over from origami and other children's projects can be used to make cut-out features – the man in the moon, on a plain dark blue wrapping for example – or bands and stripes of colour contrast to add interest to plain parcels.

COVERING
A BOX

Misapprehensions and even disappointment can result from using a discarded box and loose-covering it in gift wrapping paper. For example it would not be very tactful to pack a pottery mug in a box which advertises that it contains some very expensive piece of porcelain someone gave you as a wedding present! Cover the box and lid neatly with plain or patterned paper or, more haphazardly with a random patchwork of papers – an excellent use of leftover scraps.

YOU WILL NEED

★ a box with a separate lid
★ wrapping paper
★ pencil
★ ruler
★ scissors
★ adhesive

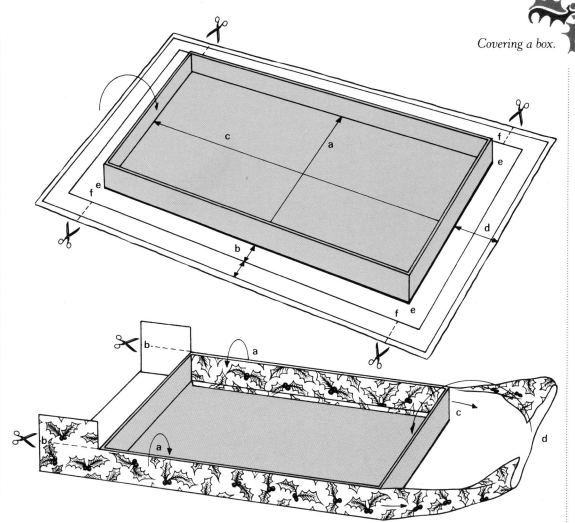

Step 1 Measure the width of the box accurately (a), and the depth of sides (b). Add together the width, twice the depth of each side (to allow for covering inside and outside) and add on another 1 cm/⅜ in at each side to allow for turning. For example, if the lid measures 10 cm/4 in across and the sides are 2 cm/¾ in deep, you will need to allow 20 cm/8 in width. Measure the length of the box in the same way (c and d). Cut the paper accurately following these dimensions.

Step 2 Place the paper, right side down, on the table. Measure from each end of the paper twice the depth of the lid plus overlap, and mark the corners (e). Place the lid in position, exactly on those marks. Make sure the paper is taut, and there are no creases.

Step 3 Draw a line from the edge of the paper to point (f), which represents the fold-over of the inside of the lid and the overlap. Cut along these lines, shown as dotted lines on the diagram above left.

Step 4 Fold the paper over neatly to cover the inside of the depth of the lid (a). Glue the paper in place.

Step 5 Cut off the excess paper at each corner (b). Pleat each corner neatly (c). Pull up the ends of the paper to cover the box and turn over the ends so that they exactly match the width of the box (d). Fold the paper over inside the lid, run your fingers along the crease, and stick the paper in place.

Step 6 Measure and cut the paper for the base of the box in the same way, allowing for about 2.5 cm/1 in fold-over inside. Cover the box in the same way.

COVERING
TRICKY SHAPES

Covering a box of regular shape is one thing. Neatly wrapping hexagonal, cylindrical or irregular-shaped gifts can be another.

HEXAGONAL BOX

Wrap the paper loosely around the box to estimate how much you need. Allow half the depth of the box for the fold-over at each end. Cut out the paper.

Place the paper, right side down, on the table and centre the box on top. Fix a strip of double-sided sticky tape along one edge (a) and seal the join (b).

At one end of the box, fold the paper towards the centre, making neat triangular folds (c). Pull the sections on each side of it (d and e) towards the centre, then those below the last two (f and g). Lastly pull up h and crease it to a triangular shape. Fold over the excess tip of that section and stick it with double-sided tape.

Repeat at the other end.

Decorate the box with a ribbon tied around the centre or towards one end and finished in a bow, with strips of contrasting paper wrapped around, or with a full ribbon bow stuck on to each end.

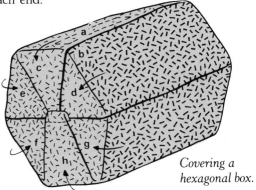

Covering a hexagonal box.

Covering a squashy parcel.

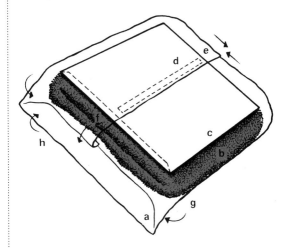

SQUASHY PARCEL

If the gift is something soft, such as a sweater, that does not have neat corners, here is a wrapping solution that obviates the need for a box.

Cut two pieces of stiff card slightly larger than the folded gift. Cover the card in wrapping paper for a specially festive effect. Wrap the gift in tissue paper. Cut the wrapping paper to the appropriate size.

Place the paper, right side down (a) and position the lower sheet of cardboard and the gift in the centre (b). Cover it with the second sheet of card (c). Fold over both sides of the paper and seal the join with double-sided sticky tape (d and e).

Fold down one flap (f) and fold in the two sides (g). Fold up the base and turn in the overlap (h). Seal the edge to make a neat join (e).

Repeat at the opposite end.

Large parcels can take large-scale decorations, such as a spray of evergreens tied with a ribbon bow, or a pleated fan in matching or contrasting paper.

ROUND CONTAINER

Many good things are packed in round boxes and jars, such as special biscuits, preserves and cosmetics. And so it pays to be adept at wrapping a neat parcel, cylinder style.

Measure the paper by wrapping it around the cylinder. Allow extra width for the pleats. The length of the paper, to allow for a neat finish at each end, should be the height of the box plus just over half the diameter at each side (a).

With the paper right side down, fold over the inside edge and make lengthways pleats along the outside edge. Stick them in place with invisible sticky tape (b).

Stick a strip of double-sided tape along the pleated edge, position the round container, roll the paper around it and seal the overlapping paper edge (b).

To seal one end, fold the paper from the top and down each side in small overlapping sections (c). Lastly fold up the pleated section, turn over the tip and seal with double-sided tape (d).

Repeat at the other end.

Decorate the top with a full ribbon bow.

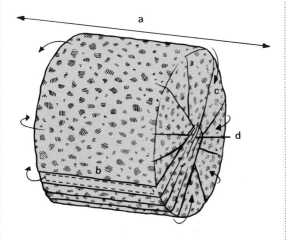

Covering a round container.

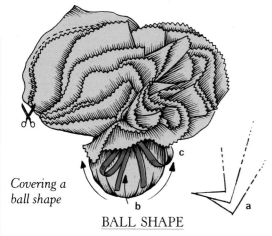

Covering a ball shape

BALL SHAPE

A basket of bathroom cosmetics, a Christmas pudding, a football – all kinds of gifts can be wrapped in this way. Use crêpe paper or tissue paper in a single colour or a mixture of colours such as red, orange and yellow. For a special effect, use Cellophane paper for the outer layer. Cut the paper into squares large enough to draw over the top of the shape and finish in a flurry of frills.

Place the squares of paper one on top of the other, but not quite meeting (a) and position the gift in the centre. Gather up the paper by joining the opposite corners and gripping all the paper tightly above the gift (b). Tie around the paper with ribbon and make a bow (c).

Use pinking shears to trim the top to a rounded shape (d). Separate the sheets to give the maximum fullness and then, if you wish, paint the papers with glue and sprinkle on glitter. Tip up the gift to shake off any excess.

PLEATED CRACKER

An example of a versatile wrapping that will visually elevate any gift – a pair of socks, a scarf, a jar of sweets, for example.

Use tissue paper or crêpe paper for the wrapping (this design is pleated) and finish the cracker with a motif all your own, such as a spray of dried flowers.

If the gift is pliable, as socks are, roll it into a sausage shape and wrap it in tissue paper. Cut a piece of card just large enough to wrap around the gift, with a slight overlap at each end (a). Seal the join along the length of the card.

Measure wrapping paper four times the length of the cylinder and wide enough to wrap around it, allowing for pleating. Cut the paper. Fold over one side and pleat the other (b). Enclose the cylinder in the paper and seal the join with double-sided sticky tape.

Grip the paper at each end of the cylinder and tie with ribbon (c). Trim the ends of the paper and tie the ribbon into a bow (d).

Add any festive motif you choose.

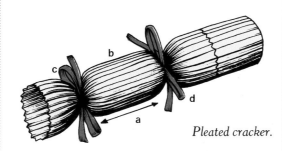

Pleated cracker.

A SEASONAL BOTTLE

Bottles feature prominently on present lists, and can be among the most problematical shapes to wrap. If possible, cheat and find a box that fits, or plan ahead and buy a bottle that is already boxed.

Otherwise, treat the base of the bottle and wrap it as any other cylindrical present. You can 'lose' the neck of the bottle by extending the cylindrical shape. Wrap and stick a piece of card around the neck, then you simply finish off the top in a similar way.

Alternatively, and if you do not mind giving the game away about the generic contents of the parcel, cut the paper long enough to extend about 7.5 cm/3 in above the neck of the bottle. Gather the paper round the neck and press it in at each side (a). Draw up the inverted pleat at the

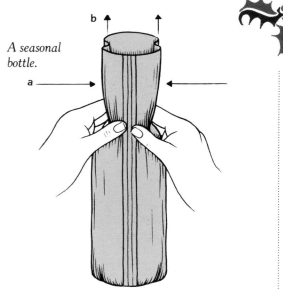

A seasonal bottle.

top of the paper (b). Tie a length of ribbon at the base of the bottle neck. At the top of the bottle, fold the paper away from you twice, then make one fold towards you, to form a horizontal pleat. Seal the top with double-sided sticky tape.

TRIMMINGS

Large parcels wrapped in plain paper, even if it is pleated, can take an exuberant trimming. A pleated paper fan is just the thing. Or a cluster of curled ribbon ends can look very dramatic.

Tie the gift box around with three strips of shiny parcel ribbon, leaving long ends for the cluster. Hold each ribbon end close to the knot, between your thumb and the back of a scissor blade. Draw the blade sharply up the length of ribbon so that it curls into a ringlet. Repeat with each of the remaining ribbons.

Full ribbon and long, slender bows are excellent for decorating any shape of box. The bows also make very attractive Christmas tree decorations.

CHRISTMAS CARDS & GIFT TAGS

—— ★ ——

*C*hildren love to make their own cards, gift tags and invitations. It is not only an absorbing occupation, and one which grandparents and other recipients greatly appreciate, it is a helpful economy in pocket money terms.
But children should not have the monopoly in card design and manufacture. Everyone, whether artistic or not, can make unique examples that convey just that little more thought than a bought card.

GIFT TAGS

The twin purpose of a gift tag is to convey a brief, bright and cheery message, and to enhance the overall design of the package. Think of the wrapping and the greetings tag as two complementary elements, and design the message accordingly.

Off-cuts from a hobby project, such as plain-coloured card in holly-berry red, holly-leaf green or starry-night blue may pick out the predominant colour of the wrapping. You could decorate them simply with cut-out silver stars, sequins, or white or gold 'snowflakes' cut from paper doilys, or with strips of the wrapping paper – the surest way to achieve a perfect match.

Used Christmas cards can be 'tagged' in two ways. Many designs are too attractive to be thrown away. A stylized motif such as a Christmas tree, or an enclosed design in a small square or circle may be cut out and used as a single-thickness tag.

The backs of used cards may yield enough plain card to cut into single or folded tags. Or you can design tags so that a strip of wrapping paper, a Christmas label or other decoration neatly conceals any printing or handwriting.

Add a ribbon loop to each card, or a sticky fixing pad to folded ones, add your personal greeting, and you have a unique work of art.

RIBBON TIE

Use a hole punch to make a hole in the corner. Cut a piece of thin parcel ribbon about 30 cm/ 12 in long, fold it in half and push the loop through from front to back (a and b). Pull the ends through the loop (c) to flatten the knot.

Ribbon tie and flat tag.

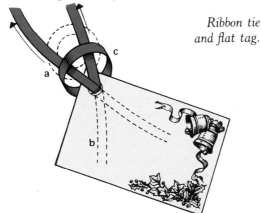

FLAT TAGS

Plain on the back, patterned on the front, a tag decorated with a narrow strip of wrapping paper – a row of chirpy robins or frosty Christmas trees for example. Outline the edge of the design with a felt-tip pen if you wish, and stick a strip of narrow ribbon to emphasize the stripe.

Shadow shape.

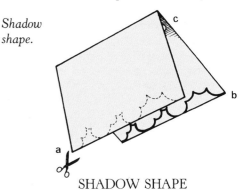

SHADOW SHAPE

A plain-folded card which relies on shape, not pattern, for effect. Draw a pencil line along the right-hand outside edge – a random zig-zag scallop or fluffy cloud effect. Cut along the line

(a) then draw around it, on to the inside back (b). Punch a hole in the top left-hand corner of the inside back.

SHORT FOLD

Fold the card not in half, but with a shorter piece on top. For example, fold a strip 17.5 cm/7 in long 7.5 cm/3 in from the left-hand edge.

Cover the front with corners of small-patterned wrapping paper and outline the edges with narrow ribbon or lines drawn with a felt-tip pen. Use the pen, too, for a cheery message in informal style.

CHRISTMAS CARDS
& INVITATIONS

Christmas cards and invitations offer even more scope for design ingenuity and imagination, and making them can become an absorbing hobby in its own right.

You can simplify the task by pasting designs cut from saved greetings cards on to folded white or coloured card, where the shape is suitable, cutting round the outline on one side to give a shadow effect.

Or you can design Christmas cards to be pictures in miniature, pressed flower compositions stuck on to the face of a card and protected with cling-film. Or make 'window' cards, with an aperture cut from the front to frame a small piece of quilting. You do not need to be an artist with a pen or paintbrush to produce attractive designs.

Children may like to decorate the face of the cards with potato-cut designs, holly leaves and berries, Christmas trees and stars, candles and brightly-coloured flames for example.

If you plan to mass-produce cards for all your friends, and not just make one or two, it is a

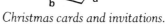

Christmas cards and invitations.

good idea to buy the envelopes first, and design and cut the cards to fit them. That way, you will achieve the best of both worlds, a hand-made and highly individual card and a professional overall appearance.

SHADOW OUTLINES

Select a wrapping paper or used card motif with a definite, easy-to-cut-out motif (or draw one for yourself). Fold the card in half horizontally to fit the motif and stick it in place. Cut around the shape, leaving a small join at the top to hold the card together. Write your message on the inside back within the outline of the design or on the back.

For a variation on that theme, cut out a simple shape in plain paper – pinking shears give an interesting outline – and stick it to the front of a card folded vertically. Cut out around the outside edge (a). Or cut out and paste only the left-hand half of the shape (b). Draw the matching outline on the right-hand side and cut it out.

FABRIC COLLAGE

Cut out the card, fold it in half and carefully measure and draw in the 'window' section. Use a craft knife to cut out the window. This piece of card may be used for a gift tag.

Cut a piece of used card – it can be from a

cereal packet – slightly larger than the aperture. Cut out strips of fabric to make a design with well-defined outlines. For the landscape scene you could use blue cotton for the sky, green and white cotton for the hill, and felt for the church and moon.

Stick the fabric to the card using multi-purpose glue and leave it to dry. Stick the collage in place in the window of the card and stick a piece of plain paper over the back to cover it.

THE ROBIN

Robins are a popular favourite with Christmas card designers, and among the brightest symbols of the festive season. But why are these perky little birds so closely associated with Christmas?

The story goes that after the birth of Jesus, Joseph went out to gather fuel for the fire in the manger. While he was gone, some small brown birds fanned the fire with their wings to keep it alight, and in doing so scorched their breasts.

The Virgin Mary noticed this, and decreed that for evermore robins should have bright red breasts, in memory of the service they performed for the Infant Jesus.

CHRISTMAS CRACKERS

★

Christmas crackers have pride of place with the family at party time. The holiday would not be the same without a cracker placed above each setting at the Christmas table, a pile of crackers to make a party go with a noisy swing, and tiny versions decorating the tree and handed out as tree presents throughout the festivities. Crackers are surprisingly simple to make from brightly coloured papers and cardboard tubes. Plan colour combinations to match your own decorative themes, trim the crackers in any way you please, and make this a cracking Christmas!

THE ORIGIN OF THE CHRISTMAS CRACKER

Pulling Christmas crackers around the dinner table has, like the Christmas tree, been a part of our celebrations only since Victorian times.

The custom is thought to have derived from France, where children were given bags of sugared almonds on all festive occasions. When pulled in a tug-of-war between rival claimants, or broken open in over-excited handling, the air-filled paper bags burst with a loud bang.

It was a London baker called Thomas Smith who developed the idea and introduced the first proper cracker. Around 1840 he started producing bags of bonbons with an added message, a romantic thought or a riddle, as a sales incentive.

His sales graph did not climb in quite the way he had hoped, and so he introduced an 'exploding strip', a piece of chemically treated card, as an extra novelty.

It was almost a question of 'invent the exploding paper strip and retire', for by the end of the century the Smith company was producing millions of crackers for sale.

By now the crackers also contained toys, games, puzzles and hats – 'cosaques', as the novelties were called – and were made in a large range of sizes, colours and designs. The largest cracker Tom Smith produced was said to be 9 m/ 30 feet long.

TO MAKE A CRACKER
YOU WILL NEED

- ★ tissue paper
- ★ crêpe paper or crinkle foil in two toning or contrasting colours
- ★ cardboard roll – from toilet rolls, kitchen roll etc
- ★ double-sided adhesive tape
- ★ scissors
- ★ pinking shears (optional)
- ★ paper adhesive
- ★ ribbon

available from cracker component firms:
- ★ 'snaps' in a variety of lengths
- ★ small gifts
- ★ mottoes
- ★ paper hats
- ★ trimmings, including gold and silver paper banding and Christmas-design sticky labels

Step 1 Wrap each small gift in tissue paper, to increase the element of surprise.

Step 2 Cut the cardboard roll to length, say 10 cm/4 in. Push a snap strip through the roll and sticky-tape it in place at one end. Insert the gift, a motto, and a paper hat inside the roll.

Step 3 Measure the decorative paper for the inner layer (a). Allow three-and-a-half times the length of the cardboard roll (in our example this would be 45 cm/18 in) and twice the circumference for each cracker. Use pinking shears if you have them to cut the decorative paper.

Step 4 Place the roll in the centre of the paper and wrap the paper firmly around it. Secure the join invisibly, using double-sided adhesive tape. This will form the back of the design.

Making a Christmas cracker

Step 5 Measure the decorative paper in the second colour for the outer layer (b). Allow twice the length of the cardboard roll (in the example, this would be 20 cm/8 in long) and the circumference of the roll plus a small overlap. Cut out the paper, again with pinking shears if possible.

Step 6 Place the cracker in the centre of the paper, right side of the cracker down and the join uppermost. Wrap the paper tightly around the cracker to seal the join with double-sided tape.

Step 7 Gather the paper tightly at each end of the roll and tie it with narrow ribbon (c). Carefully ease the ribbon knots towards each end of the cardboard roll to improve the shape (d) and cut off the ends.

Step 8 Tie a length of ribbon around each end, to cover the holding knot, and tie it in a generous bow (1e).

Step 9 Insert two or three fingers to open out the cracker ends slightly in order to improve the shape.

Step 10 Decorate the barrel of the cracker in any way you wish. You could wrap a strip of patterned acetate around it (f) to cover a paper name card (g). This is a good idea, since it enables you to match the gift inside the cracker to the recipient.

DECORATING
THE CRACKERS

Decorating the barrel of a cracker is somewhat like gilding the lily. If decorative and attractive papers are used to make the cracker, very little extra adornment seems necessary. But some other ideas are quick and easy to carry out.

* Wrap a strip of gold or silver sequin trim around the centre and sticky-tape it at the back
* wrap around a strip cut from a gold, silver or white paper doily
* stick on flowers or other shapes cut from a paper doily
* stick on a full ribbon bow or a roller bow made from parcel ribbon
* paint the barrel with paper glue and sprinkle on powdered glitter. Shake off the excess powder and, if you wish, stick a doily flower in the centre
* dab spots of glue around the barrel and stick on sequins
* stick on one, two or three dried flower heads, such as strawflowers
* stick or tie on a dried flower posy backed by a pressed leaf or a small spray of glycerine-preserved leaves
* stick or tie on a spray of evergreens, such as yew and holly laden with berries
* wrap tiny presents in complementary papers, tie them around with parcel string and tie one to the outside of each cracker.

WHAT TO PUT IN THEM

You can buy cracker 'fancies', toys, puzzles and trinkets of all kinds, from component suppliers, or you can buy your own, more personalized gifts. Here are some ideas, in a range of prices, to suit all the family.

* nail clippers
* bath cubes
* guest soaps
* key ring
* thimble
* child's brooch
* Christmas tree decoration
* rubber eraser
* plastic tweezers
* felt-tip pen
* miniature painted tin
* rolling-ball puzzle
* christmas socks
* yoyo

HAVE YOU HEARD THIS ONE?

Although everyone groans at the predictability of the 'jokes' and mottoes that are a traditional component of the Christmas cracker, we really would not want to be without them!

Instead of buying the mottoes, why not ask the children to write out their favourite 'why did the chicken cross the road' type of jokes? It might be a good idea to vet them first, since playground humour is not always suitable for the dinner table.

ENTERTAINMENTS & TRADITIONS

★

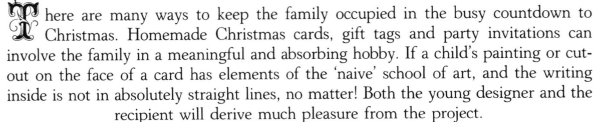

There are many ways to keep the family occupied in the busy countdown to Christmas. Homemade Christmas cards, gift tags and party invitations can involve the family in a meaningful and absorbing hobby. If a child's painting or cut-out on the face of a card has elements of the 'naive' school of art, and the writing inside is not in absolutely straight lines, no matter! Both the young designer and the recipient will derive much pleasure from the project.

There are crackers to make for the party table or the tree and the children may like to think up and write the jokes to put inside them. And there are intricate and inedible, pretty and practical play-dough-pastry decorations to make for the tree and other places around the home. Making these plaits, rings and figures involves mixing, kneading, cutting, shaping, marking and baking. It is an ideal occupation, in a warm kitchen, for a frosty afternoon.

Whether you are planning to give a party or are entertaining family and friends for a day or so over the holiday, you will need to give some thought to how (when they are not eating) they will occupy their time.

Happily, Christmas is a time of year when most people can be made to feel at home wherever they are, be relaxed enough to join in thought-provoking, merry-making or downright silly games, and emerge smiling.

Your job, as host or hostess, is to have a small itinerary of games and activities, and the wherewithal to play them, to suit all moods and all occasions. There will be times when the children will get fractious and want amusing; when people feel too comfortable to move from their chairs; when there is a slightly awkward gap in the flow of conversation, or when you feel you absolutely must point out that there *are* other things to do, besides watching television and falling asleep!

We look back nostalgically to the days when families relied on the home circle for their amusement and entertainment, but it is still possible to recreate that atmosphere in our homes this Christmas.

There are conundrums to tease the audience in a round or two of charades, and with a little ingenuity, it is possible to create an entirely impromptu knock-about-fun family pantomime.

No party would be complete without card games and conjuring tricks; pencil games to test the memory and provide a quiet interlude and team games to bring out the competitive spirit.

Just one word of advice to ensure that all your guests do have a happy time. If you sense that someone, for any reason, does not feel comfortable about joining in any of the games, do take no for an answer, and try to include them in some other way. You can always do with an extra referee or someone to present the prizes.

It is a good idea to involve the whole family in planning the leisure activities right from the beginning. Not only because many hands make light work, but because it is much more fun for everybody if a party or a special gathering has been planned as a team effort. Then, when the event is over and has been declared a huge success, everyone can feel a glow of pride.

FATHER CHRISTMAS

★

The image of Santa Claus, St Nicholas or Father Christmas, a benign old gentleman with long flowing beard and a sack full of presents, is a cherished part of the Christmas tradition in many lands. The legend long pre-dates Christianity, and the facts are deeply entwined with fiction. What matters is that for hundreds of years the warmth of the sentiment felt towards Santa Claus has contributed to the spirit of goodwill and generosity of Christmas.

THE STORY OF FATHER CHRISTMAS

When children write a letter to ask Santa Claus to bring them a toy from Reindeerland, and hang up their stockings for Father Christmas to fill when he comes down the chimney on Christmas Eve, they have in mind the same benevolent, jolly fellow. An old man with a long white beard, dressed in a fur-trimmed red suit, and always smiling, in spite of his long, cold journey and impossible deadlines.

The children are right. Santa Claus and Father Christmas have now joined forces, agreed on a practical seasonal uniform, and settled for the local mode of transport from the Frozen North, a sleigh pulled by reindeer.

But it was not always so, and the two gentlemen started with widely different characteristics, and managed to retain their separate identities until well into the nineteenth century.

The tradition of giving and anticipating gifts in wintertime dates from the earliest pagan festivals, and the legend of Santa Claus is connected with the Lord of Misrule of those festivals, the character chosen to preside over the seasonal excesses. In Roman times, people ex-changed gifts during the feast of Saturn, and in Scandinavia the Norsemen believed that their god, Odin, brought them tokens during the midwinter festival.

PERFORMING MIRACLES

With the coming of Christianity, the church took up the worthy practice of giving gifts to the poor, and eventually the seasonal benefactor was identified with St Nicholas. He was the fourth-century bishop of Lycia, a region that now forms part of Turkey. Because of a series of miraculous happenings connected with children, he became their patron saint.

One legend tells of the time when the bishop, staying at an inn, dreamt that the innkeeper was murdering three children. The bishop con-fronted the man with the crime, and miracu-lously restored the children to life.

Several European countries built on the legend of St Nicholas, and honour him, es-pecially on December 6, his feast day. In Holland he is called Sinterklaas and he is said to arrive by ship, supposedly from Spain, with his trusty servant, Black Peter. They travel from house to house on a white horse, well before December 6. Sinterklaas asks which children have been good during the past year and Black Peter takes down notes for when Sinterklaas returns.

Sinterklaas returns down the chimney on December 6, filling the shoes of the good children with presents and leaving a birch rod for bad children. It is widely known among the younger generation that even naughty children can receive presents, if they can persuade their parents to put in a good word for them.

German children are especially fortunate, because they may expect a visit from Santa Claus on his feast day, and another from the Christ-kindl, a fair-haired girl wearing a crown of candles, at Christmas.

CROSSING THE ATLANTIC

When emigrants from Northern Europe settled in New Amsterdam (later New York) in America in the seventeenth century, the legend of St Nicholas was one of the treasures of the culture that they took with them. The saintly figure led a fairly quiet life in his new surroundings until about 1820, when the Americans up-dated his image and gave him the now-familiar red uniform, sleigh and reindeers. They also stan-dardized his time of arrival, giving him the onerous task of doing all his rounds in a single night, on Christmas Eve.

DOUBLE ACT

It took about fifty years for the potential of this all-in-one benevolent character to be realised in Britain. Charles Dickens knew nothing of him when he wrote 'A Christmas Carol' in 1843. The last recorded double act, when the old-style Father Christmas and the old-style Santa Claus appeared together was a Dr Barnardo's children's party in 1886. Father Christmas, a jolly old soul crowned with holly, went about his roistering and merry-making, following the tradition of the character in the mummers' plays, and Santa Claus distributed largesse and gifts.

Soon after that, the British people had taken the new all-in-one figure to their hearts. His arrival on the scene fitted in well with the introduction of the Christmas tree from Germany, Christmas crackers, and Christmas cards.

By the 1890's men and women all over Britain were helping Father Christmas in his task, and dressing up to distribute presents to children. One charitable lady, in heavy disguise, distributed a total of 5000 presents to poor children in London, including 720 pairs of warm socks and stockings, 265 scarves, 485 dolls, 90 humming tops, 55 toy trumpets and 24 toy engines.

From time to time church members have found the commercialization of the original St Nicholas hard to reconcile. And to make matters worse, Father Christmas has been known to lend his weight to soft drinks and even soap powder advertising.

But television and technology have not harmed the tradition. Father Christmas still has his merry twinkle, and Santa Claus still travels from house to house with a sack of presents. Only now they have a corporate image!

A CALENDAR OF CHRISTMAS PRESENTS

Children in different parts of the world wait in eager anticipation for the arrival of the surprise gifts that carry on a centuries-old tradition. Here is a glimpse of the customs around the world.

Dec 6th Holland	Sinterklaas arrives by ship from Spain, accompanied by his servant, Black Peter. He rides from house to house on a white horse.
Germany	St Nicholas makes a house-to-house call.
Dec 25 Great Britain	Father Christmas arrives on a sleigh drawn by reindeer, and is very partial to a mince pie left for him in the hearth.
USA	Father Christmas carries on the tradition, as he has since the nineteenth century, of calling only once children are asleep.
Scandinavia	A man called Julemannen or Julenisse secretly leaves gifts for children under the Christmas tree. In exchange, they leave him a bowl of porridge, a symbolic Christmas feasting dish. In preparation for his arrival, homes are cleaned from top to bottom on the last Sunday in Advent, known as Dirty Sunday.
France	Children try to stay awake to catch Père Noel as he hangs a stocking by their bedside.
Germany	The Christkindl carries a basket of presents from house to house.
Jan 1 USSR	Grandfather Frost, bearing a close resemblance to Father Christmas, makes his rounds with presents.
Jan 6 Spain	Children leave out their shoes to receive gifts from the Three Kings.
Italy	La Befana, the old woman on a broomstick, climbs down chimneys to deliver her gifts.

CHRISTMAS CAROLS

★

arol singing has a long and joyous tradition as part of our Christmas celebrations. It means stamping through the frosty streets to sing carols on the village green, or in the twinkling glow of fairy lights in houses all along the street; learning new carols to sing in church or at the school play, or opening the door in response to a rousing chorus bringing seasonal cheer to your own doorstep.

THE ORIGINS

The custom of carol singing is said to commemorate the singing of the angels who, according to the Gospels, raised their voices to heaven and sang 'Gloria in Excelsis Deo' to give thanks for Christ's birth.

From at least the thirteenth century, the practice was followed by priests, choristers and monks. Gradually, carol singing spread out from the church and monasteries and was adopted by the people as a joyous way to express their own gratitude.

In Victorian times carol-singing, like other lapsed Christmas customs, enjoyed a great revival. The singers, who were known as the 'waits', sang in groups, and were usually accompanied by a musical instrument.

Some popular carols, such as 'We Three Kings of Orient Are' and 'Away In a Manger' originated in America in the middle of the nineteenth century.

TO THE LETTER OF THE LAW

It is a good idea to know where you stand, legally, before setting off to sing carols and collect money.

If you intend to donate the money collected to a charity, it is advisable to ask the local organiser for a collection box, duly labelled and sealed, and a badge or letter of authority to be carried by one member of the party. Ask for a receipt when you hand in the money.

Children singing carols to raise money for their own funds are, strictly speaking, begging, and are thus outside the law. However, the authorities usually turn a blind eye to such well-meaning activities, and are likely to intervene only if the children pester people or create an undue disturbance. Singing a raucous and hurried verse of 'Now Bring Us Some Figgy Pudding' does not usually warrant any stern action.

CHECK LIST

Carol singing has a reputation for warming the heart and lifting the spirits, but chilling the extremities. Bear in mind a few basic points before you and the children set off to sing carols in the open.

Do wrap up warmly. Thermal underwear, socks and gloves and woolly hats that pull down over the ears, were made for just this event.

Make sure that everyone in the party has a song sheet that is clear enough to read in a poor light.

Remind everyone to bring a torch, or, following the Victorian custom, make sure that there is adequate light for the gathering. A storm lantern on a pole is the traditional form of lighting.

Whether the collection is for a recognised charity, a local good cause or even the children's own funds, do have a proper collecting box with a slot for the money. You can easily make one out of a cardboard box or a coffee tin. However generous they may be, people do not like giving loose change into a collector's hand.

The purpose of singing carols is two-fold, to give thanks for Christ's birth, and to bring cheer. If your group is singing from house to house, be sure to include old people and those who are ill. A visit from a cheerfully tuneful group may be the highlight of their Christmas season. But it is best not to call, or allow the children to do so, on elderly people late in the evening. Around tea-time is the most tactful and considerate timing for all concerned.

AWAY IN A MANGER

1. A - way in a — man-ger, no— crib for a bed, The— lit - tle Lord Je - sus laid— down his sweet head. The

stars in the — bright sky looked— down where he lay, The— lit - tle Lord Je - sus a - sleep on the hay.

The cattle are lowing, the baby awakes,
But little Lord Jesus no crying he makes.
I love thee, Lord Jesus! look down from the sky,
And stay be my side until morning is nigh.

Be near me, Lord Jesus; I ask thee to stay
Close by me for ever, and love me, I pray.
Bless all the dear children in thy tender care,
And fit us for heaven, to live with thee there.

A CHRISTMAS CAROL

‘ *Foggier yet, and colder. Piercing, searching, biting cold. If the good Saint Dunstan had but nipped the Evil Spirit's nose with a touch of such weather as that, instead of using his familiar weapons, then indeed he would have roared to lusty purpose. The owner of one scant young nose, gnawed and mumbled by the hungry cold as bones are gnawed by dogs, stooped down at Scrooge's keyhole to regale him with a Christmas carol: but at the first sound of*

**"God bless you, merry gentleman!
May nothing you dismay!"**

Scrooge seized the ruler with such energy
of action, that the singer fled in terrror, leaving the keyhole to the fog and even more congenial frost.

At length the hour of shutting up the counting-house arrived. With an ill-will Scrooge dismounted from his stool, and tacitly admitted the fact to the expectant clerk in the Tank, who instantly snuffed his candle out, and put on his hat.

"You'll want all day to-morrow, I suppose?" said Scrooge.

"If quite convenient, sir."

"It's not convenient," said Scrooge, "and it's not fair. If I was to stop half-a-crown for it, you'd think yourself ill-used, I'll be bound?"

The clerk smiled faintly.

"And yet," said Scrooge, "you don't think me ill-used, when I pay a day's wages for no work."

The clerk observed that it was only once a year.

"A poor excuse for picking a man's pocket every twenty-fifth of December!" said Scrooge, buttoning his great-coat to the chin. "But I suppose you must have the whole day. Be here all the earlier next morning. ’

from 'A Christmas Carol'
by CHARLES DICKENS

SILENT NIGHT

1. Si - lent night! Ho - ly night! All is calm, all is bright; Round yon vir - gin mo - ther and child,

Ho - ly in - fant, so ten - der and mild. Sleep in heav-en-ly peace,— Sleep— in heav-en-ly peace. —

Silent night! Holy night!
Shepherds quail at the sight;
Glories stream from heaven afar,
Heavenly host sing Alleluia!
Christ the Saviour is here,
Christ the Saviour is here.

Silent night! Holy night!
Son of God, love's pure light;
Radiant beams thy holy face,
With the dawn of saving grace.
Jesus Lord, at thy birth,
Jesus, Lord, at thy birth.

ONCE IN ROYAL DAVID'S CITY

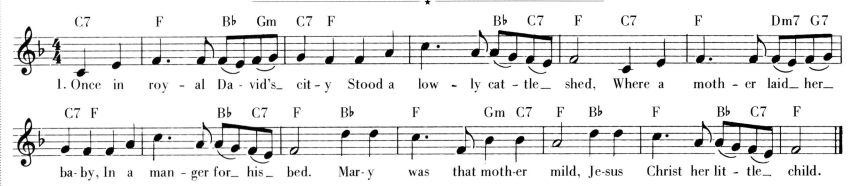

1. Once in roy - al Da - vid's_ cit - y Stood a low - ly cat - tle_ shed, Where a moth - er laid_ her_

ba - by, In a man - ger for_ his_ bed. Mar - y was that moth-er mild, Je-sus Christ her lit - tle_ child.

He came down to earth from heaven,
Who is God and Lord of all,
And his shelter was a stable,
And his cradle was a stall,
With the poor, and mean, and lowly,
Lived on earth our Saviour holy.

And through all his wondrous childhood,
He would honour and obey,
Love and watch the lowly mother
In whose gentle arms he lay.
Christian children all must be
Mild, obedient, good as he.

And our eyes at last shall see him,
Through his own redeeming love
For that child so dear and gentle
Is our Lord in heaven above;
And he leads his children on
To the place where he has gone.

GOOD KING WENCESLAS

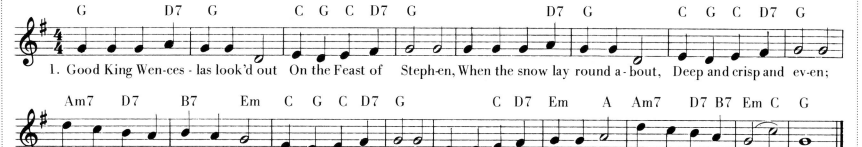

1. Good King Wen-ces-las look'd out On the Feast of Steph-en, When the snow lay round a-bout, Deep and crisp and ev-en;

Bright-ly shone the moon that night, Tho' the frost was cru-el, When a poor man came in sight Gath'ring win-ter fu — el.

"Hither, page, come, stand by me,
If thou know'st it telling,
Yonder peasant, who is he?
Where and what his dwelling?
"Sire, he lives a good league
hence,
Down beneath the mountain:
Close against the forest fence,
By Saint Agnes' fountain!"

"Bring me flesh, and bring me
wine,
Bring me pine logs hither:
Thou and I, we'll see him dine,
When we bear them thither."
"Page and monarch, on they went,
On they went together:
Through the rude wind's wild
lament,
Through the bitter weather.

"Sire the night is darker now,
And the storm grows stronger,
Fails my heart, I know not how,
I can go no longer."
"Mark my steps, be brave, my
page:
Tread thou in them boldly;
Then thou'lt find the winter's rage
Freeze thy blood less coldly."

CHORUS – In his master's steps he
trod,
Where the snow lay dinted:
Heat was in the very sod
Which his foot had printed.
Therefore Christian men, be sure,
Wealth or rank possessing,
Ye who know do bless the poor,
Shall yourselves find blessing.

WHILE SHEPHERDS WATCHED

1. While shep-herds watch'd their flocks by night, All seat-ed on the ground, The an-gel of the Lord came down, And glor-y shone a-round.

"Fear not," said he (for mighty dread
Had seized their troubled mind);
"Glad tidings of great joy I bring
To you, and all mankind.

"To you, in David's town, this day,
Is born, of David's line,
A Saviour, who is Christ the Lord;
And this shall be the sign:

"The heavenly babe you there shall find
To human view displayed,
All meanly wrapped in swathing bands,
And in a manger laid."

Thus spake the seraph; and forthwith
Appeared a shining throng
Of angels, praising God, and thus
Addressed their joyful song:

"All glory be to God on high,
And to the earth be peace;
Good-will henceforth from heaven to men
Begin, and never cease!"

FAMILY GAMES

★

It may be that Christmas presents the only opportunity of the year for the whole family to get together, and have time enough to relax. It is the ideal time to carry on the tradition of generations, to let your hair down and play games which can be inconsequential, silly, thought-provoking or witty. In the course of the festivities, there is room for them all.

CHARADES

Some experts think that the word 'charades' comes from the word *charrado* which means 'chat'. Others say it comes from the Italian *schiarare* which means to unravel or clarify. Either is appropriate, for players have to unravel the chatter of the actors and guess the hidden word.

There should be at least two in each team, five or six at most.

If there is a dressing-up box and a few old odds and ends that can be used as props, all to the good. And if the players really enter into the spirit of the game, it is without doubt one of the most entertaining of all.

One team thinks of a word of at least two syllables, and mounts short, very short, scenes, one more than the number of syllables in the word. The first scene contains the first syllable; the second syllable is mentioned in the second scene; the last syllable (if there are more than two syllables) in the penultimate scene, and the whole word is brought into the last scene.

The dictionary is full of suitable words such as airline, bystander, charisma, crisis (cry and sis), determine (debt and ermine), endless, fiddlesticks, garden (guard and hen), heartbeat, infirm,

jettison (jetty and son), kidney (kid and knee), leaflet, mainstay, needlework, operatic, orangeade (or, range and aid), particle (par and tickle), quixotic (quick, sot and tick), repository (reap, pose, sit and tory), sewage (sue and age), trireme (try and ream), uppermost, violent (vie, hole and lent), warehouse, xebec (see and beck – it's a three-masted ship used by Algerian pirates), yellowhammer (yell, low, ham and her), Zulu . . .

CHARADES IN MIME

There is another version of charades, which is played without a word being spoken.

The first player selects a word that can be split

into syllables: words like pyjamas (pie-jam-ours) or steeplejack (steep-pill-jack) or toboggan (two-bog-gone) . . . . He then mimes either the whole word or the constituent syllables. Whoever guesses the word, selects the next word and mimes it for the assembled company. If someone chose 'manoeuvres', he could mime it all in one by pretending to vacuum the carpet: man hoovers = manoeuvres! Or, if the word was 'collywobbles' the performer could get down on all fours pretending to be a dog and shake like a leaf: the dog's a collie and it's wobbling – collywobbles.

GIVE US A CLUE

This is another excellent mime game. Write the names of plays, films, television programmes and books on separate slips of paper and put them into a hat. Divide the guests into two teams. Players take it in turn to draw a slip from the hat and mime the title for their team, who have one minute to guess it. The conventions of the game are as follows:

To indicate to your team what category your title falls in mime to relevant gestures as illustrated opposite.

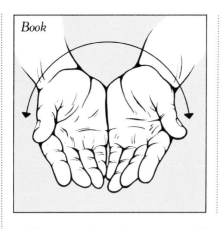

Book

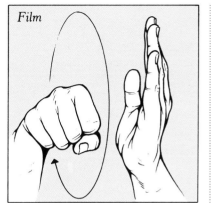

Film

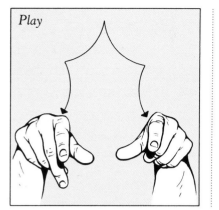

Play

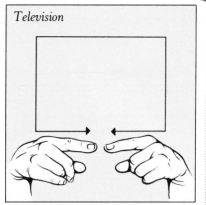

Television

If a player drew *Gone with the Wind* he would indicate that it is a book and a film. Similarly, if he drew *Singin' in the Rain* he would signal to his team that it is a song title and a film.

The number of words in the title is indicated by holding up one finger for each of them. So if *Mary Poppins* was about to be mimed, the player would hold up two fingers. If a player intends to get the title across in one mime he draws a large circle in the air with his hands.

If players cannot think of a suitable all-encompassing action they mime each word or syllable separately, indicating which word they are trying to signal by holding up the relevant number of fingers. The number of syllables in each word is indicated by placing the relevant number of fingers on the opposite forearm.

'The' is indicated by making a T-shape with both index fingers, 'a' and 'an' by holding the index finger a short distance from the thumb. If a player can't think of a suitable mime he signals to his team that he is going to mime a word that sounds like it by waggling his ear.

It is best to try to avoid titles that are easy to identify once the first one or two words have been guessed. For example, if *The* and *Diary* were mimed and identified, it doesn't take much for someone to come up with *of Adrian Mole aged thirteen-and-three-quarters* or *Ann Frank*.

CONNECTIONS

Psychologists use a similar technique to make an assessment of certain types of patient. This game is strictly a test of reaction time!

One player in the circle shouts out any word that comes to mind. The player on the right immediately calls out a word which has some connection with the first. For example: weather – forecast – outlook – lookout – post – letter – stamp, and so on. Players can challenge each other to explain the association. If there's no satisfactory explanation forthcoming, the one who called out the last word leaves the game.

★

FIRST TO LAST

Experienced players of this game will soon learn the trick of making it almost impossible for the next one to come up with the answer in time.

The first player calls out the name of a town and the player next to him shouts out another that starts with the last letter of the first. And so the game goes round and round the circle, players who can't think of a suitable town within ten seconds dropping out.

For example, Edinburgh – Hull – Liverpool – Leeds – Sunderland – Dundee – Evesham – Manchester – Rugby – York – this game will certainly improve your geography!

A MIME OF INFORMATION

This is a team game that can be as frustrating as it is creative. Its success depends on a careful choice of mime subjects, matched to the age and ability of the group.

Divide the groups into two teams. Give each team a pencil and paper. One of each team goes up to the hostess who whispers something to them. He or she returns to his team and mimes whatever was whispered. The next in line has to draw what he thinks is being mimed.

When (and if) the drawing is complete, the artist takes it to the hostess who approves the interpretation and whispers another subject to him. The artist becomes the mimer and the next member takes the pencil and paper. The first team to draw the mimes is the winner.

Subjects for mime might include: a baby piglet, a galloping horse, building a snowman, climbing a mountain, and so on.

CAT & DOG

When children in the party are feeling giggly, and ready for a really silly interlude, here it is!

It is a very simple game which is guaranteed to cause gales of laughter. One of the players is given two small objects. He passes the first to the person on his right and says, –

'Here's the dog!'

'The what?', he or she asks.

'The dog!', repeats the first player. And so the dog is passed around the circle, everyone repeating 'Here's the dog!'

'The what?'

'The dog!'

When the second player is passing the dog to the third, the first player hands the second object to the player on the left.

'Here's the cat!' he says.

'The what?', asks the player on the left

'The cat', says the first player . . .

The fun starts when the dog and the cat cross. It becomes difficult to remember what animal you have in your hand. Anyone getting the two confused leaves the circle. The faster the dog and the cat are on the move, the more difficult the game becomes.

THE
MINISTER'S CAT

A memory test, if ever there was one! Mean-minded players have a nasty habit of coming up with hard-to-remember horribly-hyphenated adjectives.

The first player calls out 'The Minister's cat is an . . .', and here adds an adjective beginning with 'a', followed by the word cat. (For example, 'an *angry* cat'.) The second player says, 'The

Minister's cat is an angry . . .', and then adds an adjective starting with 'b', before finishing the sentence. And so on around the circle, players taking it in turn to remember all the previous descriptions before adding one of their own. And when someone calls the cat an awful, black, cheeky, dead, exceptional, flighty, generous, hard, intelligent, jaundiced, kinky, lazy, mad, naughty, opulent, pretty, quaint, religious, strong, tough, unwanted, violent, Welsh, xenophobic, zany cat – the next person has to remember all that before starting over again with another 'a'! A player who takes too long or who makes a mistake drops out. The winner is the player with the best memory.

CHINESE
WHISPERS

No-one knows why this game is so-called, but it is probably because the end result of the round-the-circle whispers has as much in common with the original as Chinese has to the English language! Children, particularly, love this game – and mischievous ones have been known to cheat outrageously!

This is how it is played.

The first player whispers a message into the ear of the next person in the circle. He then whispers it to his neighbour, and so on around the circle until the message reaches the person on the other side of the one who began the whisper.

He calls out what has just been whispered to

him – it usually bears little resemblance to the original. Adults may remember hearing the story of the World War I message, 'Send reinforcements: we're going to advance', which was eventually received as 'Send three-and-four-pence: we're going to a dance.'

THE MAD
MAHARAJAH

Here is a game that gives a lie to the saying, 'Sticks and stones may break my bones, but words will never hurt me.' Just by uttering the name of a food he doesn't like, you can kill the Maharajah stone dead. Children like to add drama to the occasion by dropping down with agonising groans every time a poison food is mentioned.

'I, the mad Maharajah,' chants the player in the middle of the circle, pointing to someone in it. 'I do not like the letter 's'. What will you give me to eat?' The player being pointed to must suggest something that does not contain that letter. Cake would be quite acceptable, but biscuits would be poison to the Mad Maharajah. So would swedes, but turnip would be all right. The Mad Maharajah points to someone else and announces the next poison letter. Anything suggested must contain neither the first nor the new poison letter. Change the man in the middle after five goes. Anyone who accidentally poisons the Maharajah is out of the game.

SQUIGGLES

Still in an artistic mode: divide the groups into pairs. The first in each pair makes a squiggle on a bit of paper and gives it to his or her partner, who tries to incorporate it into a drawing.

With just a little imagination, the oddest squiggle can be turned into something interesting. And as the artistic efforts are passed round at the end of the exercise, a great deal of fun can be had by all.

KIM'S GAME

It's time for furrowed brows and deep concentration. This is a popular memory game.

Bring a cloth-covered tray into the room and make sure that everyone has paper and pencil.

Put the tray in the centre of the floor where everyone can see it and remove the cover to reveal an assortment of fifty or so small objects. After thirty seconds, re-cover the tray and give everyone three minutes to list as many of the objects as they can remember.

Anyone cheating by taking notes while the contents of the tray are being viewed is given a forfeit.

Suitable things to have on the tray include, a ring, a golf tee, a bus ticket, a rose petal, a match, a passport photograph, a pen, a hair-grip, a stamp, a cufflink, a button, a needle, a piece of cotton, a grape, a library ticket, a small ashtray, a cigarette, a cube of sugar . . . not forgetting the tray and the cloth that covered it.

Award a small prize to the winner. After all that concentration, they deserve it.

IT'S IN THE BAG

Fill a pillow-case with an assortment of about twenty odds and ends and give everyone thirty seconds to rummage in it without looking at the contents. Whoever comes up with the most complete list of what's in the bag is the winner.

SHADOW BUFF

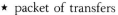

You need a large white sheet for this and two volunteers to stand on chairs, each about 2 metres (6 feet) away from the wall, stretching the sheet tightly across the area it covers. Have a bright light close to the wall behind the sheet so that whoever is between the wall and the sheet casts a clear, sharp shadow onto the sheet.

Divide the guests into two teams and sit one team in front of the sheet and send the other behind it. All the lights are put out apart from the one behind the sheet. The team behind the sheet take turns to walk between the lamp and the sheet doing whatever they can to disguise their silhouettes by limping, hobbling, putting on a false nose or a wig (if such props are available), and the audience tries to identify each one, making a list of their guesses. When everyone in the first team has cast a shadow they reveal themselves, the list is checked and the tally noted. The other team now goes behind the sheet to take their turn to disguise their silhouettes. The winning team is the one which identifies the most people in the other team.

PRIZE SUGGESTIONS

Everyone loves to receive a token prize as a reward for the skill, luck or gamesmanship it took to win a contest. Have a small box of prizes ready, wrapped as brightly and attractively as possible.

For children
* chocolate bars
* packet of sweets
* wrapped gingerbread man
* fancy pencil
* decorative rubber eraser

* packet of transfers
* picture of current pop group
* huge paper clip
* small decorative tin
* animal mask

For adults
* bar of bitter chocolate
* miniature chocolate liqueurs
* miniature bottle of sherry
* small herb cheese
* miniature jar of marmalade
* face cloth
* bath marbles
* pine-scented drawer sachet
* pocket notebook
* packet of biros

FORFEITS

There's always someone who cheats, or bends the rules a little, maybe by using hands in the Nell Gwynne game. Punishment should be swift, delivered as soon as the game has ended. What could be better than a quick forfeit?

Here are a few suggestions:
* Dress up in clothes of the opposite sex and go next door to ask the time. (Warn your neighbours first!)
* Submit to be tickled by everyone
* Drink a pint of lemonade through a straw
* Dance to some slow ballet music
* Kiss everyone of the opposite sex
* Stand on one leg with both eyes closed for half a minute
* Say 'iced ink' twenty times in quick succession
* Eat three water biscuits with no water to wash them down
* Mime to a record
* Run the gauntlet: give everyone a lightly-folded newspaper and stand them in two lines. The guilty party has to run down the lines while being pummelled by the others.

And you can surely think of many more.

CARD GAMES & TRICKS

★

With a family get-together or a party in the offing, brush up on a few favourite card games, and encourage the most dextrous and extrovert member of the group to practise some utterly amazing conjuring tricks. The best magicians accompany their tricks with amusing patter, which serves the dual purpose of (one hopes) entertaining the audience, and distracting them from the intricacies of a particularly difficult manoeuvre.

BEGGAR
YOUR NEIGHBOUR

The pendulum of luck swings backwards and forwards very quickly in this fast card game. One minute you may be holding a sizeable hand of cards; the next minute you could be out!

Deal out two packs of cards, face down, to the players. Players don't look at their cards, but sort them into neat piles in front of them. The player on the dealer's left turns over this top card and puts it into the centre of the table. The next player puts his top card on top of the first one and so on round the table. But if a court card is turned over, the next player has to pay a forfeit onto the central pile: four cards if it's an ace, three if it's a king, two for a queen and one for a jack. If, when paying a forfeit, a player turns over a forfeit card himself that player stops turning over and the next player pays the relevant new forfeit. But if only numbered cards are turned over when a forfeit is being played, whoever played the forfeit card takes all the cards in the central pile, places them face down beneath his existing pile and plays the first card of the next round. Players leave the game when they run out of cards.

OLD MAID

Remove the Queen of Hearts from an ordinary pack and deal the whole pack to the players who sort their hands into pairs of equal pip or court value and discard the pairs on the table. The first player offers his cards, unseen, to the player on his or her left. If the card taken makes a pair, the

two cards are discarded from the hand before the second player offers his hand to the third and so on round the table. Players who run out of cards stay in the game, taking a card from the player on their right and offering it to the player on their left.

As there is an odd number of queens, the last card is certain to be one of them. Whoever is left with it is the Old Maid.

★

GOODBYE!
GOODBYE!

Deal seven cards to each player (you may have to use more than one pack). The aim of the game is to collect seven cards of the same suit. Players sort their cards into suits, decide which suit they are going to collect and put one card, face down on the table. On the word 'Go!' players pass their unwanted card to the player on their left, who takes that card into his hand. And so the game goes on, players selecting one unwanted card and passing them all at the same time to the player on their left. The first to have seven cards of the same suit in hand lays them down, shouts 'Goodbye! Goodbye!' and wins the game.

CHEAT

The aim of Cheat is to be the first player to get rid of all the cards in your hand, by playing them in turn and cheating as often or as little as you want.

Deal a full pack to the players. If there are lots of people playing, use two or three packs. It doesn't matter if some players have one more card than the others. The player on the dealer's left is the first to go, putting down, in the middle of the table, as many cards as he or she wants and telling the others what has been played – two threes, for example. Cards are played face down in a pile so that no one can see how many cards there are, or if whoever plays them is telling the truth.

The next to go can play as many cards of equal pip or court value as he or she wants, or one up, again telling the others how many cards have been played. If the first player says two threes were laid down, the next to go can claim to lay down more threes or move on to fours. Players can't miss a turn. If they don't have suitable cards, they cheat by saying they are putting down the right cards when in fact the cards they play are out of sequence.

You can cheat in any way you want, by laying down one seven and two other cards and saying 'three sevens' for example, or laying down five cards and saying three of whatever! The player who has just laid down cards can be accused of cheating by any player as long as the challenge is made before the cards in question have been covered by the next player to go. If an accusation stands, whoever cheated takes all the cards played so far. If a player is accused of cheating wrongly, the accuser takes all the cards.

When a player puts down the last cards in his or her hand, he or she announces what's been played and says 'And out!'. He or she will, of course, be accused of cheating because the other players have nothing to lose. If there was cheating going on, whoever said 'And out!' will have to take the cards in the central pile. If he or she had been honest, that round is over.

★

THE ASTONISHING CARD TRICK

Ask a spectator to take a card, any card, from a pack. Give the other 51 cards to someone else and ask whoever drew the card to put it on the top of the pack. Now ask the second person to cut the cards as often as he or she wants until the drawn card is completely lost among the others. Now collect the pack and fan the cards out face up on a table. Study the spread, divide it in to two and put one half under the other. Next produce a small self-adhesive label and stick it on the back of the top card. Shuffle the cards and spread them once more face upwards on the table. Give whoever drew the card another label and ask him or her to stick it onto the face of the card he or she drew. Amazing! It's the very card you have already stuck the adhesive label on to.

You start this trick by fanning the cards out face upwards on the table and ask someone to draw a card while you look away. Make sure that you know what the card on the far left is, for when you give the 51 cards to someone else, that card will be on the top of the pack. The cards can be cut again and again and it is still 99 percent certain that when you fan the cards out for a second time, the card drawn will be the one immediately to the right of the 'locator card'.

When you have spread the cards out face up for the second time and have identified the drawn card, you must divide the pack between the locator card and the drawn one, putting the left hand stock under the right so that the drawn card is on the top of the pack. After a little practice, splitting the pack at the right point can be done with professional smoothness. The pack can now be shuffled as often as you want: you have stamped the drawn card and when the pack is spread out again and the spectator who drew the card sticks his label on the face of the card he drew, it is certain to be the one already bearing a label on its back.

★

BANK RAID

Before starting this trick, secretly take out the four jacks and any other four cards. Place the jacks in a fan and hide the other four cards behind. Place the remaining cards on a table in front of you. Start the trick by holding up the four jacks saying that here you have four robbers who are going to break into the bank and steal its contents. Then place the jacks (and, of course, the other four cards) face down on the top of the pack.

Take the top card, keeping its face hidden, and place it into the pack saying 'This is the first robber and he is entering the bank on the first floor.' Take the second, third and fourth cards in turn placing them on the 'second', 'third' and 'fourth' floors. Next tap the pack on the top several times and produce the jacks from the top saying that they are now escaping with their ill-gotten gains. Magic!

★

THE BALANCING GLASS

Hold a card in your right hand and place a non-breakable tumbler on the top edge of the card. Naturally it falls off. 'Ladies and Gentlemen. I can balance this tumbler on top of this card. . . .' and next time you try you succeed to the surprise of your audience. In fact, you are holding two cards in your hands. One has been folded lengthways and one half pasted to the back of the other to create a flap. Show the audience both sides of the 'card' making sure that the flap is closed. Keep it closed while you make your first, unsuccessful attempt to balance the glass, but on the second try use a free finger to open the flap. The tumbler will balance very easily on the card and the strut, but to the audience in front it will look as if the tumbler is balanced on the card.

The balancing glass trick.

IT'S WRITTEN IN THE CARDS

Shuffle a pack of cards and then spread them out, face-down on a table. Take one card at random, write something on it and drop it into a box. Then ask a spectator to pick any one of the face-down cards and drop it into the box also. Remove the two cards from the box. Across your card is written 'Three of Diamonds', and when the spectator's card is shown – surprise, surprise – it is the three of diamonds.

You will have to use a whole pack of cards to do this trick, and you will need a new pack each time you show it. But the effect is so fantastic that the expense is well worth it.

Remove the Three of Diamonds from the pack (or whatever card you decide to use). Put a small pencil mark on the back of it so you can identify it later. On the face of every other card in the pack write 'Three of Diamonds'. Write near the bottom edge of each card so you can fan out the cards but keep the writing hidden. The pack thus appears quite ordinary. Re-assemble the pack, find a suitable box, and you are ready to perform.

Shuffle the cards – if you are really brave you can get one of the audience to shuffle them – and then spread them out, face-down, on the table. While you are spreading them, search for the card marked Three of Diamonds.

Casually remove it and pretend to write on it, in fact you write nothing on the card. Place it, without showing its face, into the box. Now ask for any one of the other cards to be selected. Since they all have 'Three of Diamonds' written on the face, it doesn't matter which card is chosen. Drop this card, sight unseen, into the box. Gather up the rest of the cards, making certain that no-one sees that they have something written on them.

Take the two cards from the box, and hold up

the one on which is written 'Three of Diamonds'. Show it as if it were the card on which you made your prediction. Emphasize the fact that the spectator had an absolutely free choice. Now turn other the other card (which everyone will think was the one that the spectator chose) and reveal that it is the very card you predicted – the Three of Diamonds!

THE CONVERTIBLE ACE

It gives the magician a wonderful feeling of superiority, to gaze at the astonished and admiring faces of his or her puzzled audience. Here is a trick to work that particular magic for you.

You will need to doctor the ace of spades and the ace of hearts before you can do this trick. Fix a red coloured heart to the ace of spades, and a black coloured spade to the ace of hearts. Use *soap* to do this. Display the two doctored aces to the audience and lay them face down on the table. Ask someone from the audience to put one hand on top of one ace: ask a second person to do the same with the second ace and then tap their hands with your magic wand, commanding the cards to change places as you do so. When the cards are upturned the aces are seen to have obeyed your command. What you have done is surreptitiously removed the false facing on both cards before putting them face down on the table. This takes some practice, but it is worth the effort.

READING
THE CARDS

Gypsy Telfutura reaches deep into the pockets of her voluminous gown, draws out a pack of playing cards, shuffles them and beckons her first subject to her.

She gives him or her the cards and requests that they be shuffled again. Taking them back, she spreads the cards out in a semi-circle, face down on the table. Her client selects five cards and the rest are laid on one side.

Gypsy Telfutura now turns the cards over one by one and interprets them. Here is what the cards foretell.

CLUBS

Ace: Illness. If the next card is a heart, the illness will afflict someone in the family circle.
King: A dark, tall stranger will render a great favour.
Queen: A dark lady will give a piece of advice it would be wise to follow.
Jack: A dark young man will soon become a friend and offer new opportunities.
Ten: A legacy or money from an unexpected source.
Nine: A long and happy marriage is in store.
Eight: An invitation will be issued which should be well considered before being accepted.
Seven: Be alert and a good business opportunity will be offered.
Six: Be prepared to welcome a new friend.
Five: A letter from abroad will give cause for concern.
Four: A friend who has promised to be of assistance will be found lacking.
Three: A young acquaintance will become ill, but will recover.
Two: something depressing will happen but should be shared.

HEARTS

Ace: A love card: a meeting with an old friend will lead to love.
King: If the subject believes he has something to offer the world now is the time to do something about it.
Queen: A fair lady will assist socially and in business.
Jack: An unexpected meeting will solve a lot of problems.
Ten: Be wary of a proposal.
Nine: A life-long wish will come true but not in the immediate future.
Eight: A recent acquaintance is about to become a life-long friend, perhaps a spouse.
Seven: A little effort is needed for a smooth-running home life.
Six: News of a great achievement by a young friend.
Five: A romantic invitation will be a memorable event despite initial hesitation in accepting it.
Four: The client will strive to be surrounded with beautiful things.
Three: It's time to let others shoulder self-imposed burdens.
Two: This card signifies two big love affairs.

DIAMONDS

Ace: Some news about money: if followed by a heart card it is good news: if the next card is a spade, beware.
King: Be on the look out for someone who seems sincere but who will turn out to be dishonest.

Queen: A slight female acquaintance wants to become better friends.
Jack: A gentleman in uniform will want to ask you questions.
Ten: Consider carefully before accepting an invitation to go on a long journey.
Nine: Be prepared to do a lot of extra work concerning a new business.
Eight: A new love is on the horizon.
Seven: There may be arguments concerning business that could cause trouble unless great care is taken.
Six: An unexpected gift is on its way.
Five: There is likelihood of an important loss.
Four: A request for a loan from a fair-haired man should be thought about carefully.
Three: There could be a disappointment in store.
Two: If it is followed by the ace of hearts it signifies two marriages.

SPADES

Ace: When facing up, a birth in the family. If facing down, it signifies news of a death.
King: Someone, probably a dark gentleman, is likely to cheat or deceive.
Queen: Learn from someone else's experience but do not be dominated.
Jack: Listen to and benefit from the words of a younger person.
Ten: News is about to cause great concern.
Nine: A seemingly bad occurrence turns out to be a blessing in disguise.
Eight: A disappointment at work is only a temporary setback.
Seven: A trusted friend is not what he appears.
Six: An unexpected telephone call.
Five: A family argument could blow up ending in a long rift.
Four: News of a long lost friend.
Three: A close friend's strange behaviour causes mistrust.
Two: Without great care, there could be an argument.

TEAM GAMES
★

There is a competitive spirit in most of us, a willingness to pit our wits, skills or dexterity against the best in the room and also to have some fun in the process. The ideas for team activities are many and various from writing and performing an impromptu pantomime, and creating and playing a tuneful assortment of musical instruments, to passing a pin or an orange from one team member to the next in the most improbable of ways.

PANTOMIME TIME

Divide guests into teams of four or five and give each team the title of a different pantomime and three objects that are utterly irrelevant to the story. Each team must have the same three objects. The teams have about 20 minutes to write the script for a short, five-minute pantomime in which they have to include the three objects. When time is up, teams take it in turn to entertain the assembled company with their dramatic efforts.

If teams really enter into the spirit of the game, it is usually hilarious. Imagine a situation at which the objects may be an old gas mask, a packet of disposable nappies and a picture of an Edwardian matron.

The team faced with making these objects part of Cinderella might decide to update the story to the Second World War. The Ugly Sisters may have incontinent dogs (which never appear) and so Cinderella would be forever rushing off stage clutching one of the nappies to prevent a nasty accident. At the ball, Cinderella would drop her gas mask and when Prince Charming comes to look for the love of his life,

the mask would fit one of the Ugly Sisters.

But just in time, the Prince would notice the picture. 'That's our dear mother, sadly no longer with us,' sobs the Ugly Sister through the gas mask. The Prince is struck by its likeness to his own mother, and is told that the Ugly Sisters' mother had been one of a pair of twins, and that she had been kidnapped by gypsies.

'Mother was brought up by gypsies,' sobs the Ugly Sister. 'Then,' says the Prince in obvious relief, 'it seems that we are first cousins and forbidden by law to marry.' Just then Cinderella comes on to tell everyone there is an air raid and she cannot find her gas mask . . .

★

& THE BAND PLAYED

If you have a large gathering of 12 or more people, and can form at least three bands, this game can be fiercely and noisily competitive. With fewer people, it can just be fierce and noisy.

Form teams of four or five players and give each one the following equipment:

* at least eight empty milk bottles
* a jug of water
* spoons
* rubber bands
* one or two rulers
* one or two combs
* tissue paper

The teams have five minutes to create their own musical instruments and five minutes to rehearse. Then they entertain the other teams, who vote for the best band. Teams cannot vote for themselves.

Rubber bands tightly stretched around the ruler at different tensions will produce various notes when plucked.

Bottles filled to different levels will produce a

different note when struck by a spoon, resembling a xylophone.

Paper wrapped round the comb will make a mouth-organ.

Spoons tapped together sound like castanets.

PASS THE PIN

Stand players in two lines facing each other and about 1 metre/3 feet apart. Put a small table at each end of each line. On the table at the head of each team, scatter as many pins as there are players in the team. Tell everyone to stand with their wrists crossed in front of them.

On the word 'Go!' the first player in each line takes the right hand of the player standing next to him and uses it to pick up a pin. The second player passes it to the third player in the same way and so on down the line, when the last player deposits it on the table at the end.

In the meantime, more pins have started their journey down the line. If a pin is dropped, the umpire picks it up and puts it back on the table at the top of the line to restart its journey.

The first team to have transferred successfully all its pins from one end of the line to the other wins the game.

NELL GWYNNE

This is an excellent game to get guests acquainted at the beginning of a party!

Divide the group into two teams and ask them to stand in line, alternating men and women if possible. Give the leader of each team an orange, which he or she tucks under the chin.

On the words, 'Ready! Steady! Go!', they try to tuck their orange under the chin of the next in line, who continues by passing the orange under the chin of the third in line and so on.

If an orange falls, or if anyone is seen to cheat by using his or her hands to put the orange under a chin, it has to go back to the front again. The winning team is the one whose orange is the first to be safely transferred from the last in line back to the leader.

THE CHOCOLATE RACE

Divide the group into two teams and ask each one to form a circle. On a chair in the middle of each circle put a huge bar of chocolate, an old plate (preferably tin if you have one), a knife and some forks, a hat and a scarf.

Players in each team take it in turn to throw a die. The first to get a six runs to the chair, puts on the hat and scarf and tries to eat the chocolate, using the knife to cut off a piece and a fork to get it into his mouth. Next to throw a six runs to the chair, helps the player already there to take off the hat and scarf and puts them on before starting to eat the chocolate with the knife and a fork. The game goes on until one team has eaten the last crumb of chocolate.

If you don't mind the mess, you can play this game with a large bowl of Spaghetti Bolognese and pairs of chopsticks!

KEEP A STRAIGHT FACE

Divide everyone into two teams and seat them facing each other. The first team does its utmost to make players in the other team laugh – using whatever means they want, short of tickling or any physical contact. They can pull faces, tell jokes ('Did you hear about the tap dancer who broke her leg when she fell into the sink?') or use any other legal ploy. Anyone in the second team who laughs, giggles or gives even the merest flicker of a smile is out. The winner of the first round is the last player to keep a straight face. Now the roles are reversed: the laughter-makers become the stooges and the other team try to make them laugh. When that round is over the two winners are subjected to the jokes and comic antics of all the others. The loser is the one who smiles first.

SCAVENGING

Divide players into two or three teams depending on numbers and give each team a list containing twenty objects they have to find, and a box in which to put them. Each list should be totally different from the others: most things on the list should be somewhere in the house, or items that guests are likely to have in their wallets, pockets and bags. Give teams ten minutes to find as many articles on their list as they can.

Articles on the list might include a bus ticket, a tin of baked beans, a book by Charles Dickens (or any other author on the bookshelf), the telephone number of the local library, a sprig of holly, a theatre programme, a lipstick, a five pound note, a foreign coin, a book of matches from a restaurant, a pair of spectacles, a photograph, a paper handkerchief, a letter, a piece of headed writing paper, a biro, a salt cellar, a Trivial Pursuit question card, a credit card, a cheque for £10,000 made payable to the host (which he is honour bound to return as soon as the scores have been totted up), a hard-boiled egg, a cassette, a needle and cotton, a library card, a pin cushion, a candle, a paper knife, a stamp, a postcard . . . .

PENCIL GAMES

★

It may be that everyone is exhausted after a spell of team games, or not yet feeling energetic enough to get on to their feet. It may be that conversation starts to flag, or there is nothing good on television. Be ready with a pile of paper and a handful of pencils, and judge just the right moment to suggest a pencil game. Some of these will make people laugh, others provide a quiet interlude.

THE BEETLE GAME

This was a very popular family game, so popular in fact that people used to hold private and community Beetle Drives, organized rather like whist drives, and taken just as seriously. But the Beetle Game is purely one of chance. It is entirely dependent on which numbers you throw on the die, whether you can draw the head, legs, antennae, tail and eyes of your creature, and be first to shout out 'Beetle!' at the top of your voice.

Everyone takes it in turn to throw the die. A six allows the player to draw the body of his or her beetle. Once the body has been drawn, the other parts of the body are filled in as follows:

A five for the head;
One four for each leg;
One three for each of the two antennae;
A two for the tail;
A one for each of the two eyes.

Legs and tail can be drawn before a five is thrown for the head, but eyes and antennae cannot be filled in until the head has been added to the body.

The winner is the first to complete the beetle:

to do so he or she must have thrown one six, one five, four fours, two threes, one two and two ones (although not necessarily in that order).

★

CONSEQUENCES

This is one of the best-known and most popular of all 'pencil' games. And just the thing to suggest when people are tired after activity games, or the evening is starting to flag a little.

Everyone is given a pencil and a sheet of paper on the top of which they write an adjective or two. Each person then folds his paper so that what they have written cannot be seen, and passes it to the person on their right. Everyone now writes the name of a gentleman, folds and passes as before.

The game goes on until everyone has written:

1 one or more adjectives
2 the name of a gentleman
3 another set of adjectives
4 the name of a lady
5 a place where they met
6 an object that he gave to her
7 something he said to her
8 what she said to him
9 the consequence
10 what the world said.

When everyone has written down whatever it was that the world said, they pass their papers on one more time and take it in turn to read out the papers they receive. Because most players plump for the ridiculous or offensive, the results are usually quite amusing.

'The swarthy, but vapid Conrad Rothbart *met* the avian and garrulous Jennifer Ambleside *in* the jungle that passes for a garden in that part of London. He *gave* her a look that suggested he would like to get to know her better. He *said* 'I wonder if I could use your telephone, please.' She *said*, 'My father-in-law passed away doing that,' The consequence was that the canary never sang again, and the world said, 'We told him he'd be fined if he carried on like that.'

★

ALLITERATION

The Victorians loved 'letter' games, and a great favourite – a quiet, sitting-down-and-chewing-your-pencil type of game – was one called

Old Christmas comes, commanding Christian charity; causing cordial congratulations; creating cheerful conviviality. Circling country-cottage casements, clean, chubby, cherry-cheeked children cluster, chanting Christmas celebration carols.

Dingledale, Dromore,
December 3.

Dear Dr. Dodd, –

Do drive down directly! Darling David's dying – drowned (doubtless doing Dan's dreadfully dangerous duty, draining damaged dykes during Dan's dinner-hour.) Dash, devoted dog! darting down, did daring deeds, dived, discovered, dragged, drylanded dripping David. Dear Doctor, *do* despatch doses distinctly directed – don't delay! – Deeply distressed, & c.,

DORA D'ARCY.

Alliteration's Artful Art.

Each person around the circle draws a letter out of a hat. Lucky ones may draw, B, C, D or M, not-so-lucky ones have to puzzle over J or K. It is probably best not to include the real brainteasers, such as Q, X, Y and Z.

The idea is that, within a given time, everyone has to write a letter, a news item, an essay, any piece of prose – or even a poem – using only words that begin with their chosen letter. Adjectives, verbs, nouns, proper names, they all have to conform. Children are amazingly inventive in this way, and can often beat their elders hands down.

The winner is the player whose composition consists of the highest number of approved words.

THE KEY WORD

A short, sharp game to fill in a small gap in the proceedings.

Provide each player with paper and pencil. Call out any three-letter word. Players have three minutes to list as many words as they can that contain the key word. If the key word was *rip*, for example, suitable words would be *trip*, *tripper*, *tripe*, *stripe*, *stripped*, *ripping*, *strip*, *stripping*, *stripper*, *frippery* ... Gripping stuff!

LIMERICKS

This is played in a similar way to a game of consequences but the consequence of this game is a five-line rhyme of the kind that Edward Lear immortalized. The first, second and fifth lines have to rhyme, and the third and fourth lines make a rhyming couplet.

You need between three and five players in each group. Each one has a piece of paper and a pencil. Everyone writes down the first line of a limerick. If there are four players the first player completes both the first and fifth lines.

Having written the first line, the players pass on the sheet of paper and add the second line to rhyme with the one they have been passed. Pass on the paper again; add the third line; then the fourth and fifth lines.

The hilarity comes when each player, trying to keep a straight face, reads out the completed rhyme in his or her hands.

An example may be something like this:

A young man went lately from Oz,
And couldn't recall where he was;
So he questioned his collie,
Who chided his folly
And told him, this island's called Kos.

Whizz-kids at Limericks may, by pre-arrangement with the other players, like to try the version inspired by W. H. Gilbert's spoof verse that goes something like:

There was a young man from Tralee,
Who was stung one day on the elbow
The wound he did clasp
As he looked at the hornet,
And thanked God it wasn't a scorpion.

PICTORIAL CONSEQUENCES

After such exhausting literary masterpieces as Consequences and Limericks, the party will be in the mood for something rather more artistic.

Each player needs a pen or pencil and a piece of paper. A selection of coloured felt pens can add to the bizarre effect of the completed work of art.

Each player draws a head at the top of a piece of paper. It can be human, animal or fantasy.

They then fold the paper over so that only the necks are visible and pass the papers on to the person on their left. He or she adds arms and a body down to the waist, folds so that only the belt can be seen, and passes the paper to the next player who draws in legs down to the knees. The papers are folded for the last time and passed on for the lower legs and feet to be added. The completed drawings are then unfolded, and usually raise a laugh or two.

☆ 151

CONJURING TRICKS

★

It is now time to baffle the guests with a selection of amazing conjuring tricks. Practice makes for perfect prestidigitation, but no matter how well you do a trick, it's best not to repeat it. It's also best not to tell the secret of a trick after it has been performed. Not only will younger members of the audience be disappointed if they know how a trick is done, but next time everyone settles down for an evening of fun and games, you won't be able to do it again.

THE BALLOON
THAT WON'T BURST

'Ladies and Gentlemen I will now inflate this balloon, stick this pin into it and, I swear to you, it will not burst. And so saying, you inflate a balloon, stick a pin into it and express great astonishment when it bursts.

'Forgot the magic words!' And this time when you stick a pin into a balloon you have just blown up in front of the audience – it doesn't burst. Why? Because you secretly inflated the second balloon before you started your act and while it was inflated you stuck a piece of clear Sellotape somewhere on it. Then you deflated it. When you blow it up, prick it on the Sellotape which no one in the audience can see and it stays intact.

★

'MIND READING'

Red, White & Blue You need an assistant for this game of deception. Leave the room while the audience selects any three objects around

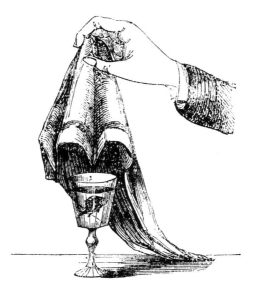

them. Your assistant takes no part in the choice, he or she simply lists the three objects.

When you come into the room, your assistant points to various objects and asks you if they were included in the selection.

'No!' you say, until he points to the first selected object . . . then, after a few more choices, to the second . . . and the third.

All that happens is that the assistant points to the first object on the list immediately after he has pointed to a red object; the second object on

the list is pointed to after a white one and the third after a blue one. If, of course, the game takes place in an all-grey room, or one furnished only in shades of green, you will have to agree to adapt the 'rules' accordingly!

★

TYING
THE KNOT

Challenge your audience to tie a knot in a large handkerchief, holding one corner of the handkerchief in one hand, the opposite corner in the other, and keeping hold of the corners while trying to tie the knot! When a few vain attempts have been made, it's extremely easy for you to do what the audience assumes to be impossible.

Fold the handkerchief in two diagonally and lay it flat on the table. Fold your arms across your chest, your left hand on top of the right arm and the right hand under the left arm.

You should be able to pick up the two corners without changing the position of your arms: and now simply by slowly uncrossing your arms you make a knot without letting go of either corner of the handkerchief.

LOVERS' HANDCUFFS

Secure two people together with string attached to their wrists as in the illustration. The object is to set themselves free without unfastening or cutting the knots. To do this, A must gather up the string which binds his or her hands into a loop, pass it under the string fastened around either of B's wrists and then slip it over B's hands. This done, both will be set free. The string may be replaced by a reversal of the same procedure.

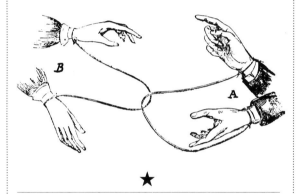

★

THE
VANISHING COIN

You need an empty matchbox and a small coin – a one penny piece is ideal. Drop the coin into the box in front of your audience and shake it so that everyone can hear the coin moving around inside the box. You must hold the box by one end between the base of your thumb and your forefinger. As you shake, discreetly turn the box upside down and squeeze the box gently. The box gapes open just enough for the coin to slip out into the palm of your hand, concealed from view. Stop shaking.

Ask a member of the audience to take the box, and open it. Lo! and behold! The coin has disappeared, having been slipped surreptitiously into your pocket.

THE
BALANCING COIN

The idea of this trick is to balance a ten pence piece on its edge on the point of a needle. Impossible? Not so. Simply get a bottle with a cork in its neck and insert a middle-sized needle upright in the cork. Cut a nick in another cork and fix a ten pence piece into it. Stick a couple of forks into the cork, opposite each other as illustrated. Next balance the rim of the coin on the point of the needle. If may then be made to rotate without falling off as the centre of gravity is below the centre of suspension.

★

THE
DISAPPEARING COIN

Ask someone in the audience for a fifty pence piece and place it in the centre of a large handkerchief. Fold one corner to the one opposite, making sure that the coin is hidden in the centre of the handkerchief.

Fold the left corner upwards so that it is slightly to the right of the apex. Fold the right

The disappearing coin.

corner over to the top so that it is slightly to the left of the apex. The coin is in the bottom fold. Take the corner that is to the left of the apex in your right hand and the corner that is to the right of the apex in your left hand and pull your hands apart and upwards. The coin seems to have vanished into thin air. Practise throwing the handkerchief in the air and catching it so that the coin doesn't fall out of the fold, and stuff it into your pocket. You are now fifty pence better off!

★

THE
MAGIC CROSS

You need a long-stemmed wine glass and a cross shape cut from a sheet of newspaper. Place the cross over the top of the glass and bend the ends over the rim to prevent the cross slipping off. Announce to the audience that you are going to make the cross revolve on top of the glass without touching it in any way.

As you are saying this, fill the glass with water almost to the brim, taking great care that the cross, the outside of the glass and the rim remain quite dry.

When your audience have scoffed at your claim, hold the base of the glass firmly with the fingers of one hand. Now rub the tip of one finger on any part of the glass that lies between any two arms of the cross and it will move. Rub round the rim and the cross with revolve as well.

NEW YEAR'S EVE

★

New Year's Eve, or Hogmanay, the threshold between one year and the next, is a time for a mixture of customs; for silent contemplation or noisy revelry; for traditional processions and expressions of good luck; for feasting and toasting and, most of all, for looking to the future with hope and confidence.

WASSAILING

Wassailing, which is sometimes wrongly confused with carol singing, is an ancient custom especially associated with New Year. The word comes from the Anglo-Saxon *Waes-Hail*, a toast which means 'Be whole', to which the reply was *Drink-Hail*, or 'Good Health!'

In some parts of the country, villagers and townspeople celebrated the New Year with wassailing processions, when the wassail bowl, containing hot spiced ale and sliced or whole apples, was decorated with greenery and carried from house to house. The inhabitants were invited to drink from the bowl, to ensure good luck for the year ahead, and then to refill it.

Sometimes children went wassailing to collect fruit – especially apples – and gifts of money. The words of one traditional wassail song were quite explicit:

'Wassail, wassail through the town,
If you've got any apples,
throw them down;
If you've got no apples,
money will do,
If you've got no money,
God bless you.'

People who had neither apples nor money used to take an empty wassail bowl from door to door in the hope of getting it filled with ale and, like the children, being offered food and money.

It might seem as if the whole population was on the move on New Year's Eve. But that was not so. In England, it was the custom for people to get together in their homes and pass round the wassail bowl as they waited for the procession to call on them. Then they would have some hot, spiced ale ready to pour into the visitors' bowl.

Tree wassailing, the crop fertility ritual which was carried out in fruit-growing regions, usually took place on Twelfth Night (see page 156).

WASSAIL SONG

*❛ Here we come a-wassailing
Among the leaves so green,
Here we come a-wandering,
So fair to be seen:*

*Love and joy come to you
And to you your wassail too,
And God bless you, and send you
A happy New Year,
And God send you
A happy New Year. ❜*

ANON.
From a traditional North of England song.

SCOTS VERSION

The Scots have their own version of the wassail bowl, as Sir Walter Scott reminded us:

'. . . it was uncanny and would certainly have felt very uncomfortable not to welcome the New Year in the midst of his family, and a few old friends, with the immemorial libation of a het pint.'

The het pint was carried through the streets

several hours before midnight on Hogmanay, in large copper kettles known as toddy kettles. The steaming (at least, when it left the kitchen) brew consisted of mild ale, whisky, sugar, spices and beaten eggs.

HOGMANAY FARE

The traditional Scots black bun has taken a step back in time, and is now served at Hogmanay instead of on Twelfth Night. The bun is a rich, dark fruit cake baked in a pastry case. Like Christmas cake, it should be made several weeks before Christmas, so that it has time to mature.

Haggis is *the* food with which to celebrate Hogmanay in Scotland. It is usually served with clapshot, mashed potatoes and turnips mixed with herbs. Haggis (the name is thought to derive from the French *hachis* meaning 'chopped') is made of chopped offal, oatmeal and suet boiled inside the bag of a lamb's stomach. The finest haggis is said to be made from deer's liver.

And it is *always* eaten to the accompaniment of the skirl of the bagpipes and washed down with neat whisky.

FIRST FOOTING

The tradition of first footing on New Year's Eve goes back a long way in both England (where it has now almost lapsed) and Scotland, where it is still an important part of the Hogmanay ritual.

The responsibility for whether a household will or will not be blessed with good luck in the coming year rests on the shoulders of the first person to cross the threshold after midnight has struck.

Opinions differ as to whether the 'first footer' should be dark or fair, but there is general agreement that the first visitor of the New Year should be male, and bring with him the traditional gifts of a piece of bread, a lump of coal and some salt. His reward, of course, is a wee dram of whisky.

GOOD LUCK OMENS

New Year's Eve is all about trying to ensure good luck for the coming year, and finding out what it holds in store.

People used to sprinkle their homes inside and out with water freshly drawn from the well, in a combined act of symbolic cleansing and good luck. It is a domestic version of 'tree wassailing' (see page 156).

In Spain, at midnight on New Year's Eve, people eat twelve grapes, one for each stroke of the clock ringing in the New Year.

In the Channel Islands a figure of old Father Time is buried in the sand with due ceremony. This done, the people are ready to greet the New Year, full of hope.

In Britain, people used to try to discover their fate in the coming twelve months by all kinds of means. One was to drop molten lead into cold water, and then try to analyse the shape it formed as it set and hardened.

The New Year was a busy time for people who possessed the ability to read fortunes in the tea leaves left in the cup. This was a favourite way of gazing into the future.

Another was to shuffle the Runes, a collection of marked stones derived from an ancient method of Chinese fortune telling. According to the patterns on the stones selected and the 'readings' they gave, the person's fortune could be mapped out for the coming year.

WATCH NIGHT

For nearly 200 years it has been the custom to hold a Watch Night vigil in many churches, a practice begun by the Wesleyans.

A thanksgiving service is followed by a period of silent vigil, during which the congregation waits for the church bells to ring out, and signal the start of the New Year.

In the last century it had been the tradition, on the way home from the service, to take gifts of food and drink to the less well-off.

LATE NIGHT REVELRY

New Year's Eve is often the excuse for the biggest and most boisterous party of the season. 'Eat, drink and be merry' seems to be the by-word.

People wait to hear the bells 'ring out the old, ring in the new'. Then it is time for balloons to pop, paper sirens to be blown, streamers to be thrown and people to link hands and sing 'Auld Lang Syne'.

OUT OF STEP

Not everyone in the British Isles celebrates New Year's Eve on the same day. It depends which calendar you go by.

In the Scottish fishing port of Burghead they still adhere to the old calendar, the one used throughout the country until 1752, which means that the annual festival falls on January 11.

Two ancient local families construct a fire basket, which in Gaelic is known as a clavie, from whisky casks or barrels. This is borne around the town by runners, while onlookers scrabble for the falling pieces of charred wood, which are thought to bring luck for the new year.

TWELFTH NIGHT

★

The feast of Epiphany, which falls on the twelfth day after Christmas, was celebrated for its religious significance, as the day the Three Kings brought their gifts to the Infant Jesus, and because it marked the end of the long winter festival. That was excuse enough for feasting and fun, parties and pantomimes, bonfires and bonhomie. There are several traditional customs associated with Twelfth Night.

CELEBRATING EPIPHANY

There used to be more to Twelfth Night than taking down Christmas decorations, reading through the Christmas cards for the last time, and putting the tree outside.

The day brought the long Christmas festival to a close and, as such, was looked upon as the last excuse for a round of merry-making.

First and foremost the day has a religious significance, for January 6 is Epiphany, the day when the Three Kings, Caspar, Melchior and Balthasar, arrived from the East with their gifts of gold, frankincense and myrrh for the Infant Jesus. To commemorate this date, a church service is still held in St. James's Palace in London, when members of the royal household present the Chapel Royal with similar gifts in honour of the first Epiphany; and special church services are widely held.

In the past, there were both religious processions and revelry and the feast day was notable for its rituals and good humour. Farmers lit bonfires in the fields and danced, sang and drank around the blaze to drive away evil spirits. Guessing games were a popular pastime, the sillier the better. Revellers might be asked, for example, to guess what was cooking on the rotating spit in the farmhouse kitchen. And they would be barred the door until they had guessed correctly. If the object was something obscure, like an old shoe or a tin bucket, they might be destined to spend several more hours around the bonfire.

PRACTICAL JOKES

Twelfth Night was the ideal time to play practical jokes of all kinds, too, a practice which began at court and was copied all the way down the social scale. Court jesters, and Morris men with their hobby horses toured the streets playing tricks on the revelling crowds, and collected money for the next round of drinks.

The feast of Epiphany is still celebrated in many parts of Europe, with family parties, pantomimes and presents for the children. In Spain children leave their shoes outside on Twelfth Night, hoping that the Three Kings will pass that way and fill them, if not with gold, frankincense and myrrh, then with small presents.

HUNT THE BEAN

Twelfth Night cake was a traditional part of the feasting, in Britain as elsewhere. The cake was baked with a hidden bean inside – a custom similar to that of putting charms in the Christmas pudding. Whoever was lucky enough to be served the slice with the bean was king or queen for the day and, with a chosen consort, ruled over the day's festivities. The custom is retained in France, with the Galette des Rois, cake of kings.

In London, the cast of the play running at the Theatre Royal, Drury Lane, on Twelfth Night enjoys a link with tradition. As directed in the will of the eighteenth-century actor Robert Baddeley, the cast is served Baddeley cake.

In the apple-growing counties, in Kent and the west of England the ceremony of wassailing in the orchards took place on Twelfth Night. This was seen as a make-or-break event, to ensure a bountiful harvest in the coming year. The trees were sprinkled with cider from the wassail bowl then (each region had its own tradition) the wassailers would fire shotguns into the trees, or whip the trunks. To finish off the ceremony, and the festive season, the wassail bowls were refilled with cider, and the health of the next harvest drunk.

QUITE A STRUGGLE

A tradition that dates back to the thirteenth century keeps villagers of Haxey, in Lincolnshire, on their mettle all day long on January 6. In the old days, so the story goes, peasants fought to retrieve a landowner's leather hood which was blown away in a gale, and were rewarded with parcels of land for their trouble.

The custom continues, as the 'boggins', two rival teams from local pubs, struggle for possession of a symbolic piece of rolled up leather. The victorious team line up for their free drinks at the winning pub.

TWELFTH NIGHT
CAKE

fat for greasing
150 g/5 oz margarine
75 g/3 oz soft dark brown sugar
3 eggs
300 g/11 oz plain flour
60 ml/4 tbsp milk
5 ml/1 tsp bicarbonate of soda
30 ml/2 tbsp golden syrup
2.5 ml/½ tsp mixed spice
2.5 ml/½ tsp ground cinnamon
pinch of salt
50 g/2 oz currants
100 g/4 oz sultanas
100 g/4 oz cut mixed peel
1 dried bean

Line and grease a 15 cm/6 inch round cake tin. Set the oven at 180°C/350°F/gas 4. In a mixing bowl, cream the margarine and sugar until light and fluffy. Beat in the eggs, one at a time, adding a little flour with each. Warm the milk in a saucepan, add the bicarbonate of soda and stir until dissolved. Add the syrup.

Mix the spices and salt with the remaining flour in a bowl. Add this to the creamed mixture alternately with the flavoured milk. Lightly stir in the dried fruit and peel. Spoon half the cake mixture into the prepared tin, lay the bean in the centre, then cover with the rest of the cake mixture. Bake for about 2 hours. Cool on a wire rack.   MAKES ONE 15 CM/6 INCH CAKE

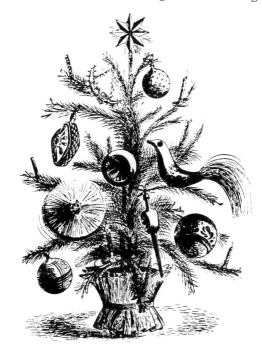

COOKERY INDEX

A

Almond paste, 58–59
Aloo, 80
Anchovy
    butter, 14
    tartlets, 69
Apple(s)
    and cranberry jelly, 13
    ham slices with, 92
    peppers with, 37
    salad, red cabbage and, 65
    sauce, 13
    snow, 81
Apricot
    dried, in Madeira, 16
    glaze, 58
Atholl brose dessert, 93
Avocado,
    smoked salmon and, 25

B

Bacon
    peas with, 39
    rolls, 29
Bananas in rum, 93
Bean salad with tuna, 64–65
Beef, 33
Bombe mould, lining, 49
Brandy butter, 14
Bread
    Irish soda, 92–93
    puris, 80
    sauce, 29
Brussels sprouts with
        chestnuts, 38
Bûche de Nöel, 93
Butters
    anchovy, 14
    brandy, 14
    Cumberland rum, 14
    orange, 14
Butterscotch sauce, 89

C

Cabbage, red, and apple salad,
    65
Cake(s)
    carrot, 88
    chestnut Christmas log, 93
    Christmas, 58
    covering with paste, 60–61
    crunchies, 84
    icing, 61
    Paris–Brest, 77
    peanut butter slices, 85
    tipsy, 65
    Twelfth Night, 157
    Victoria sandwich, 82
Candied peel, quick, 12
Carrot(s)
    cake, 88
    glazed, 38, 76
Cauliflower with mushroom
        sauce, 92
Celery, braised, 39
Cheese
    potted, 19
    straws, Mrs Beeton's, 69
Chestnut(s)
    brussels sprouts with, 38
    Christmas log, 93
    roasting, 20
    sauce, 14, 29
    stuffing, 28
Chicken liver pâté, jellied, 17
Chick-pea dip, 86
Chocolate, 89
    fruit fondue, 89
    sandwich cake, 82
    sauce, 89
    truffles, 52
Choux pastry, 77
    Paris–Brest, 77
Christmas
    cake, 58
    log, chestnut, 93

pudding, rich boiled, 40
sandwich shapes, 85
Cider cup, 89
Claret jelly, clear, 65
Clementines in vodka, 16
Cocktail
    sausages, 84
    vols-au-vent, 68
Coffee, 57, 73
    chiffon pie, 72–73
    Irish, 77
Conserve, kumquat, 13
Consommé jardinière, 70
Cranberry
    and apple jelly, 13
    and rice stuffing, 28
    sauce, 13
Cream
    anchovy, 69
    horseradish, 36
    praline, 77
    soured, 69
Crudités, 69
Crunchies, 84
Cumberland rum butter,
    14
Curry, 78, 80
Custard
    pouring cup, 44
    sauce, cornflour, 44
    cream, 45

D

Dal, 80
Dates, stuffed, 53
Devilled turkey, 92
Drinks, 20–21
    for children's party, 84
    Irish coffee, 77
    measures, 68
    non-alcoholic, 68
    party, 66–68
    for teenage party, 89

Duchesse potatoes, 76
Duck, terrine of, 19

E

Eggs, 49
    stuffed, 62

F

Feather icing, 83
Figs in sherry, 16
Fillings
    for sandwiches, 85
    for vols-au-vent, 68
Fish and corn chowder, 90
Fondue, chocolate fruit, 89
Fool, Scandinavian fruit, 81
Fruit
    bombe, glacé, 49
    cocktail, 24
    fondue, chocolate, 89
    fool, Scandinavian, 81
    glazed, 52
    punch, 84
        non-alcoholic, 21
    salad in a melon basket,
        76–77
    in syrup and alcohol, 16

G

Gâteau with praline cream,
    77
Giblet stock, 29
Gingerbread, 101
Glacé
    fruit bombe, 49
    icing, 61
        feather, 83
Glazed fruits, 52
Goose, 32
Grapefruit cocktail, 24
Gravy, thickened, 29

H

Ham
    boiled, 62
    slices with apple, 92
    stuffing, 75
Hazelnuts
    praline cream, 77
    rissoles, 36–37
Herb forcemeat, 28
Herring fillets, potted, 19
Horseradish cream, 36
Hot water crust pastry, 64
Hummus, 86

I

Icing
    bag, 61
    for carrot cake, 88
    feather, 83
    glacé, 61
    Royal, 60
Indian spiced lentils, 80

J

jelly
    clear claret, 65
    cranberry and apple, 13

K

Kebabs, lamb, 88
Keema, 78
Kumquat Conserve, 13

L

Lamb Kebabs, 88
Lemon sorbet, 48–49
Lentil(s)
    Indian spiced, 80
    turnovers, 37

CUSTOMS, DECORATIONS & GAMES INDEX

★